The Floral Dictionary of Anna Maria Campbell

Language of Flowers series
Volume 3

With an introduction and notes by
RACHEL HENRY

Sphinx House

The Language of Flowers Series by Rachel Henry:

The Language of Flowers 1550-1680
The Language of Flowers 1810-1816
The Floral Dictionary of Anna Maria Campbell

Published by Sphinx House Publishing, Norfolk
Copyright ©Rachel Henry 2025
All rights reserved. No portion of this book may be reproduced in any form or by any means - graphic, electronic or mechanical, including photocopying, recording, taping or information storage and retrieval systems, without the prior permission in writing of the publishers. The author, Rachel Henry, has asserted her right under the Copyright, Designs and Patent Act, 1988, to be identified as the author of this work.

Contents

INTRODUCTION	1
NOTES	5
BOOKS & AUTHORS REFERRED TO IN THE TEXT	7
GLOSSARY	11
ORIGINAL PREFACE TO THE FLORAL DICTIONARY	17
A	21
B	36
C	59
D	103
E	114
F	124
G	141
H	150
I	176
J	180
K	183
L	185
M	209

N	236
O	244
P	254
Q	277
R	279
S	294
T	319
V	330
W	338
X, Y & Z	344
GROUPS AND MESSAGES	347
BOTANICAL NAMES	349
ACKNOWLEDGEMENTS	350

INTRODUCTION

On holiday in Cornwall some years ago, I was browsing around a small antique shop when I found, laid carelessly upon a shelf, a copy of Anna Maria Campbell's *Floral Dictionary or Language of Flowers*. Measuring only three and a half by four inches, it would have been easy to miss. In its original binding of mottled boards and a simple morocco leather spine, it had seen some wear in its time. But it had a certain charm – and so I bought it. And so began my fascination with the language of flowers.

AUTHOR, PUBLISHER, & DATE OF PUBLICATION

I have been unable to find a record of any other books written by Anna Maria or to find out anything about her.

The title page of the book tells us that it was published by a London firm, Rock Brothers and Payne. Although Anna Maria's surname is a Scottish one, I felt it was unlikely that she lived in Scotland, since she had chosen to submit her work to a London publisher – and a small one, at that – rather than one of the Scottish firms that were thriving in the 19th century.

The volume's binding and style of printing show that it dates from the nineteenth century – but there is no date anywhere in the book. On investigation, I discovered that Rock & Co., which later became Rock Brothers and Payne, was founded, as a printer of engraved views, fancy stationery, books and booklets, in the 1820s by William Frederick Rock. In 1833, his brother became a partner and the company name was changed to William & Henry Rock. Eleven years later, in 1844, his brother-in-law joined the firm, which then became Rock Brothers & Payne. And it remained in existence, and prospered, until 1884 when William Rock retired and sold the company to Dickinson & Co.

So this book must have been published between 1844 and 1884. By this period, it seems, Rock was more a publisher than a printer, since on the reverse of the title page it states *Printed by H. Kemshead, Lower Kennington Lane, Lambeth*. With some help from the Printing Historical Society and the *British Book Trade Index*, I was able to discover that one Henry Kemshead was active at 6 Portsmouth Place, 23 Lower Kennington Lane from 1844 until 1849 when he moved just down the road, to 46 Lower Kennington Lane. And he is shown still to be at this address in the Commercial Directory for 1891, so this did nothing to narrow down the possible date at which Anna Maria's book was published.

However, the book's simple binding suggested something closer to the middle of the century than to the end of it. So I started to do some more research into the Kemshead printing works. It seemed that mostly it printed Acts of Parliament, sale catalogues, journals and other ephemera, with only a few books. For my purposes, though, this didn't matter because all these items bore the printer's imprint. And of the dozens of pieces that I looked at that were dated later than 1864, all bore the postal district of 'S' or, from about 1869, 'SE'. So we have, for example, 'London: H. Kemshead's Steam Printing Works, Kennington, S' and 'H. Kemshead, Printer, Kennington Lane, SE'. But in AMC's little book, the imprint states 'London: Printed by H. Kemshead, Lower Kennington Lane, Lambeth'. This, together with the style of binding, convinces me that we can confidently place the publication of AMC's book between 1844 and 1864.

MORE THAN ONE EDITION?

Floral dictionaries were very popular in Victorian times and many can still be found in antiquarian bookshops and at auction. However, Anna Maria's version seems to be very scarce. There is no copy in the British Library nor in any of the major libraries in the UK. The only copies I could trace were in the library of the University of Delaware and the library of Ohio State University. These are not American editions – both libraries show the book as having been published by Rock Brothers and Payne However, the University of Delaware has noted its copy as being a 10th edition. This strikes me as being very odd – I know enough about antiquarian books to expect a book that went into ten editions to have rather more copies in existence, even after 170 years. Its scarcity suggests it was not a best-seller – so why would it have gone into 10 editions? Did the publisher perhaps bring out a second printing with '10th edition' added to try to suggest that it was more popular than it actually was?

ANNA MARIA CAMPBELL & HER LANGUAGE OF FLOWERS

When I bought my copy of Anna Maria's book, I knew next to nothing about the language of flowers and, as I looked through it, certain questions arose. It occurred to me that it would have been all very well for a young Victorian man to send his sweetheart a message in a bouquet, but it would be in vain if she didn't know how to read it. This led me to wonder how many floral dictionaries had been written.[1] And that, of course made me curious as to whether the information in all of them was interchangeable or whether both sender and recipient would need to have a copy of the same version.

I started to look for other dictionaries and, as I read them, it became clear that Anna Maria's has several important differences from most of them. For a start, she is very precise with her listings. She doesn't just give a meaning for 'auricula', for example. She gives a meaning for 'Auricula, *purple edged white*'. Some other authors will give an occasional colour (such as different meanings for red roses

---

1. By the time I had finished writing *The Language of Flowers and the Victorian Garden*, I had unearthed 15 different floral dictionaries. Now that number has risen to 130.

and yellow roses) but with Anna Maria there is a colour for almost every plant named. In addition, some of Anna Maria's meanings are quite different from those found in other books. And she lists some plants that I have not found in any other floral dictionaries. Researching the plants she lists, I began to suspect that she had got some of her information from books, since not all the plants were common in Britain at the time – indeed, some didn't grow there at all.

The more I thought about it, the more I wanted to know and, as I researched, I started to get a clearer idea of the Victorian garden, to learn a little of the folklore associated with some of the plants, and discover the different uses various plants had been put to in the past. The more I read, the more fascinated I became by the social context of Anna Maria's *Floral Dictionary*. And, out of that, my book *The Language of Flowers and the Victorian Garden* was born.

NOTES

Throughout the book, I have referred to the author, Anna Maria Campbell, as AMC.

While I have not given English plant names initial capitals, where these are used in the works quoted, I have retained them in the quotes.

I have made a few corrections to AMC's original work – where entries are simply duplications of others, I have omitted them, and where a plant is listed under two different names, I have combined them. However, I have not corrected AMCs mis-spelling of some of the plant names.

Botanical names and knowledge are constantly changing. Older names have been retained when they occur within a direct quote from another book but, other than this, I have endeavoured to give the current accepted botanical names for plants. In a quotation, an asterisk next to a plant name indicates that the current accepted botanical name can be found in the Appendix.

Where a plant mentioned in an entry for another plant has its own separate listing elsewhere in the book, its name is shown in small capitals – for example, under 'Pink' you will find '"The pink, the CARNATION, and the SWEET-WILLIAM, are in every garden, and are universal favourites" says Mrs. Loudon.' indicating that there are separate entries for 'carnation' and 'sweet William'.

Some of the colours that AMC assigns to plants are incorrect and, while unable to say definitely why this should be, I suspect that it may be because she obtained a lot of her information from books. Chromolithographic printing was not introduced until the 1830s. Before that, and for some time thereafter, illustrations were hand-coloured. Given that paints may fade, darken or change in other ways, it is possible that AMC, using books with hand-coloured illustrations, misread the colour. (In her introduction, she mentions John Lindley's books on botany, several of which have hand-coloured illustrations.) Another possibility is that she was using books in which several flowers were organised into one illustration and she misidentified the one that she was trying to describe.

The illustrations for this edition are all based on photographic originals. The creators of those photographs are listed at the end of the book.

BOOKS & AUTHORS REFERRED TO IN THE TEXT

While investigating the plants listed, I have endeavoured to use only reference books that would have been available to AMC. On the odd occasion when I have referred to a modern source, this is because I could find no contemporary information.

There is a core of books to which I refer frequently throughout this volume. When I quote them, I just give a single author's name as a reference, the key to which is shown below, together with the titles of the books that those quotes came from. The dates given for each are those of first publication. Other books that I quote are given their full author and title in the text, and the date that follows each is that of the edition which I am quoting.

Barton: Benjamin Barton & Thomas Castle: *British Flora Medica*

Culpeper: Nicholas Culpeper: *The Complete Herbal* (1653)

Dixon: George Dixon: *Handbook to the Herbarium* (1845)

Dolby: Richard Dolby: *The Cook's Dictionary* (1830)

Don: George Don (ancestor of TV gardener Monty Don): *General System of Gardening and Botany* (4 volumes, 1831-1838)

Glenny: George Glenny: *Handbook to the Flower Garden* (1851)

Ildrewe: Miss Ildrewe: *The Language of Flowers* (1865)

Kent: Elizabeth Kent: *Flora Domestica* (1825)

Loudon: J.C. Loudon: *Encyclopaedia of Trees and Shrubs* (1842)

Mrs. Loudon: Jane Loudon: *Gardening for Ladies* (1843); *The Ladies' Flower Garden of Ornamental Annuals* (1840)

Maund: Benjamin Maund: *The Botanic Garden* (1827); *The Botanist* (1836)

Phillips: Henry Phillips: *Flora Historica* (1824); *The Companion for the Kitchen Garden* (1831); *Floral Emblems* (1825)

Prior: R.C.A. Prior: *On the Popular Names of British Plants* (1863)

Tyas: Robert Tyas: *Popular Flowers* (1843); *Handbook on the Language & Sentiment of Flowers* (1840)

Wilkinson: Lady Caroline Wilkinson: *Weeds and Wild Flowers* (1858)

OTHER PEOPLE OF NOTE

A few other people of note are referred to in various places throughout the book. They are:

DUCHESS OF BEAUFORT

Mary Somerset, Duchess of Beaufort (1630-1715), one of Britain's earliest distinguished women gardeners, began to collect plants in the 1680s. Seeds were sent to her from the West Indies, South Africa, India, Sri Lanka, China and Japan and she became an expert at identifying exotic plants grown from unidentified seeds. She is acknowledged to be the first person to bring a number of species to England, including the globe amaranth, the geranium, the blue passion flower, the white pine and oriental persicaria.

EVELYN
John Evelyn (1620–1706) was an English diarist and gardener, and author of *Sylva or a Discourse on Forest Trees* as well as other books on a wide variety of subjects.

GERARD
John Gerard (c. 1545–1612) was a botanist and herbalist who is best known as the author of a great *Herbal* which was the most influential English book on botany of the 17th century. Based on an earlier *Herbal* by the Flemish physician and botanist, Rembert Dodoens, Gerard's book included listings of numerous plants growing in his London garden as well as others imported from North America.

LINNAEUS
Carl Linnaeus (1707-1778) was a Swedish biologist and physician who devised a system of classifying plants and animals which is still in use. This has seven sections and it is the last two of these that are used to give a plant or animal its scientific name (such as *Dianthus caryophyllus*, the carnation).

MILLER
Philip Miller (1691–1771) was an English botanist and, for nearly 50 years, chief gardener at the Chelsea Physic Garden. His correspondence with other botanists resulted in him introducing plants into England from all over the world. A Fellow of the Royal Society, he was the author of two major works on gardening, *The Gardener's and Florist's Dictionary* and *The Gardener's Dictionary*.

NUTTALL
Thomas Nuttall (1786-1859} was an English botanist who travelled extensively in America between 1808 and 1841, collecting many plants that were previously unknown.

PARKINSON
John Parkinson (1567–1650). Described as the last of the great English herbalists and one of the first of the great English botanists, he was Royal Botanist to King Charles I and was the keeper of a botanical garden in Covent Garden as well as being the author of two great treatises on plants.

PLINY
Gaius Plinius Secundus (AD 23–79) was a naturalist, commander in the Roman army and author of a major work on natural history. He is usually referred to as Pliny the Elder, to distinguish him from his nephew, the lawyer and author, Pliny the Younger.

TURNER
William Turner (1508-1568), who is known as the 'father of English botany', was an English naturalist, botanist, theologian and the author of a three-volume *Herbal*.

GLOSSARY

A number of horticultural and medical terms (many of them archaic) are to be found in the text. Since some of these may not be familiar to the reader, I offer a short glossary.

HORTICULTURAL TERMS

ALGA, or ALGAE: non-flowering and, usually, aquatic plants that range from seaweed down to microscopic organisms

ANTHER: the part of the flower where pollen is produced

CARPEL: the female reproductive organ of a flower

COROLLA: the petals

CULTIVAR: a plant variety that has been produced by selective breeding

FLORIST: a term first used in 1623. For many years it meant someone who grew flowers – either amateur or professional. By the 19th century, it had come to mean a nurseryman, particularly one who was interested in improving plants and developing new varieties.

FRONDS: the leaves of a fern or similar plant

GENUS (plural GENERA) & SPECIES: living organisms are traditionally classified into groups. The kingdom (animal kingdom, plant kingdom) is subdivided into phyla, then into classes, then into orders, followed by families, genera and species. The botanical name of a plant consists of its genus and species – for example, *Helianthus annuus* is the common sunflower, *Helianthus* being the genus and *annuus* the species.

GENERIC & SPECIFIC: in the context of plants, generic refers to the genus and specific to the species. For example, *annuus* is the specific name of the common sunflower.

PARTERRE: this is described by Wikipedia as "a formal garden constructed on a level surface, consisting of planting beds, typically in symmetrical patterns, separated and connected by gravel pathways".

PINNATED: having leaflets on either side of the stem

SEPALS: green, leaflike parts of a flower that enclose the petals

SPORT: a naturally occurring mutation that changes a plant's appearance

STIGMA: the part of the carpel (qv) that collects pollen

STOVE PLANT: a plant native to a warm climate that, in temperate climates, needs to be kept indoors or in a heated greenhouse.

TUBER: a thickened underground part of a plant stem, such as a potato

UMBLE: a cluster of small flower stalks that radiate out from a common point, like an umbrella.

MEDICAL TERMS

AGUE: fever associated with shaking

ALOPECIA: abnormal hair loss

ANTIPHRODISIAC: The opposite of an aphrodisiac. Described by Dr. O. Phelps Brown in *The Complete Herbalist* (1865) as something that "composes the genital organs" and "quiets" erections

APERIENT: something used to relieve constipation

CARMINATIVE: something that relieves flatulence (wind)

CATHARTIC: purgative

CERATES: medicated ointments

CEREBRAL: relating to the brain

CHOREA: involuntary and irregular muscle movements

CONSUMPTION: tuberculosis
CONTUSION: a bruise
CUTANEOUS: relating to the skin
DISTEMPER: a disturbance in the balance of the body's 'humours', causing illness
DIURETIC: promoting urine output
DROPSY: swelling of the tissues from water retention; oedema
DYSPEPSIA: indigestion
EXCORIATION: abrasion
EXPECTORATION: coughing up phlegm
FALLING SICKNESS: epilepsy
GOITRE: enlarged thyroid gland
GRAVEL: small kidney or bladder stones
HYDROPHOBIA: rabies, a deadly virus spread by animal bites
KING'S EVIL: swelling of the lymph nodes of the neck, often due to tuberculosis
NEPHRITIS: inflammation of the kidneys
PALSY: paralysis, particularly if associated with involuntary shaking
PSORA: scabies and other itchy skin conditions
PULMONARY: relating to the lungs
PUTRID: rotting
SCORBUTIC: relating to scurvy (see below)
SCURVY: disease due to lack of vitamin C
SOMNIFEROUS: sleep inducing
STUPOR: a state close to unconsciousness
VERTIGO: giddiness
WHITLOW: an infection of the fingertip, causing redness, pain and swelling

WARNING

Some of the entries contain information about therapeutic uses of the plants. You should NOT try using any of these. Herbal remedies should only be taken on the advice of a qualified herbalist or if generally available in a proprietary and over-the-counter form.

ANNA MARIA CAMPBELL'S
FLORAL DICTIONARY

WITH NOTES BY
RACHEL HENRY

ORIGINAL PREFACE TO THE FLORAL DICTIONARY

Floral Language, which originated in Eastern climes, where for centuries the loving and the loved have "told in a garland their loves and cares,"[1] has of late received much attention throughout Europe. The "Oriental Love-letter,"[2] which originally was a simple tulip, implying a declaration of love, or which conveyed by an Aenothera[3] an assignation for evening, has now received such additions, not only from Legends and Poetry, but also from Science, as to be expanded into a volume, and to assume the important title of a Floral Dictionary.

In the present compilation, the Editor has consulted every authority which was entitled to consideration, from the Romantic Legends which amuse the favorites on the shores of the Bosphorus, to the more sedate but more pleasing records of

---

1. This is a quotation from a poem called *The Language of Flowers* by American geologist and poet, James Gates Percival (1795-1856) and is also used in the introduction to Robert Tyas' earlier work, *The Sentiment of Flowers* (1836).

2. The so-called Oriental love letter was described in depth by Lady Mary Wortley Montagu. See the introduction to Rachel Henry's *The Language of Flowers 1550-1680*.

3. *Oenothera* (mis-spelled here by AMC) is the evening primrose.

the accomplished Professor of Botany, Mr. Lindley.[4] No historical allusion to a flower has been neglected – no scientific exposition of a flower's qualities has been disregarded; and, in the numerous instances in which conflicting opinions have hitherto disturbed the lovers who "telegraph with flowers," the compiler of the Dictionary has endeavoured to decide so impartially, as to establish his[5] book as an authority. Since precision is at length so nearly attained, that in future

"token-flowers will tell
"What words can ne'er express so well,"[6]

it is expected that it will become a matter of reproach for a Lover to be without this little Lexicon of Flowers; and (who knows) by study and a happy combination of love, wit, and fancy, the reader may, by and bye, rival that accomplished Floral Linguist, Leigh Hunt[7], and produce something to compete (excellence can no higher go) with his delicious trifle –

THE ALBANIAN LOVE LETTER

An exquisite invention this,
Worthy of love's most honied kiss,

---

4. John Lindley (1799-1865), Professor of Botany at University College London and author of numerous works on botany.

5. The use of 'his' rather than 'her' here is puzzling.

6. A slight misquotation from Byron's *Maid of Athens*. The correct quote is:
By all the token-flowers that tell
What words can never speak so well;

7. Poet and essayist, 1784-1859.

This art of writing billet-doux
In buds and odours and bright hues,
In saying all one feels and thinks,
In clever daffodils and pinks.
A letter comes, just gathered, we
Doat on its tender brilliancy,
Inhale its delicate expression
Of Balm and Sweet-pea; its confession,
Made with as sweet a Maiden's Blush
As ever morn bedew'd in bush.

And then, when we have kissed its wit
And heart, in water putting it,
To keep its remarks fresh; go round
Our little eloquent plot of ground
And with delighted hands compose
Our answer, all of Lily and Rose,
Of Tuberose and Violet,
And little darling Mignonette,
And Gratitude and Polyanthus,
And flowers that say "Felt never Man thus!"

A

ACACIA

White – **Friendship, esteem**
Rose – **Taste, elegance**
Yellow – **Jealousy, fear**

Acacias are confusing. There are the 'true' acacias, commonly known as wattle, many of which are to be found in Australia. And there are the false- or pseudo-acacias, which belong to the genus *Robinia*. Here, though, AMC seems to have lumped them all together.

The white flowered acacia in AMC's list is most likely to be *Robinia pseudo-acacia*, a false acacia which has white, sweet-scented flowers and is also known as the bastard acacia or the LOCUST tree. The yellow flowered version could be any one of the thirty or so Australian wattles (all with yellow ball-like flowers) that, according to Mrs. Loudon, were in cultivation in British nurseries around this time. As to the rose-coloured version, this may be the bristly locust (*Robinia hispida*), a false acacia, or the silk tree (*Acacia julibrissin*), a true acacia, which Mrs. Loudon describes as having flowers that "are like long silk tassels, [which] vary from a pale pink or rose colour, to a delicate lilac".

The true acacia is a source of gum Arabic which Don tells us is highly nutritious: "During the whole time of the gum harvest... the Moors of the desert live almost entirely upon it and experience has proved that six ounces are sufficient for the support of an adult during twenty four hours." It has also been used, since the time of the ancient Egyptians, in cosmetics, inks and dyes, and in medications to treat catarrh, hoarseness, cough, smallpox, and gonorrhoea.

According to Tyas, the wood of the false acacia is "more valued by the [American] cabinet-maker than any other native timber" and has been used for ship-building, for fencing and, by early settlers in Boston, Massachusetts, for building houses.

The name acacia is thought to have been derived either from the Celtic *ac*, meaning a point, or from the Greek *akazo*, to sharpen, since many of the species have spines. *Robinia* was named after Jean Robin, a 17th century French botanist whose son was the first person to cultivate this plant in Europe.

ACANTHUS

Yellow – **Deceit**

Acanthus is a genus of about 30 species of flowering plants, many of which have been grown in English gardens since the start of the 16th century. Most of them have white, blue or purple flowers, and AMC's yellow variety probably refers to hairy bear's breech (*Acanthus hirsutus*) whose flowers are pale yellow.

Over the centuries, acanthus has been used medically to treat a variety of complaints including cramp, gout, and fevers and, used as a poultice, was applied to broken bones, burns and abscesses.

The acanthus leaf was a popular motif for the decoration of columns in ancient Greek architecture. Legend says that the sculptor Callimachus, who lived in the fifth century BCE, saw an acanthus which had grown up round a basket of flowers left on a grave, and this influenced him to use it in his work. It became popular again in the 19th century when William Morris incorporated it into designs for wallpaper and fabrics.

Other names for the plant are bear's breech (or breeches) and brank ursine. The generic name derives from the Greek *akantha*, meaning a thorn.

ACONITE. HELMET FLOWER, MONKSHOOD

Dark blue – **Misanthropy**
Purple – **Chivalry, knighthood**

AMC gives the meaning of "misanthropy" to aconite (dark blue) and, later in the book, "chivalry, knighthood" to helmet flower and monkshood (purple), so it is possible that she did not realise that these names all refer to the same plant.

Mrs. Loudon describes aconite as "tall-growing handsome plants, producing an abundance of dark-blue, purple, or yellow flowers". The common aconite (*Aconitum napellus*), according to Barton, was first cultivated in English gardens around 1596.

Aconite is a poisonous plant, and Don warns us that "Some persons, only by taking in the effluvia of the herb in full flower by the nostrils, have been seized with swooning fits, and have lost their sight for two or three days".

According to Barton, some people believe the generic name comes from the Greek *akonitos* meaning 'devoid of dust', and referring to the rocky soil in which the plant grows, while others think it comes from *akon* a javelin which, in ancient times, would have been dipped in its poison. However, the most likely derivation is from Acone (or Acona), a town on the Black Sea which was famed for growing poisonous herbs.   The plant is also known as wolfsbane.

ALL-HEAL or HERCULES'-WOUNDWORT

Yellow – **Consolation, I will help you**

Hercules-all-heal (*Opopanax chironium*) grows up to ten feet tall and has large flat umbles of yellow flowers. The stem produces an unpleasant smelling resin which has been used in the past to induce vomiting and to treat a variety of complaints including asthma, chronic infections and hysteria.

Culpeper's Complete Herbal (1832) tells us that it is called Hercules' woundwort because the Greek hero Hercules is said to have learned about its medical uses from the centaur Chiron, from whose name the specific name of the plant is derived.

ALMOND BLOSSOM

Pink & white – **Early hope, promise**

Loudon tells us that the almond tree (*Amygdalus*) is a native of North Africa, Asia, Russia and the Levant. It was known to the ancients and was probably introduced into England in the mid 16th century. William Woodville, in his *Medical Botany* (1810), comments that almonds "are said to be difficult of digestion" but that almond oil has been used to treat a variety of complaints including coughs, hoarseness and kidney pain. The German physician Adam Christian Thebesius (1686–1732) even claimed to have cured 12 cases of rabies by administering bitter almonds.

Although English almond trees were cultivated more for their flowers than for their fruit, the nuts seem to have been very popular in the Victorian era. Dolby offers numerous recipes ranging from almond soufflé and almond fritters to almond pickle, and including almond hog's pudding which consists of beef marrow, almonds, orange or rose water, white bread, currants, sugar, spices, wine, cream and egg yolks, all boiled together in pig guts.

ALOE

In bloom, white – **Grief, sorrow**
Out of bloom – **The fulfilment of long hoped-for joy**

Mrs. Loudon distinguishes between true aloes, which are members of the day-lily family (*Asphodelaceae*) and the American aloe, or agave which belongs to the *Amaryllis* family. Unlike the true aloe, which is a succulent that flowers every year, the American aloe only ever flowers once.

Most true aloes have red, orange or yellow flowers, so it is possible that AMC was thinking of the American aloe, which can have cream-coloured flowers. John Frederick Wood, a Fellow of the Horticultural Society described a particularly spectacular one in an 1852 issue of *The Midland Florist*: "A specimen of this aloe (*Agave Americana*) is now in bloom, at Moreby Hall, York, where it forms a very stately and conspicuous object . . . Previous to the formation of the flower-stem, the leaves extended between forty and fifty feet in circumference [and] the heart or central part of the plant . . . [was] two and a half feet in diameter . . . The flower scape is twenty feet in height; and at the elevation of about ten feet the side flower branches, which are twenty-eight in number, commence diverging horizontally from the main column . . . forming an elegant candelabra-like pyramid or outline. . . . It is calculated that the aggregate number of blossoms contained in the twenty-eight fasciles[1] is between four and five thousand."

---

1. Presumably a misprint for fascicles – bunches of flowers growing closely together.

AMARANTH, LOVE LIES BLEEDING

Red – Everlastingly the same
Crimson – Immortality, everlasting

Amaranth and love lies bleeding are both names for the same plant. However, AMC lists them separately describing amaranth as red and love lies bleeding as crimson.

Mrs. Loudon tells us that "The most common species are *Amaranthus hypochondriacus*, the prince's feather, and *A. caudatus*, love-lies-bleeding, both old inhabitants of British gardens", and both having dark crimson flowers. The former, introduced from Virginia in 1739, is the smaller of the two. Its specific name, according to Mrs. Loudon, "signifies melancholy [and] is supposed to allude to the dull reddish-green of the leaves".

Love-lies-bleeding is a native of the East Indies and, says Phillips, was cultivated by Gerard during the reign of Queen Elizabeth, under the name of 'branched flower gentle' while livid amaranth (*A. blitum*) "was cultivated in our gardens previous to 1564".

Mrs. Loudon comments that "The leaves of all the species may be used as spinach, and they are so employed in China".

The generic name comes from the Greek *amarantos*, meaning everlasting, possibly because the flower retains its colour for a long time. The ancient Greek poet Homer tells us that crowns of amaranth were worn by mourners at the funeral of the Greek hero Achilles.

AMARYLLIS (DAY LILY)

Yellow – **Pride with jealousy**

AMC seems to have confused the yellow amaryllis (*Sternbergia lutea*) with the yellow day lily (*Hemerocallis lilioasphodelus*). Phillips tells us that the former "is frequently called the Autumnal Narcissus, or the Star Lily" and it "was brought to this country . . . [in] the time of Queen Elizabeth . . . yet it still continues rare in our parterres".

As to the yellow day lily, in 1596 Gerard reported that "these Lillies do growe in my garden, and also in the gardens of herbalists and lovers of fine and rare plants".

ANEMONE, WIND FLOWER or ZEPHYR FLOWER

Pale pink – **Expectation, coyness, sickness**

The anemone has been grown in English gardens for centuries. Gerard, writing in 1597, describes them as being "without number". AMC may be referring to either the poppy anemone (*Anemone coronaria*) or the star anemone (*Anemone hortensis*) since both include varieties with pink flowers. Glenny comments that the poppy anemone "is imported in large quantities from Holland, grows very dwarf, and comprises many varieties of colour", while Phillips describes the star anemone as "amongst the most elegant as well as the most showy of our early flowers".

The generic name comes from the Greek word *anemos*, meaning wind, and this, says Phillips, is "because it flowers both in a windy season, and in exposed windy situations".

The association of the anemone with sickness comes from ancient times. According to Pliny the 'wise men' of his time advised people to pick the first anemone they saw each year and keep it as a safeguard against illness.

ANGELICA

Light green – **Imagination**

The garden angelica (*Angelica archangelica*) was being grown in English gardens before 1568, and by the early 19th century was, according to Barton, completely naturalised. It has greenish flowers.

Barton says that the stem and roots were eaten raw with butter by Icelanders and that "the fresh stalks of the Angelica are made by confectioners into an agreeable sweetmeat". Nowadays, it is still possible to buy candied angelica, but it is not nearly as popular as it once was. Dolby offers us recipes, among others, for angelica cakes, jelly, paste and a liqueur which involved soaking the angelica in brandy and water, with mace, cinnamon and cloves and, after a week, distilling it, adding sugar and more water and, finally, straining it through a 'jelly-bag'.

The wild angelica (*A. sylvestris*) has been used in tanning, and a tincture made from the leaves will dye wool a golden yellow.

The name comes from the Latin *angelicus*, meaning angelic, because the plant was thought to be protective against contagious diseases. Gerard believed that it would also protect against "witchcraft and inchantments" and would cure "the bitings of mad dogs and all other venomous beasts". The specific name, *archangelica*, implies the superiority of that species over all the others in the genus.

APPLE BLOSSOM & APPLE

Blossom, pink & white – **Beware**
Apple (a fine one) – **Temptation**

Don comments that it is not known where the cultivated apple (*Pyrus malus*) came from originally, although it was probably introduced into England by the Romans. By the first century CE twenty two varieties were known.

In 1664 John Evelyn published a brief work entitled *Pomona ... Concerning Fruit Trees, in Relation to Cyder*, in which he wrote that "it was through the plain industry of one Harris, a fruiterer to Henry VIII, that the fields and environs of about 30 towns in Kent only, were planted with fruit from Flanders, to the universal benefit and improvement of the county." Later in the same volume there is a *Kalendarium Hortense or Gardener's Almanack* which lists large numbers of varieties of apples, many with wonderful names such as leather coat, chestnut apple, fennel apple, go-no-further, cat's head, greatbelly, belle-et-bonne, honey-meal, cinnamon apple, violet apple and sheep's snout.

Edmund Gibson, in *Churches of Dove and Homelacy* (1727) attributes the Hereford cider orchards to Lord Scudamore who, when he was ambassador to the French court in the early 17th century, took cuttings from Normandy cider apple trees for the farmers of Herefordshire to graft onto root stock.

Loudon considers the apple tree to be less handsome in form than the pear tree, but its blossom to be much more ornamental and fragrant. He also reminds us of the many culinary uses of the apple – including the manufacture of wine, cider, marmalades, jellies, fritters and tarts. Boiled apple pulp, baked with flour, and fermented for twelve hours, is "said to make an excellent bread, very palatable and light". Therapeutically, boiled or roasted apples can be used as a laxative. The bark of the tree can be used to form a yellow dye and the wood "being fine-grained and very compact, is well adapted for turning and for staining, so as to be used as a substitute for ebony".

APPLE, THE CRABB

Green – **Sourness**

Mrs. Loudon describes the crab apple as "very ornamental" and mentions two species whose fruit is green when ripe, the Chinese crab (*Pyrus spectabilis*) and the sweet crab apple (*Malus coronaria*). Her husband, J. C. Loudon, comments that the fruit of the Chinese crab "is only fit to eat when in a state of incipient decay, at which period it takes the colour and taste of the medlar".

The fruit was made into a drink, and also a vinegar, in both France and England, while a yellow dye was produced from the bark.

APPLE, THE THORN APPLE

Pink – **Deceitful charms**

The thorn apple is not an apple but, rather, the name given to a number of plants in the genus *Datura*. Its prickly seed pod contains highly toxic seeds. The flowers are white or, less commonly, yellow, lilac or purple. However, seven species of very similar plants, originally classified as *Datura*, were transferred into a new genus, *Brugmansia*, in 1805. Known also as angel's trumpet, these are shrubs with attractive, scented flowers and, since some have pink flowers, it may be that AMC was confusing the two genera.

The common thorn apple (*D. stramonium*) is a native of the USA and was first grown in England around 1590, when Gerard raised some plants from seed. By the early 19th century, it had become naturalised and was frequently found growing wild. Its common names include devil's trumpet, devil's apple, and Jamestown-weed or jimson weed.

Phillips calls the thorn apple a "dangerous narcotic plant" and tells how "Indian princes have been known to make use of it to render their rivals stupid, and then to expose them to the people, to show how incapable they are to govern".

ASPEN LEAF

Dark green – I tremble

The European aspen is a member of the poplar family, *Populus tremula*. John Aikin, in *The Woodland Companion* (1815) writes "This species is remarkable for the constant tremulous motion of the leaves with the lightest breeze, which is owing to the length and slenderness of their foot-stalks". The tree, he says, is large "and its roots spread so near the ground, throwing out numerous shoots, that they suffer nothing else to grow near it".

The wood, which is very white, light and soft, was used to make milk-pails and wooden shoes.

Phillips tells us that the aspen was sometimes called rattler by country people, because of the noise made by its leaves. The name aspen is derived from *espe*, the German word for the poplar. A legend that the aspen leaf trembles from shame and horror, because the cross on which Jesus was crucified was made from its wood, is probably why, in other floral dictionaries, it has been given the meanings of groaning and lamentation.

ASPHODEL

Yellow – **Unceasing regret**

The most common yellow-flowered asphodel is king's spear (*Asphodeline lutea*). Surprisingly few gardening books of the period mention it, although Mrs. Loudon describes it as ornamental and an article an 1877 issue of *The Journal of Horticulture and Cottage Gardener* declares the double flowered variety to be very desirable.

Phillips tells us that the asphodel root, roasted with salt and oil, was, to the ancient Greeks and Romans, what the potato is to us now. However, the Greek poet Hesiod (born in 776 BCE) liked the root mashed with figs.

Pliny asserted that asphodel roots boiled with barley was the perfect diet for people with consumption. Other therapeutic claims over the centuries have included the belief that the plant was an antidote to snake bites and scorpion stings, that the roots, burnt to ashes and mixed with duck fat, would cure alopecia, and that various preparations of the plant would act as a diuretic and would cure ringworm and gout.

Phillips tells us that "The asphodel is said to be useful in driving away rats and mice, which have so great an antipathy to this plant, that, if their holes be stopped up with it, they will die rather than pass it".

The ancients believed that the asphodel was the food of the departed and, for this reason, it tended to be planted round graves. In the *Odyssey*, Homer wrote of the meadows of asphodel where the "souls and shadows" of the dead dwelled. The Romans would sometimes plant it to protect their houses against sorcery.

AURICULA

Purple-edged white – **Painting**

A native of the Swiss Alps, the auricula was first cultivated, says Phillips, by Flemish gardeners, after which it "was eagerly sought after by all the florists of Europe". By 1597, Gerard reported it as growing in London gardens. In the first half of the 19th century, Lancashire was the centre of auricula-growing, supplying most of the florists in the London area. Both Mrs. Loudon and Phillips express their admiration of the range of colours available.

The leaves of the plant are said to resemble the ears of a bear and Gerard refers to it as "beare's-eares, or mountaine cowslips" and "*Auricula Ursiflora*".

SEE ALSO POLYANTHUS AND PRIMROSE

AZALIA

White – **Temperance**

Mrs. Loudon comments that several attempts have been made to naturalise these "beautiful flowering plants" which are native to North America, Turkey and China, "particularly at High Clerc, near Newbury, the seat of Lord Carnarvon". The first Chinese azalea was imported into England in 1808 and was soon followed by other species.

B

BACHELOR'S BUTTON

With stalk & leaves, yellow – **Single from choice**
Without leaves, yellow – **Single from necessity**

Bachelor's button is the name given to several members of the BUTTERCUP family (*Ranunculus*) as well as to a variety of other flowers. Barton says that the name refers to a cultivated variety of *RANUNCULUS* with double flowers, while Don identifies the white double *Ranunculus platanifolius* as both the bachelor's button and FAIR MAIDS OF FRANCE. Mrs. Loudon mentions "*Ranunculus aconitifolius*, the white-flowered bachelor's button, an old inhabitant of British gardens" and "*Ranunculus acris flore pleno*, the double-flowered yellow bachelor's button", which may be the one that AMC is thinking of.

BALM

Light green – **Compassion, sympathy**

Several species of *Melissa* are called balm, but the best known of these is the common or lemon balm (*M. officinalis*). A native of southern Europe, it has been cultivated in English gardens "from time immemorial" according to Barton. Kent describes *Melissa* as a "darling of the bees . . . very pretty when in flower; particularly that which is called the great-flowered balm, which has large purple flowers", and she bemoans the fact that it is seldom found in flower gardens. The beauty of the lemon balm, however, is in its lemon-scented leaves, while its flowers are small, white and fairly insignificant. So it seems likely that AMC, in describing the plant as green, is referring to this species.

A seemingly unique property of balm was discovered by Nehemiah Grew (1641-1712), known as 'the Father of Plant Anatomy'. He observed that if the leaves of the lemon balm were put into water they would turn it purplish red, while putting them into alcohol would give "a pure and perfect green".

Over the centuries *Melissa* has been used to treat a wide variety of complaints and Barton tells us that it is often used "more or less successfully" in cases of dizziness, fainting and paralysis, while the Arabs have used it to promote cheerfulness. Kent says that it was "formerly considered as an efficacious remedy in hypochondria, but it is not so highly esteemed by the physicians of the present day. It proves, at least, an innocent substitute for foreign tea".

The generic name is the Latin word for a honey bee, and Kent tells us that the plant "was one of the herbs directed by the ancients to be rubbed on the hive, to render it agreeable to the swarm".

BALM OF GILEAD

Light green – **Succour, relief**

The traditional balm of Gilead, according to Don, was the tree *Commiphora gileadensis* which, before being introduced into Palestine, was known as the balsam of Mecca.

Barton cites the balm of Gilead fir (*Abies Balsamea*), describing it as "an elegant tree which . . . yields the Canada balsam". But an article in *The Family Magazine*, published in Cincinnati in 1837, says that, while the resin of the silver fir is sold under the name of balm of Gilead, "every body knows" that the true balm of Gilead is produced by *Commiphora gileadensis*.

Despite these assertions, it seems likely that AMC is referring to *Cedronella canariensis,* a close relative of *Melissa officinalis* (described under BALM). Given the name of balm of Gilead because of its aromatic leaves, it was, according to the anonymous author of *The Garden* (1831), used in nose-gays because of its "delightful fragrance".

BALSAM

Variegated – **Pettishness**
Red – **Impatience**
Yellow – **Jealous resolves**
White – **I forgive you**

The *Balsamina*, also known as *Impatiens,* were popular with the Victorians and still find favour as a garden and house-plant in the 21st century, one species being the busy Lizzy.

William Turner, in his *New Herball* (1564), reports that balsams are to be found in English gardens and, over 200 years later, Mrs. Loudon says they have "long been great favourites in our greenhouses", while Phillips comments on their "petals of scarlet, crimson, brick red, purple white, variegated, parti-coloured or delicate blush."

There are various possibilities for AMC's red balsam. Mrs. Loudon lists several, including the common balsam (*Impatiens balsamina*) and the scarlet balsam (*I. balsamina var. coccinea*), as well as the Nepaul balsam (*I. glandulifera*) which was introduced in 1837, and the three petal balsam (*I. tripetala*) a very showy species, introduced in 1825.

Don tells us that the common balsam has some white flowered varieties. As to the yellow balsam, AMC may have been referring to jewelweed (*I. capensis*) which was introduced from North America in 1818 and which Mrs. Loudon describes as "the handsomest species of the genus, having dark yellow flowers".

The Garden Flowers of the Year, published by the Religious Tract Society in 1799, describes the variegated balsams which "with their . . . spikes of delicately-tinted flowers, bloom in July". The balsam grows wild, it says, in India, China, Japan, and the West Indies "and is used in Cochin China by the ladies, who make of its flowers an infusion, with which to cleanse and perfume the hair. The great attention paid by the females of the east to personal decoration, renders this a valued flower, for they tinge their nails with the deep pink dye which its petals, when mixed with alum-water[1], will furnish. The flowers are white, red, or purple or variegated and striped with all these hues".

---

1. Water containing aluminium sulphate

BARBERRY

Red – **Sourness**

The barberry is the fruit of the *Berberis vulgaris* shrub. Don says of it: "The berries are so acid that birds will not eat them. The Barberry, however, is cultivated for the sake of these, which are pickled and used for garnishing dishes; and being boiled with sugar they form an agreeable rob[2] or jelly, they were formerly used as a dry sweet-meat as well as in sugar-plumbs and comfits".

Mrs. Loudon declares *B. vulgaris* to be a most elegant plant, with "rich yellow blossoms and . . . long red fruit, which at a distance might be mistaken for the flowers of a scarlet Fuchsia". All *Berberis* species have yellow flowers so, clearly, AMC is referring to the fruit.

The common barberry is native to the British Isles – Barton reports that "it is found in woods and hedges in many parts of England and Scotland, and near Fermoy in Ireland".

Preparations of barberry were, in the past, credited with curing various inflammatory diseases, urinary tract infections, typhus, and even the plague.

---

2. Syrup

BASIL, SWEET

Olive green – **Good wishes**

Basil (*Ocimum basilicum*) is a member of the MINT family. Don comments that "The leaves . . . are gathered for culinary purposes . . . to be used in highly seasoned dishes. A few leaves are sometimes introduced into salad, and not infrequently into soups".

In her *Flora's Dictionary* (1830), Elizabeth Washington Gamble Wirt describes basil as a hardy annual and a native of India and Persia. Several species of basil, she says, "are held in superstitious veneration by the Hindoos, and are used in their religious ceremonies", while all the species are valued "for their fragrant, aromatic, and sweet scent".

Many floral dictionaries give basil the meaning of 'hatred'. Why a sweet smelling plant should be associated with such a meaning is not entirely clear, although it has been suggested that it is because of an association of its name with the basilisk – a mythical reptile that could kill a man simply by looking at him.

BAY

Leaf, dark green – **I change but in death**
Wreath, dark green – **Reward of merit**
Branch, dark green – **A poet's glory**

It is not know when the bay tree (*Laurus nobilis*) was first cultivated in England, but Phillips believes it to have been during the Roman occupation. In the 16th century, he says, it was customary "to strew the floors of distinguished persons … with bay-leaves" but, even so, it doesn't seem to have been a common plant at that time. Phillips goes on to say that the most handsome bay he had seen had been planted "by a lady at Tarring, in Sussex, on her wedding-day [and which] sent up its spiral top higher than her dwelling, in less than twenty years; affording ample shade to her playful and numerous offspring . . . to say nothing of the aromatic taste its leaves give to her baked herrings".

Mrs. Loudon calls the bay "a very handsome evergreen shrub or low tree" and mentions that the leaves are used to flavour custards.

The ancients believed that the bay protected against lightning and it is said that the Roman Emperor Tiberius, who was frightened of thunder storms, when they occurred, would lie under his bed with branches of bay over his head. Phillips says that, even in the 19th century "we have known it planted by our own villagers as a protection from fire".

The bay was also credited with cleansing the air and protecting against contagion so that, during a plague, the Emperor Claudius moved his court to Laurentium where many bay trees grew.

In the time of the Greek philosopher Theophrastus (c. 371 – c. 287 BCE) people sucked bay leaves to protect themselves against misfortune and believed that the death of bay trees heralded a catastrophe. Before the death of the

Emperor Nero all the bay trees in the area are said to have withered and died (although, given the reputation of Nero, it may only have been the trees who saw his death as a catastrophe).

Several words and phrases derive from the ancient use of the bay. The crowning with a wreath of *Laurus* of those who had distinguished themselves in the arts gives us the expression "poet laureate". The French word *baccalaureat*, referring to an academic achievement comes from the Latin *bacca* (berry) and *Laurus*. From this, the word bachelor (as in Bachelor of Arts) was derived.

BEE ORCHIS (clover)

Red – **Industry**

Although originally in the *Orchis* genus, the bee orchid (along with others whose flowers resemble insects) was transferred to the *Ophrys* genus in the late 18th century. Its full Latin name is *Ophrys apifera* and it is pink, not red as AMC states. Presumably AMC has included "(clover)" as that flower, too, has a meaning of 'industry'.

Phillips describes the flower as resembling "a small humble bee" in shape and colour. It is, he says, a native of several parts of Europe, and grows in England near woods and in meadows. Maund tells us that "In districts where chalk or limestone prevail, it is not uncommon; but is scarcely ever met with elsewhere". It has, he says, "always been an object of admiration, as one of our native plants".

Pliny maintained that the generic name, *Ophrys*, which comes from the Greek word for eyebrow or eyelash, was given because the plant was used by women to darken their eyebrows. Maund thinks it more likely that the name relates to "the fringe of the inner sepals being like an eyelash". The specific name comes from the Greek *apis*, a bee.

SEE ALSO ORCHIS

BEGONIA

Pink with yellow centre – **Flower of the heart, so called from the shape of the leaves**

The begonia was introduced into England in 1777 and, 60 years later, in his *Floral Cabinet*, Frederic Westcott wrote that probably all of the 50 or so known species had now been imported to Europe and most "may be procured in England from the nursery-men and florists, with whom they have always been favourite objects of culture for their beauty and singularity".

The *Begonia* genus, says Westcott, is made up of deciduous shrubs and herbaceous plants, all native to tropical countries. The *Annals of Horticulture* for 1847 lists 19 species with pink flowers, native to Jamaica, South America, China, Mexico and Nepal. These include the pennywort begonia (*B. hydrocotylifolia*) and the hollyhock begonia (*B. gracilis*), which the writer declares to be among the most beautiful, and the common Rex begonia vine (*Cissus discolor*) which, he says, "may be cultivated to considerable perfection in sitting-rooms". So it may be that this is the species to which AMC is referring.

Westcott also believes that the therapeutic properties of the begonia deserve to be better known since the astringent, slightly bitter roots "have been used successfully in haemorrhages, in scorbutic affections, and in certain fevers".

One of the pink-flowered species, *B. minor*, has leaves that are used in cooking in the same way as sorrel and, in Jamaica, it is known as sorrel of the woods, while the root is called wild rhubarb.

The generic name was given in honour of Michel Begon (1638–1710) a French plant collector.

BELLADONNA LILY

Orange & pink – Silence

The belladonna lily (*Amaryllis belladonna*), also known as the Jersey Lily, has pink flowers, not orange and pink. However, I wonder whether AMC, although listing it as 'Belladonna Lily', was thinking of it more in terms of a 'Jersey Lily'. If so, she might have believed that it was the same plant as *Nerine sarniensis*, which is also known as the Jersey lily (although more often as the Guernsey lily) and which has red or orange flowers.

A native of South Africa, the belladonna lily was introduced into Britain in the early 18th century. Kent tells us that it grows "on shady hills, and by the margins of streams . . . and is very common in the Italian gardens, particularly in the neighbourhood of Florence". She describes it as being very fragrant and flowering around the end of September or the beginning of October.

BILBERRY or WORTLEBERRY

Dark purple – **Treachery**

Mrs. Loudon describes this plant, *Vaccinium myrtillus*, as a dwarf shrub "with pretty drooping heath-like flowers and generally showy fruit". Culpeper says that two sorts are common in England, having either black or red berries. Since the flowers of the bilberry are white, it seems that AMC's 'dark purple' is referring to the black fruit.

Maund believes that fresh bilberries "possess a flavour of flatness that prevents their becoming favourites with many" but, used in tarts, they are "superior, in the estimation of many persons, to the Gooseberry or Currant". Don tells us that in the north and west of England and in Scotland the berries are "eaten in tarts or with cream, or made into jellies" while, perhaps unsurprisingly, "In Devonshire the berries are eaten with clotted cream".

Other names for the bilberry include bleaberry, whortleberry, whorts, windberry, black-whorts, hurts, and hurtleberry.

BIRD'S FOOT

Pale yellow – **Light as a bird**

Culpepper writes about a plant which he calls bird's foot, describing it as a "small herb [which] grows not above a span[3] high with many branches spread upon the ground, set with many wings of small leaves. The flowers grow upon the branches, many small ones of a pale yellow colour being set a-head together, which afterwards turn into small jointed pods, well resembling the claw of small birds, whence it took its name". This seems to be a description of what is usually called bird's foot trefoil (*Lotus corniculatus*) which is probably what AMC is referring to.

In 1785, which was a summer of drought, William Marshall recorded his thoughts on bird's foot trefoil in *The Rural Economy of the Midland Counties*: "This plant, notwithstanding the extreme dryness of this season, flourishes in a singular manner, in the most exposed situations. On bowling greens and mown lawns, it is almost the only green herbage left (the daisey excepted) . . . In meadows and pasturegrounds, it is, this year, particularly abundant, or perhaps more accurately speaking, particularly conspicuous. A very strong deep tap root is evidently the cause of its thus resisting drought."

---

3. Approximately 9 inches

BIRDWEED

White – **Protect me, insinuation**

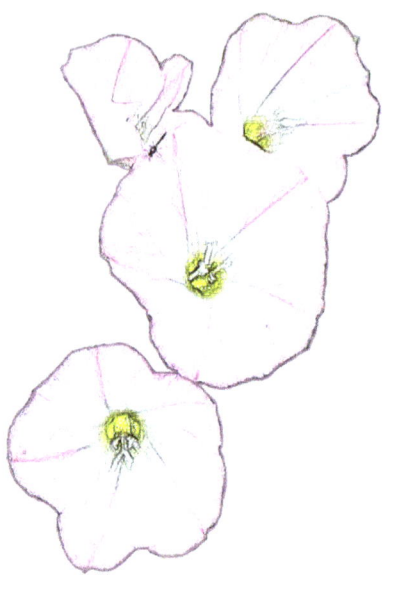

Although birdweed is another name for KNOT GRASS, here it is probably a misprint for 'bindweed' since one of AMC's meanings (insinuation) is given to bindweed by other floral dictionaries.

Wilkinson describes bindweed (*Convolvulus*) as a "beautiful plant; which wreathes in the most graceful festoons over our hedgerows, or around the gooseberry and currant-bushes in our gardens, opening its large tender white or rose-tinted blossoms in the bright sunshine". Phillips, however, is less enamoured with it, describing the white CONVOLVULUS (*C. arvensis*) as "more formidable .. than the great bindweed, which principally confines itself to the hedgerow, whereas the *Arvensis* travels over the whole field, entwining itself around the stalks of corn for support, or upholding itself by the blades of grass, or whatever comes in its way, not even refusing to embrace the nettle".

Gerard calls *Convolvulus* "unprofitable weedes, and hurtfulle unto each thing that groweth next them" and denounces those who use it therapeutically as "runnagat physick-mongers, quacksalvers, old women leeches, and abusers of physick, and deceivers of people!"

Bindweed's unattractive features led to its being known by some as devil's-guts. Other popular names included cornbind, withbind, barebind, and hedge-bells.

BITTER-SWEET or nightshade

Purple with yellow spot – **Truth**

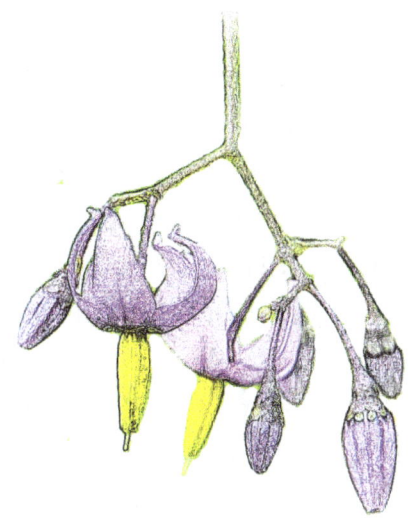

Bittersweet (*Solanum dulcamara*) is also known as bitter nightshade, climbing nightshade and woody nightshade, and is in a different genus from deadly NIGHTSHADE (*Atropa belladonna*). Mrs. Loudon describes it as a "climbing shrub, with pretty flowers and red berries, common in hedges".

The plant has been used as a herbal remedy but Culpeper warns: "Have a care you mistake not the deadly Nightshade for this; if you know it not . . . let them both alone, and take no harm." Barton reports that the berries "are looked upon with terror by the peasantry" who call them "poison-berries."

The name bitter-sweet and the specific name (from the Latin *dulcis*, sweet, and *amara*, bitter) have been given because, if any part of the plant is chewed, it produces first a bitter and then a sweet taste.

BLACKTHORN

White – **Danger, difficulty**

The blackthorn (*Prunus spinosa*) is a shrub or small tree, otherwise known as the sloe or wild plum. Barton tells us that it is frequently found in hedges and coppices, has pure white blossoms and "flowers earlier than most other plants".

The plant has had numerous uses. The wood was used for "turnery-ware, teeth of rakes, and walking sticks". The bark, which was said to stop cheese from going rotten, was also made into a red dye and was used for tanning leather. The young leaves "form one of the most popular substitutes for China tea" and the berries can be "made into a pleasant wine". The juice of the fruit "makes a good marking-ink for linen or woollen cloth," and if iron sulphate is added it turns into a good quality permanent black writing ink. However, Barton warns, sloes are also used "by fraudulent dealers to adulterate port wine".

Its English name relates to the spines found on its branches. A country name for it, according to Barton, is scroggs.

BLUE BELL (CAMPANULA)

Bright blue – **Constancy**

Two plants have, for centuries, laid claim to the title 'bluebell'. One is *Hyacinthoides non-scripta*, the 'English' bluebell, and the other is the HAREBELL (*Campanula rotundifolia*), the 'Scottish' bluebell. Perhaps AMC's note that she is referring to *Campanula* indicates that she is Scottish in more than just her surname. But, even among those who purport to be experts, there is a great deal of confusion between the two plants – Phillips writes that "The English Hyacinth, *Nutans*, or *Non Scriptus* [is] commonly called the Harebell".

However, the author of *A Botanical Ladder for the Young* (1845) is clear that the bluebell is "this pretty little flower [which] is found throughout Europe. Its root is a white bulb: it bears generally blue flowers, but now and then we find them white or pink. It is a different flower, you see, from the hare-bell, and found in a different class".

Don, writing about *C. rotundifolia*, says that "the juice expressed from the flower makes a very good blue ink . . . The roots are eaten by children in many parts".

BLUE BOTTLE (CENTAURY)

Light blue – **Delicacy**

The blue-bottle or corn-bottle (*Centaurea cyanus*) is one of the many flowers known by the name of 'BACHELOR'S BUTTON'.

Phillips tells us that "the art of the florist has multiplied its florets, and varied its colour so much, that it is now become one of the summer favourites of the parterre . . . In its natural wild state the flowers are of a fine ultramarine blue". Mrs. Loudon comments that the varieties "most generally grown in gardens are the lilac, the pink, and the dark purple" so it seems likely that AMC is referring to the wild flower.

In the 16th century, the blue bottle was also known as blueblow, baptisecula and – because it was believed to blunt the sickles used for harvesting the corn – hurt-sickle. In Scotland it was called blue bonnets.

According to Barton, *Centaurea* received its generic name "because its virtues were supposed to have been discovered by the centaur Chiron, one of the earliest cultivators of botany and medicine".

BORAGE

Light blue – **Bluntness**

Mrs. Loudon describes borage as "annual and perennial plants with blue, white, or pink flowers" and Glenny recommends planting it in order to attract bees. Don tells us that it came originally from Aleppo, but has now become naturalised and can be found growing wild on dunghills and heaps of rubbish. Wilkinson, however, identifies common borage (*Borago officinalis*) as a British species.

Barton tells us that young leaves can be used in salads or as pot-herbs and, combined with lemon, sugar, wine and water, will make "the old English beverage, called a 'cool tankard'". In Gerard's time it was customary to use the flowers "in sallads to exhilarate and make the mind glad. There be also many things made of them . . . for the driving away of sorrowe".

Barton believes that the English name is related to this property of gladdening the mind, being derived from the Latin *cor*, heart, and *ago*, to bring.

BRAMBLE

White – **Envy**

The term 'bramble' can relate to many species of *Rubus*, most of which have white flowers. Don identifies the common bramble as *R. vulgaris* while Barton names it as *R. fruticosus*, "a sturdy shrub, common in every hedge in this country".

Barton tells us that the bramble is used to form hedges, while the shoots are used by thatchers and by makers of mats and straw beehives. The fruit, he says, "is made into pies and puddings by the cottager", and Don adds sweetmeats, jams, tarts and sauces to the list. Both mention the drinks that can be made from blackberries – "a cordial spirituous liquor" and "a good and pleasant wine". Barton adds that they also make "an excellent gargle in sore throats, especially where there is ulceration".

BRANCH OF THORNS

Brown – **Punishment**

A 'branch of thorns' could, of course, mean a branch from any one of a hundred common thorny plants, such as the BRAMBLE. However, AMC's meaning (which differs from that in many other floral dictionaries) makes me wonder if she is relating this to Christ's crown of thorns.

There are two plants which are said to have been the source of the crown of thorns – the jujube tree (*Ziziphus spina-Christi*), a native of North Africa, Palestine, and Ethiopia, and the Jerusalem thorn (*Paliurus spina-christi*), a native of southern Europe and western Asia. Opinions as to which was actually used for the crown of thorns are divided. The jujube tree is common in the East, and has large numbers of sharp spines but Don tells us that "many travellers of credit" have affirmed that the Jerusalem thorn "is one of the most common shrubs in the country of Judaea, and from the pliability of its branches . . . may easily be wrought into any figure".

We can never know who is right but, more relevant, is the fact that Don calls the Jerusalem thorn "these handsome shrubs . . . well fitted for shrubberies", suggesting that they were to be found in some 19th century English gardens.

BROOM OF THE HEATH

Yellow – **Meekness**

This is the common broom (*Cytisus scoparius*). Barton refers to it as an "ornamental shrub [that] grows abundantly in dry sandy pastures".

The plant had many uses, and presumably got its common name because it was frequently made into besoms[4]. The twigs were used for thatching while cabinet makers used the older wood for veneering. The branches were used in the tanning of leather and – in France and Italy – as a source of fibre from which paper or a

---

4. Traditional broomsticks consisting of a bundle of twigs tied to a stout pole

coarse cloth could be made. The flower buds were sometimes pickled like capers and the roasted seeds used as a substitute for coffee. Broom also made a useful winter fodder for sheep.

An alternative name for *Cytisus* is *Genista* and it is often said that the English house of Plantagenet took its name from the nickname given to Geoffrey of Anjou (the father of the first Plantaganet king, Henry II) who wore a sprig of broom (*'planta genista'*) in his hat. But Wilkinson maintains that it was, in fact, Geoffrey's father Fulke, who started the tradition, by wearing the plant as a symbol of humility, when he made a penitential pilgrimage to the Holy Land.

BUGLOSS

Red – **Falsehood**

Several plants in the *Anchusa* genus are known as bugloss. Most have blue or purplish flowers. AMC may be referring to the common bugloss (*A. officinalis*) which sometimes has dark pink flowers. But it is also possible that she is thinking of viper's bugloss which is the name given to a number of species in the *Echium* genus, some of which have red flowers.

Another possibility is that she is thinking of the rouge which used to be made from bugloss roots. Phillips tells us that it is this use that has made bugloss the emblem of falsehood, and he describes the use of rouge as "the barbarous practice of disfiguring ... the countenance by ... an unnatural stain." Rouge was being made from bugloss as far back as the second century and was popular because it did not easily rub off and was kinder to the skin than other sorts of rouge. However, Phillips warns that "all kinds of paint for the face are dangerous, for, however delicately it may be used in the first instance, it is sure to increase . . . We have remembered several ladies, who, from having been accustomed to the use of rouge from an early age increased the colour from year to year until their cheeks were but a few degrees behind those of Grimaldi[5] in a Christmas pantomime".

The English name is derived from the Greek *bouglossos*, meaning ox-tongue, which the leaves are said to resemble.

BULLRUSH

Brown - **Docility**

It seems that, even in large gardens with ponds or streams, bulrushes were not popular in the 19th century. Loudon in *The Suburban Gardener* (1838) writes of having them in his own garden, growing in pots, with other aquatic plants, "the bullrush growing several feet higher than the end of the hot house". But, other than this, the earliest reference I can find is in George Bentham's *Handbook of the British Flora* (1858). Bentham lists the great bulrush (*Typha latifolia*), also known as cat's tail or reedmace and the lesser bulrush (*Typha angustifolia*). The former

---

[5]. Joseph Grimaldi (1778 – 1837), English actor and comedian, developed the role of the clown in pantomimes and created the whiteface make-up still used by circus clowns

he describes as growing wild "On the margins of ponds, lakes and watery ditches nearly all over the globe [and] . . . abundant in England, Ireland and southern Scotland but not in the Highland districts" and the latter as less common and probably confined to England and Ireland.

J. T. Boswell in his *English Botany* (1870) list four other species known as bulrushes. One, the lakeshore bulrush (*Schoenoplectus lacustris*) "grows in clear stagnant water, throwing up numerous round stems". Large quantities, says Boswell, were imported from Holland "for making the bottoms of chairs, mats, and hassocks, . . . for thatching buildings . . . [and] by coopers for placing between the staves of casks." The old name for the plant, he tells us, was "bumbles".

Boswell also mentions the triangular bulrush (*S. triqueter*) and the keeled bulrush (*Isolepis carinata*), both of which were to be found on river banks in the south east of England, and the great bulrush (*S. tabernamontani*) which was common around the coasts of England and Ireland.

Other than Loudon's brief comment, none of these plants is described as being grown in gardens, and it is impossible to say to which of them AMC is referring.

BUTTERCUP, or, as Shakspeare calls them, King-cups

Golden yellow – **Youthful joy**

Don tells us that the meadow buttercup (*Ranunculus acris*), the creeping buttercup (*R. repens*) and the bulbous buttercup (*R. bulbosus*) are "called vulgarly butter-flower, or butter-cup under a notion that the yellow colour of butter is owing to these plants. It is richness of the pasture that communicates this colour and not these flowers, which the cattle seldom eat".

All buttercups are acrid, particularly the roots, and Don says that they are used to treat gouty joints since they "raise blisters with less pain and more safety than Spanish flies[6]". They had also been known to be used by beggars "to blister their skin, with a view of exciting compassion".

To the popular names already given, Don adds gold-cups, and "the cuckoo buds of yellow hue of Shakspeare". Barton notes that the generic name is derived from the Latin *rana*, a frog, "because many of the species delight in damp situations where frogs abound".

SEE ALSO KINGCUP, RANUNCULUS

BUTTERFLY ORCHIS

Brown & pink – **Pleasure, gaiety**

Several plants are known as butterfly ORCHIS but the only pink one is *Anacamptis papilionacea* (formerly known as *Orchis papilionacea*), which grows in dry, stony ground in southern Europe and northern Africa. Barton claims the lesser butterfly orchis (*Platanthera bifolia*) as a British native "not unfrequent in moist copses and pastures in June, and . . . celebrated for the delicious fragrance of its flowers", but its flowers are white.

---

6. An irritant made from crushed Spanish fly beetles.

C

CABBAGE

Green – **Gain, profit**
Red – **Advantage**

An Encyclopaedia of Plants (1829) tells us that "The cabbage tribe is of all the classes of cultivated culinary vegetables, the most ancient as well as the most extensive." It was, says *The Edinburgh Encyclopaedia* (1830), "a favourite vegetable with the Romans" who probably introduced an Italian variety into Britain, although "to the inhabitants of the north of Scotland, cabbages were first made known by the soldiers of the enterprising Cromwell". According to Gilbert White's *Natural History of Selborne* "our Saxon ancestors certainly had some sort of cabbage, because they call the month of February sprout-cale".

The *Edinburgh Encyclopaedia* assures us that the original, or wild, cabbage (*Brassica oleracea*) which grows around the English coast is "good to eat early in the spring . . . [but] must be boiled in two waters to remove the saltness". It also lists some popular varieties of the time, including "Small early dwarf, Large early Yorkshire, . . . Early Battersea, Imperial, . . . Hollow sugar-loaf, and Long-sided".

There seems no doubt that cabbage was a popular vegetable in the 19th century. Dolby includes no fewer than 37 recipes for preparing it, including cabbage à la creme, cabbage and milk soup, cabbage pudding, syrup of red cabbage, cabbage stewed à l'espagnole, and cabbage en surprise, which consists of chestnuts and sausages, wrapped in boiled cabbage leaves, then stewed in stock with root vegetables, onions and herbs, and served with "a good butter sauce".

CACTUS

Brilliant pink – **Warmth of affection**
Grandiflora, brilliant crimson – **Warmth of gratitude**

Mrs. Loudon tells us that cacti "have been distributed by modern botanists over numerous genera, which they are still continually changing and rearranging". The influx of cacti (mainly from the tropical regions of the Americas) was comparatively recent, very few being known in the 18th and early 19th centuries "but now [1846] above five hundred living species are to be found in a single collection; and numbers of new species are being sent home by collectors every year".

Perhaps one of the reasons for the large numbers being introduced to Britain was the ease of transport. According to Mrs. Loudon "if collectors cut off the top of any of the Cacti which they may find in flower, and send it with the flower on it . . . [the seeds will] ripen on the passage home, from the supply of moisture contained in the divided part".

With so many cacti available, it is hard to say which species AMC is referring to. There was a *Cactus grandiflorus* (now *Selenicereus grandiflorus*) but this has white flowers. And there are numerous species with bright pink or bright crimson flowers.

Don mentions the rat tail cactus (*Aporocactus flagelliformis*) which, he says, is very common in gardens, with red or pink flowers that are "so beautiful, and are produced in such profusion, that the plant is worth being conveyed into the house whilst in flower, to adorn any of the rooms". He also describes a species of torch thistle, the scarlet-flowered sun cactus (*Disocactus speciosus*), as "a most splendid plant when in flower, and . . . now very common in the gardens". Glenny is somewhat less enthusiastic about torch thistles, saying that they are "grotesque-looking objects when out of flower" but he agrees that *D. speciosus* is "the most gaudy of the genus . . . [with] large splendid blossoms of a rich crimson scarlet".

CALYCANTHUS

Light blue – **Benevolence**

It seems likely that AMC had never seen a calycanthus, since it is not light blue. Two species are mentioned in the books of the period – the Carolina allspice (*Calycanthus floridus*), whose flowers Mrs. Loudon describes as dark brownish purple, and Don as "lurid purple", and the Japanese allspice (*Chimonanthus praecox*) whose flowers are yellow.

Philip Miller, in the 1759 edition of his *Gardener's Dictionary*, tells us that the Carolina allspice is the only species of the genus at present in England. He lists it under the name of basteria, saying "As this plant had no proper Title given to it . . . I have given it this in Honour of my worthy Friend Dr. Job Baster, FRS of Zurick Zee, in Holland, who is a Gentleman well skilled in Botany, and has a fine Garden stored with rare Plants". The plant, he tells us, was first introduced by Mark Catesby (c. 1682–1749), an English botanist and author of *The Natural History of Carolina*, who had found it "some hundred Miles on the Back of Charles Town, in Carolina".

Carolina allspice, says Miller, was very scarce in England until about 1755 when the number of plants being imported from Charleston started to increase. Miller seems to have a poor opinion of allspice: "It seldom rises more than four Feet high in this Country . . . the Flowers . . . are of a sullen purple Colour, and have a disagreeable Scent". However, Glenny considers them "remarkable for the fragrant spice like odour of their brownish blossoms". The bark also has an aromatic scent, says Miller, "from whence the Inhabitants of Carolina gave it the Title of All-spice, by which it is generally known in the Nurseries near London".

Japanese allspice was introduced from Japan in 1766. *The Botanical Cabinet* (1822), published by the London nurserymen Loddiges, Conrad and Sons, tells us that it "was first cultivated in perfection by the late earl of Coventry, in whose conservatory at Croome . . . the original plant is still growing. By his lordship's liberality we were favoured with a specimen raised from it many years since, from which we have propagated great numbers . . . the blossoms have a delicious fragrance."

CAMELLIA JAPONICA or JAPAN ROSE

Red – Unpretending merit, beauty is all your attraction
Camellia carrose, yellow – Pity

Camellias were introduced into England some time before 1742. Mrs. Loudon describes them as "Evergreen shrubs with splendid flowers, from China, of which *C. japonica*, and its numerous garden varieties, are in general cultivation in all the greenhouses of Europe and America".

Don tells us that, in its native country, *C. Japonica* "grows to a large tree [and] is in high esteem . . . for the elegance of its large flowers, which exhibit a great variety of colours". He goes on to list a large number of red varieties but says that the crimson shell camellia (*C. J. imbricata*) is "without doubt the best variety that has been brought from China. The flowers are upwards of 33 inches in diameter. The colour is of a fine crimson-red and remarkably shewy".

As to 'Camellia Carrose', I can find no mention of this in any reference work, Victorian or modern. The website of the International Camellia Society says that the term "yellow-flowered Camellia" is usually taken to refer to *Camellia nitidissima*. But this has only been available in Britain since the 1960s so, unless AMC had visited China, she would have been unlikely ever to have seen a yellow camellia. It is impossible, therefore, to know to what plant she is referring.

The generic and English names were given in honour of George Joseph Kamel (1661-1706) a Moravian Jesuit missionary who was the first person to describe the flora of the Philippines.

CAMOMILE

Straw color – **Energy in adversity**

The true camomile – sometimes spelled 'chamomile' – (*Chamaemelum nobile*) is a white daisy-like flower. However, when its flower heads are dried for herbal use, they become straw coloured, and it could be this to which AMC is referring. Barton tells us that "Much of what is brought to the London market is grown about Mitcham, in Surrey".

The English name is derived, according to Barton, from the Greek *chamai*, 'on the ground', and *melon*, 'apple' "because the plant smells like apples".

CAMPION, THE ROSE

Pink – **Polite, graceful**

Mrs. Loudon describes the rose campion (*Silene coronaria*) as a "joyful-looking little plant". The 1810 edition of Philip Miller's *The Practical Gardener* tells us that "the single Rose Campion has three varieties which are sometimes admitted into gardens . . . [but] the double Rose Campion is a finer flower". Sixty five years later, in an issue of *The Garden,* the author of an article entitled *My Wild Garden* agrees that "A double form crimson is very good" although "one seldom sees it now-a-days".

CANARIENSIS (Tropeolium)

Yellow – I want kindness, help me

The name *Canariensis* implies that this plant comes from the Canary Islands but this, says Mrs. Loudon, is wrong. It is a native of Peru, introduced into England in 1775 and its correct name is *Tropaeolum peregrinum.* She describes it as a very beautiful hardy annual with "fringe-like pale-yellow flowers". Its Spanish name is *Paxaritos Amarillos,* meaning yellow birds "and it has been cultivated from time immemorial as an ornamental climber in the gardens of Lima, and other cities of Peru".

CANDYTUFT

White – **Indifference**
Purple – **Carelessness**

The first species of candytuft to be cultivated as a garden flower was *Iberis umbellata* which was brought from Candia (Crete) resulting in its English name. Gerard was growing it from seed in about 1590. "From that time to the present," says Mrs. Loudon, "Purple Candy Tuft has been a general favourite in British gardens". Phillips comments that "Few plants are more conspicuously ornamental in the borders of the flower-garden".

The bitter candytuft (*I. amara*) is, according to Mrs. Loudon, "a native of England, and is found . . . wild in corn-fields in nearly every part of Europe". It is, she says, a pretty little plant, with small tufts of white flowers.

Glenny lists several white species including the evergreen candytuft (*I. sempervirens*) which, according to Phillips, arrived in England in 1731 and was being cultivated at the Chelsea Physic Garden by 1739. The broad-leaved candytuft (*I. semperflorens*), with which it is often confused, was brought to England in 1679, and was being grown at the Botanical Garden at Oxford in 1680.

Commenting on the use of this plant to symbolise indifference, Phillips suggests that it is because "*Iberis semperflorens* . . . remains in blossom nearly the whole year . . . braving all the inclement seasons with such an apparent negligence of the changes in the weather".

In the past, leaves and young stems of candytuft were boiled as a vegetable, while their seeds were eaten with meat, like mustard.

CANTERBURY BELL

Blue – **Faithful, constant**
White – **Gratitude**

Mrs. Loudon calls the Canterbury bell (*Campanula medium*) "one of the most ornamental of biennials". Don describes blue, purple, and white, single and double varieties.

Wilkinson tells us that its name came about from its abundance around Canterbury, from where it was gathered by pilgrims "and treasured in evidence of the task they had completed". She gives it the alternative name of steeple-bells. In Gerard's time, it was known as "Haskewoort, Throtewoort, and Vuula Woort" and was believed to be useful in treating inflammation and swelling of the throat.

CARDINAL FLOWER

Scarlet – **Rank, distinction**

Don identifies this as the scarlet lobelia (*Lobelia cardinalis*) a native of Virginia, Carolina and Mexico. Sir James Justice (1698-1763), Scottish horticulturalist and author of *The Scot's Gardener's Director*, calls it "a flower of most handsome appearance, which . . . excells all other flowers I ever knew in the richness of its colour".

Mrs. Loudon regards it as a very beautiful species and tells us that it is the oldest lobelia in our gardens, having been sent, in 1629, to Henrietta Maria, the wife of Charles I. "It is said that when the Queen saw it she laughed excessively, and said that its colour reminded her of the scarlet stockings of a cardinal, whence the learned botanist Parkinson called it the cardinal's flower in his *Paradise*, a work which he afterwards published and dedicated to her Majesty". It is thus the oldest lobelia in our gardens, says Mrs. Loudon.

CARNATION

Clove scented, white – **Woman's love, a blush**
Striped red &white – **Refusal**
Yellow – **Dislike**

Don tells us that *Dianthus caryophyllus* is thought to be the species from which all the many varieties of carnation have arisen. In a wild state, it can be found "on old ruinous walls, particularly on Rochester, Deal, Sandown, and other old castles, [and] on walls in Norwich, and other old towns", with flowers that are single or double, white, yellow, purple, and variegated.

Phillips says that "The name of Clove, as well as that of *Caryophyllus*, was given to this species of *Dianthus* from the perfume being similar to that of the spice". In the reign of Edward III, he says, "it was used to give a spicy flavour to ale and wine, and from hence it was called Sop in wine". In the time of Elizabeth I, the poet Spenser called the flowers "Coronations . . . and from hence the name of Carnation seems a corruption".

Don believes that the carnation in its cultivated state was "unknown to the ancients" but that it has "been cultivated from time immemorial in Europe". In the time of Charles I, there were 49 types of carnation in cultivation but it seems that most of these were lost during the Civil War and subsequent Commonwealth. During this period, says Phillips, the Dutch had "taken up the cultivation of the Carnation, and we renewed our gardens with these flowers from Holland during the reign of Charles the Second". At the beginning of the 18th century, nearly 400 named varieties were known while, by the time Don was writing, the carnation had become "the principal florist's flower in Germany and Italy, from which countries the British florists procure their best Carnation seed".

Although AMC and some other floral dictionaries offer a meaning specifically for a yellow carnation, Phillips notes that even though Gerard, in the 16th century, reported having a yellow carnation in his garden "which, a worshipfull marchant of London, Master Nicholas Lete, procured from Poland" it is, in the 1820s, "still scarce in this country".

CASSIA

Dwarf, yellow – **Abundance**

The cassia is a large genus, mostly consisting of shrubs, with a few annuals, some of which, says Glenny "furnish the senna of commerce". Over 200 species are known "of which about eighty have been introduced", all having yellow flowers.

Writing in *The Botanical Magazine* (1790), William Curtis tells us that dwarf cassia is a native of the West Indies and Virginia, and is "not common in our gardens, though cultivated as long ago as 1699, by the Duchess of Beaufort".

CATCH FLY

Scarlet – **Deception**

The catch fly belongs to the genus *Silene*, most of whose species produce on their stalks a sticky liquid in which, it is said, flies can get trapped. Many species of *Silene* (including those found growing wild in England) have white flowers, but there are also a number that are bright red or crimson including *S. muscipula* which was introduced into English gardens from Spain before the end of the 16th century.

CEDAR LEAF (fennel)

Green – **I live only for you**

At first glance, there seems to be no connection between cedar and fennel. However, the solution seems to lie with Robert Tyas who, in his *Hand-book of the Language and Sentiment of Flowers* (1845), lists the two plants together with a meaning of 'strength'. It would seem that AMC copied this from Tyas but gave it the meaning assigned only to cedar in several other floral dictionaries.

A modern source says that the name 'cedar' can refer to a number of plants, including trees of the *Pinaceae, Cupressaceae, Meliaceae* and other families. Indeed, several floral dictionaries list 'cedar of lebanon' and 'cedar' separately, giving them different meanings, while some specify 'cedar (*Juniperus*)' or 'red cedar' (*Juniperus virginiana*). And, in an article in the *Journal of the Royal Horticultural Society* for 1848, J. F. Schouw, professor of botany at the University of Copenhagen, points out that "when Pliny talks of the great Cedar ... it is not quite clear whether he means the Cedar of Lebanon or *Juniperus Phoenicea*". So it may be that AMC is referring to one of the taller species of JUNIPER.

In the past, juniper was thought to be an antidote to poison and to protect against plague. The berries were believed to cause abortion and assist childbirth and, as late as the mid 20th century, the myth persisted that an abortion could be caused by sitting in a hot bath while drinking gin (which is flavoured with juniper berries).

CELADINE

Yellow-green – **Happiness to come**

Mrs. Loudon tells us that there are two plants known as celandine (AMC has mis-spelled it) – the lesser celandine or pilewort (*Ficaria verna*) and the common celandine or swallow-wort (*Chelidonium majus*). Both have yellow flowers.

Don says that the common celandine is found "in shady places along the sides of walls in hedges and thickets" and that the lesser celandine has been reported "about Wimbledon in Surrey".

The root has been used to treat jaundice, gout and stones, and the juice was believed to combat dropsy, warts, ringworm, itching, ulcers and, diluted with milk, to remove "white opaque spots on the eyes". But Dr. William Woodville in his *Supplement to Medical Botany* (1794) writes "We have little doubt but that the virtues of celandine have been greatly exaggerated".

The generic name of the common celandine, and the English name, come from the Greek *chelidon*, a swallow, which, according to Barton, is "either because it flowers about the time of the arrival of those birds, or from an ancient tradition, that they used it to open the eyes of their young".

CHICKWEED

White – **A day appointment, if the day is fine as the flower closes when it rains, and at night**

Don lists 82 species of chickweed, both wild and cultivated. Among these are three that he describes as being plentiful in Britain – the common mouse-ear chickweed (*Cerastium vulgatum*) which is found in fields and on waste ground, walls and dry banks, the semidecandrous mouse-ear chickweed (*C. semidecandrum*) found in waste and sandy ground and on walls in the outskirts of towns or villages, and the water mouse-ear chickweed (*Myosoton aquaticum*) which grows on the margins of rivers and ditches and other wet places.

CHINA ASTER

Single, purple – **Disappointment**
Variegated – **Variety**
Double, purple – **I think with you**
Single, pink or white – **I will think of it**

Although originally put in the *Aster* genus, Mrs. Loudon tells us that the china aster was later placed in the genus *Callistema*, but "it and its varieties . . now form the new genus *Callistephus*".

The China aster first appeared in Europe in 1730 when a Chinese missionary, Father D'Incarville, sent some seeds to the Royal Garden in Paris. The following year, seeds from the Jardin des Plantes in Paris were sent to Philip Miller, the head gardener at the Chelsea Physic Garden. The earliest seeds yielded single red and single white flowers. In 1736 Miller obtained seeds for the single blue. However, in 1752, according to Phillips "he received seeds of the double flowers, both red and blue, and in the following year Dr. Job Baster, of Zirkee, sent him seeds of the double white sort; since which time the varieties have been infinitely increased . . . and thus we are presented with . . . flowers in red and white, blue and white, purple and white, pink and purple, two reds, two blues". (It may have been in gratitude for Baster's generosity that Miller gave the name *Basteria* to the newly introduced CALYCANTHUS.)

CHINA, or INDIAN PINK

Red – Dislike, aversion
Dark pink – Always lovely

Seeds of the China pink (*Dianthus Chinensis*) were sent to Paris by French missionaries in China in 1705, and gardeners in England first received some in 1713. Mrs. Loudon tells us that even though "it is entirely destitute of the fragrance of . . . the carnation and common pink" and its colours "only vary from a rich dark crimson to pink and white . . . the various manners in which these colours are combined and varied almost exceed belief".

The double variety was a later development and Phillips states that "this flower has been greatly improved by the cultivation of European gardeners since its first arrival from China".

CHRYSANTHEMUM

Rose – Cheerful, though unfortunate
Red – I love
White – Truth
Yellow – Slighted love

At the time that AMC was writing, two types of flowers were known as chrysanthemums. The first was a member of the daisy family with white or yellow flowers, (*Glebionis coronaria*), while the second, which we now refer to simply as a chrysanthemum, in the early and mid 19th century was known as a Chinese chrysanthemum.

It was introduced to Europe in 1764, and grown by Philip Miller at the Chelsea Physic Garden. In 1789, three cultivars were brought from China to France by a merchant, Pierre Louis Blanchard, but only the purple variety survived. At the end of the French Revolution, in 1795, the chrysanthemum reached England where, according to Phillips, "being then considered a new plant, it was sold at a high price by the nurserymen in the neighbourhood of our metropolis until its easy propagation became known; but it is only within these last few years that its cultivation has attracted the notice of florists in general". By Phillips' time there were some thirty varieties which had "rapidly spread themselves over every part of the island, filling the easements of the cottagers and the parterres of the opulent".

The English name and the generic name come from the Greek *chrysos*, gold, and *anthos*, a flower, This, says Phillips "shows the error of forming the generic name of plants from [a] colour, since, in one species of Chrysanthemum, we have all the colours of the rainbow, [but all are] indiscriminately styled golden flowers".

CINQUEFOIL (clover grass)

White – **Beloved daughter**

Here, AMC becomes confused. The term cinquefoil refers to the genus *Potentilla*, whereas CLOVER is known as trefoil. The meaning of 'beloved daughter', however, is given by other floral dictionaries to cinquefoil, Glenny describes *Potentilla* as "a very large family of hardy perennials" and Don lists around 40 species that are either white or white tinged with red, including the strawberry leaved cinquefoil (*P. sterilis*) which is found growing wild in woods and dry pastures, and the rock cinquefoil (*P. rupestris*) which is found in mountainous regions of Montgomeryshire in Wales, although it is probably not a British native.

CITRON

Green – **Beauty with ill humour**

The citron (*Citrus medica*) belongs to the same genus as the lemon and the lime. Contrary to AMC's description, it is yellow. John Stephenson in his *Medical Botany* (1834) tells us that it is a native of "all the warmer parts of Asia" and was formerly believed to be a variety of lemon "differing chiefly in the form and qualities of the fruit".

Don lists three varieties – large, monstrous and florence (small) – and tells us that "Unless the season be warm, and the trees well managed, the fruit rarely ripens in England". It's possible, therefore, that AMC was basing her colour on that of the unripe citron. The fruit, which can grow to six inches long, has an acid pulp and so, says Don, "is seldom eaten raw, but is generally preserved and made into confections".

Clearly the citron was a well known fruit in the early 19th century. Dolby's *Cook's Dictionary* contains no less than 13 recipes for using it including a citron pudding for which a pint of cream and the yolks of six eggs must be mixed with sugar, finely shredded citron, two spoons of flour, and some nutmeg, and baked.

The citron was also well known in Roman times, according to Stephenson, "though their propagation and culture were then but little understood". He quotes Pliny as saying that the citron, which was a "singular antidote against all venom" was "not good to be eaten as a fruit" but was "very odoriferous, as are the leaves, which are . . . put in wardrobes among apparel, to give a perfume, and to drive away moths and spiders". And, according to Pliny although many people had tried to grow the trees in other countries, no one had yet been successful.

Other names for the tree were Assyrian tree and median apple.

CLARKIA (PULCHELLA)

Pink & white – **Refinement, elegance**

Clarkia pulchella is a member of a genus of hardy annuals. The flowers tend to be pink *or* white and not, as AMC implies, pink *and* white. Glenny comments that "The Clarkia is a popular annual, though not one that everybody admires; some think it has too much foliage for the quantity of flower".

Don disagrees, telling us that it "is one of the most showy border annuals ever introduced to the gardens, and is on that account to be seen in every flower-garden and nursery, although but a few years since its first introduction".

Mrs. Loudon tells the story of how it was discovered by Captain William Clarke in 1803. The American President, Thomas Jefferson, had sent his private secretary, Captain Lewis, together with Clarke, to explore the American West. During the three year long expedition, Clarke sent back dried specimens of this newly-found plant and it was described by the naturalist Fredrick Pursh in his *Flora of North America*. However, it was 1826 before Clarkia seeds made their way to England. Mrs. Loudon tells us that "It was one of the first Californian annuals imported".

CLARY, or cleary

Purple top – **Welcome news**

Clary is a somewhat confusing term as, sometimes, it has been used interchangeably with 'sage'. However, Charles Macintosh in *The Book of the Garden* (1855) tells us that only two species of SAGE can truly be called clary – *Salvia sclarea* (common clary) which was introduced into Britain from Italy in 1562 and *Salvia viridis* (annual clary) which came from southern Europe in 1596.

Since the annual clary has two varieties, one of which is known as purple-topped, it would seem that this is the species to which AMC is referring. According to Mrs. Loudon the varieties of annual clary "are not cultivated for their flowers at all but merely because the points of the shoots are so deeply tinted as to have the appearance of flowers".

Thomas Green in *The Universal Herbal* (1820) tells us that "An infusion of the leaves is a good gargle for putrid spongy gums; and the powder of them snuffed up the nose excites sneezing, and a discharge of watery humours from the head; the leaves or seed put into the vat with ale while fermenting greatly increase its inebriating quality."

Dolby includes two recipes for clary wine. Another, in James Robinson's *The Whole Art of Making British Wines* (1848), requires 45 lbs. of raisins, 10 gallons of water, 2 lbs. of beetroot, 3 pints of brandy and a peck (equal to 2 gallons in volume) of clary tops in flower.

CLEMATIS

Flowering, white – **Mental superiority**
Evergreen – **Poor, yet in hope**
Traveller's joy, white – **Safety**

Mrs. Loudon is a great fan of clematis, telling us that it is "among the handsomest of conservatory climbers". She, Glenny and Don, give the names of a number of white species including *C. florida*, and the sweet-scented *C. flammula* and *C. erecta*. The last of these was used therapeutically to treat many "obstinate complaints", including "syphilitic diseases".

Don tells us that "The English name of this genus, Virgin's-Bower, is given to it on account of several of the species being used for covering bowers. It is also called Traveller's-joy, because several of the species grow in hedges by way-sides, as well as from the beauty and the scent of their flowers, or more probably from their affording a grateful shade." Since AMC distinguishes between white flowering clematis and white traveller's joy, it suggests that the former relates to the cultivated variety while the latter is the one found growing wild.

CLOVER GRASS

Red flowered – Industry
Trefoil, green – Unity

Loudon tells us that there are 159 species of clover (*Trifolium*), "all more or less ornamental", and that their colour varies "from dark crimson, and sometimes scarlet, to purple on the one hand, and to white, cream-colour and pale yellow on the other".

However, the primary use of clover (and particularly the red variety) was as animal feed. Don tells us that the white, red, and yellow clover are "the most valuable herbage plants adopted in European agriculture," and he remarks that "One acre of red clover will go as far in feeding horses or black cattle as 3 or 4 of natural grass".

Glenny mentions two species with red flowers, ruddy clover (*Trifolium rubens*) and crimson clover (*T. incarnatum*). Among the English species, Don lists the pale red sea clover (*T. squamosum*), found "on the east and south coasts . . . from Norfolk to Somersetshire", and two that are "rose-coloured" – clustered clover (*T. glomeratum*) found "in gravelly fields and pastures" around London and in East Anglia, and strawberry clover (*T. fragiferum*), found "in moist meadows and pastures in black boggy soil".

In his 1884 book *Plant lore – legends and lyrics*, Richard Folkard tells us that clover can remain dormant for many years and "if lime is powdered and thrown upon the soil, a crop of white Clover will sometimes arise where it had never been known to exist" which, he says is "an infallible indication of good soil". Clover can also predict the weather, feeling "rough to the touch when stormy weather is at hand".

According to Miss Carruthers, the author of *Flower Lore* (1879), clover was believed to ward off witchcraft and the evil eye, thanks to the "magic mark of the horse-shoe" at the centre of the triple leaflet.

Richard Folkard tells us that in ancient times, Hope was depicted as a little child holding a clover flower, while clover is used to decorate churches on Trinity Sunday, as a symbol of the Trinity. And in Cambridgeshire, Norfolk, and Suffolk, young people use a sprig of clover with two leaves "as a charm to enable them to ascertain the names of their future wives and husbands".

Folkard tells us that, in olden times, clover was known as honey-suckles. Its current name, he says, is derived from the Anglo Saxon word, *clafre* – and the club on modern playing cards "is so named from its resemblance to a Clover-leaf".

The generic name comes from the Latin *tres*, three and *folium*, leaf, relating to the fact that all the species have leaves composed of three leaflets.

CLOVES

Dark crimson – **Dignity**

Cloves are the flower-buds of the aromatic or common clove (*Syzygium aromaticum*) and derive their name from the French *clou*, meaning a nail, since that is what they resemble. The buds, when ready to harvest are bright red, so AMC's 'dark crimson' is likely to be describing the colour of the dried cloves.

Don tells us that it is hard to say when cloves first appeared in Europe, but they seem to have come into common use early in the 16th century. And by the time he was writing, cloves were "cultivated in almost every part of Asia . . . and several of the West India Islands".

Don says "The cloves are gathered by hand, or beaten with reeds, so as to fall upon cloths which are placed under the trees to receive them, and dried by fire, or . . . in the sun. The fully-formed berries are preserved in sugar, and eaten after dinner, to promote digestion". They are used as "a seasoning in various dishes, and to give flavour to wines and spirits". They have been used as a tonic and to stimulate the muscles, but Don warns that they are "dangerous to bilious persons". Oil of cloves has been used to cure toothache, and by perfumers.

COBOEA SCANDENS

Blue – **Scandal, gossip**

Although named after the Spanish Jesuit missionary Father Bernabé Cobo (1582-1657)[1], the correct spelling of the generic name is Cobaea.

Don says that *Cobaea scandens* is "a great favourite with most gardeners; it is a quick-growing, and profuse-flowering climber". However, he describes its flowers not as blue but as "dark, dirty purple".

Maund waxes lyrical about the plant. Against a south wall, he says, "it will grow from thirty to forty feet in a season [and] flower abundantly".

---

1. Father Cobo lived for 61 years in South America and was one of the first people to introduce cinchona bark (and thus quinine) into Europe.

COLCHICUM

Yellow – **Adversity**
Meadow saffron, yellow – **My best days are over**

Colchicum is the botanical name for meadow saffron, or autumn crocus, but AMC lists them separately and with different meanings, as she did with aconite and monkshood. And, although she identifies the flower as yellow, it is in fact either white or purple. Did she, perhaps, just assume that something called 'saffron' must be yellow?

Mrs. Loudon describes *Colchicum* as a hardy bulbous-rooted plant, with crocus-like flowers which "come up through the ground without the leaves in autumn" to be followed by the leaves in spring. (It is because they come up without leaves that they are sometimes called naked ladies.)

Gerard records *Colchicum* growing in Wiltshire and Northampton, while Phillips says it is "indigenous to our moist meadows . . . particularly in Essex and Suffolk". Barton adds several other southern counties to the list.

According to Phillips, the name *Colchicum* comes from the fact that it grows abundantly "in the vicinity of Colchis, a city of Armenia, celebrated for its numerous poisonous plants, and as the birth-place of Medea[2]". He goes on to relate the legend that Medea had prepared a magic liquor "to restore the aged Aeson[3] to the bloom and vigour of youth" and spilled a few drops, from which the flowers sprang. "On this account," says Phillips, "the Colchicum was anciently regarded as a preservative against all sorts of maladies. The Swiss

---

2. An evil sorceress in Greek mythology

3. The father of the Greek hero Jason

peasants tie the flower of this plant around the necks of their children, with a firm belief that it will render them invulnerable to all diseases".

Mrs. Loudon reports that an extract of the plant was used to treat rheumatism and gout. (A synthetic version, colchicine, is still used by doctors in the treatment of gout.)

COLLINSIA (BICOLOR)

White with violet spots – **Give to me**

Mrs. Loudon describes the genus of *Collinsia* as "Californian annuals, of great beauty". She, Glenny and Don all praise *C. heterophylla* as 'handsome' and 'showy'.

C. grandiflora was brought to England in 1828. Maund describes it as one of the "great number of beautiful plants that have been introduced to this country from North America . . . lowly and modest, it reclines on its home, and invites the hand to raise it, the eye to inspect its party-coloured flowers, which are disposed in whorls, as rustic damsels were wont to garnish the village May-pole".

However, Maund acknowledges that *C. grandiflora* was perhaps incorrectly named, since *C. heterophylla* (introduced in 1833) excels it "in the size of the flowers, in general showiness, and also in height". Somewhat ruefully, he writes "Names founded on comparison will always be subject to the same inconvenience till that time when all the plants on the face of the earth shall have been collected and arranged – a period, by the bye, of which it is impossible for the human mind to catch the least conception". Don, also writing about *C. bicolor*, tells us that "notwithstanding its recent introduction, seeds are already common in all the seed-shops".

Collinsia was named after the botanist Zaccheus Collins (1764-1831), who was vice-president of the Academy of Natural Sciences of Philadelphia.

COLUMBINE

White – **Peace, innocence**
Blue – **Love with anxiety**
Purple – **Resolved to win**
Red – **Folly, fear**

By the 19th century, columbine (*Aquilegia*) had been in cultivation for many hundreds of years and many garden varieties were available, in a large selection of colours. Phillips writes of "this gracefully rustic flower, which forms a principal ornament to most of our village gardens [and] is . . . principally found in the open spaces of our forests or large woods". Wilkinson tells us that "a tradition exists, that it is not a native plant, but a Roman introduction, only occurring in a really wild state in localities at some period occupied by these colonists".

According to Gerard, the seeds were used to make a gargle to "cleanse the teeth and gums", while Wilkinson records that candied seeds were used to treat giddiness and, when mixed with saffron, were "supposed to cure the jaundice and to 'expel poison'".

Its generic name, says Barton, is derived from the Latin, *aquila*, an eagle, because "the spurs of the petals . . . were thought to resemble the claws of that bird" and the name columbine derives, similarly, from *columbus*, a pigeon or dove.

CONVOLVULUS

Major, purple & pink – **Extinguished hope**
Minor, light blue – **Hope for the future**

Like several other floral dictionaries, AMC has separate entries for convolvulus and for its wild variety, BINDWEED. Mrs. Loudon describes the convolvulus as "well-known splendid climbing plants", while Don tells us that *Convolvulus major* "has long been a favourite in our gardens . . . [and] appears to have been introduced into England at a very early period, as it is mentioned in 1629 by Parkinson, who calls it the greater blue Bindweed, or Bell-flower". The flowers vary greatly, says Don, with "combinations of white, reddish purple, bluish purple, and violet".

COREOPSIS

Yellow & brown – **Love at first sight**
C. tinctora, bright gold & brown –
Always merry

In 1792, William Curtis, writing in *The Botanical Magazine* describes one species, the whorled coreopsis (*C. verticillata*), as a native of North America, with "uncommonly shewy" flowers. It grows, he says, to a great height and the petals will dye cloth red.

C. tinctoria was first discovered in 1819 in Arkansas by the English botanist Thomas Nuttall. In *The Botanic Garden* (1825), Maund describes it as "a very pretty slender-growing annual [which] having been lately introduced amongst us, is by no means common".

The generic name comes from the Greek *koris*, a bug. The specific name *tinctoria* is derived from the Latin *tinctura*, a colour or dye, and refers to the property of its petals.

CORIANDER

Yellow – **Concealed merit**

Barton tells us that coriander (*Coriandrum sativum*) "has long been cultivated in Essex . . . for the sake of its seeds". Don explains how the ripe seeds are harvested: "Women and children are employed to cut plant by plant, and to put it immediately into cloths, in which it is carried to some convenient part of the field, and there threshed upon a sailcloth". The seeds are used "by the distillers for flavouring spirits; by the confectioner for incrusting with sugar; and by the druggists for various purposes ... [and] in spices as currie powder, and seasoning for black puddings".

The name, Don tells us, is derived from the Greek *koris*, a bug, because of the plant's foul-smelling leaves. Barton comments that "Although the leaves in their recent state have a strong disagreeable smell, yet when dried they are pleasant and aromatic. In some countries they are eaten in soups and salads, and the inhabitants of Peru are excessively fond of the flavour".

CORONELLA

Pink – **Success attend you**

The correct spelling of this plant is *Coronilla* but AMC's is not the only floral dictionary to get it wrong. The genus includes shrubs and perennials, many of which have yellow flowers. AMC may be referring to the pink-flowered crownvetch, *Securigera varia*, which was previously known as *Coronilla varia*. *The Horticultural Register*, published in Boston in 1836, describes this species as producing "an immense number of its pretty coronets of purple and white, or pink flowers, in long succession". But it warns that the juice of the plant is poisonous.

The name, says Don, derives from the Latin *corona*, a crown and relates to the configuration of the flowers.

COWSLIP

Pale yellow – **Languishment, pensive**

Barton tells us that the cowslip (*Primula veris*) "though so frequent in England, especially in a clayey soil . . . is very rare in Scotland, and is only found about Edinburgh and Glasgow".

Phillips says that the flowers are frequently mixed with tea and, as an infusion, were formerly thought to be useful for easing joint pains and palsy, giving the plant the name of palsy-wort. Barton says that in some countries a drink is made from an infusion of the flowers fermented with sugar or honey, and lemon juice. In addition, the flowers are "often used to make wine, which is flavoured like muscadel, and is very sparkling and pleasant, but considered somniferous" and the roots are "put into casks of wine or beer to impart additional strength and flavour".

The leaves, says Phillips used to be eaten in salads, "but the ease by which we now procure lettuce and other exotic salad plants in our kitchen gardens, has banished those of our fields from the table".

The name of the plant, according to Phillips, was given either because the flowers smell like the breath of a cow or because it is "pressed away by the lip of the cow in the pastures, where it is considered an injurious weed that occupies a space which clover or other nutritious plants should fill".

COXCOMB

Red – **Foppery**

Phillips tells us that the name of cock's comb (the usual spelling) was given to the crested amaranth (*Celosia argentea var. cristata*) because of "the resemblance which the crested head or mass of flowers has to the crest or comb of a cock. The flowers of this plant are so numerous and small, and so closely set together on an irregular flattish surface, that it frequently looks more like a piece of rich velvet than a vegetable substance".

The cock's comb has been known in England since the 16th century but, says Phillips, "The most perfect plant of this kind that has been raised in England . . . was grown by Thomas Andrew Knight . . . [in] 1820 . . . The flower of this extraordinary plant measured seven inches in height and eighteen inches in width; it was. . . of a most intense purplish red colour". A drawing of the plant was sent to the Horticultural Society of London and was preserved in its library.

However, Mrs. Loudon tops this story by telling us that in 1834, an "enormous Cockscomb . . . perhaps the largest ever grown, measured in height two feet four inches; one of the leaves was one foot long and five inches broad: and the flower was very nearly two feet in length, and fifteen inches in breadth".

CRANBERRY

Red – **Cure for the heart-ache**

Don describes the common cranberry (*Vaccinium oxycoccos*) and the American cranberry (*Vaccinium macrocarpon*) at length, and he mentions the "exquisite taste" of the scarlet-berried erect cranberry (*Vaccinium erythrocarpum*).

The common cranberry, says Don, could be found in Switzerland, Russia, Scotland, Ireland, Lincolnshire, Norfolk and the north of England. Large numbers of berries were imported for culinary use from Russia although "not long since, cranberries from Lincolnshire and . . . Norfolk were sold in the streets of Norwich by cart-loads; but the extensive inclosures have in many parts destroyed and drained their native bogs . . . On the borders of Cumberland, not less than £20 or £30 worth[4] were sold each market day, for five or six weeks together, and dispersed over different parts of the kingdom". Don comments that in Sweden cranberries were not grown as a fruit, but were used for whitening silver plate.

The berries of the American cranberry are larger and brighter red than the common cranberry. They, too, were exported to Europe but Don believes that, by the time they reached Britain, they were inferior in quality to the Russian berries. "The best way of having American cranberries in Europe", he says, "is by cultivation in an artificial bog . . . If allowed to hang until they are full ripe . . . they are even better than the common cranberry, and may be kept dry in bottles throughout the year".

The specific name comes from the Greek *oxys*, sharp, and *kokkos*, a berry.

---

4. Equating to between £1650 and £2500 in today's money

CRANE'S BILL (wild geranium)

Violet – **Envy, covetousness**

Barton tells us that there are about thirteen native species of wild GERANIUM. The commonest is probably herb robert, but this has pink flowers, not violet. Don lists several that are violet and native to Britain. These include the knotted cranesbill (*G. nodosum*), found in thickets in Cumberland and Hertfordshire, the wood cranesbill (*G. sylvaticum*), found by the sides of rivers in the north of England and Scotland, and the hedgerow cranesbill (*G. pyrenaicum*), found in meadows and pastures around London and in Yorkshire, Norfolk, Oxfordshire and Scotland. The lilac-coloured Bicknell's cranesbill (*G. bicknellii*) is a garden species.

Wilkinson quotes Pliny who described crane's bill as "a rare hearbe" which could help those "weakened and decaied in nature by long sicknesse". The juice of the roots, says Wilkinson, was thought to be effective for ear problems, while the seeds, mixed with pepper and myrrh, were used for treating cramp. "In our own days," she says, "the crane's bills are successfully given in nervous complaints".

Crane's bill is so called because its seed pod resembles the head and beak of that bird.

CROCUS

Yellow – **Sunshine, youthfulness**

Mrs. Loudon tells us that "There are nearly a hundred named kinds of Crocus, including hybrids and varieties; but there are only about thirty distinct species" and she names two with yellow flowers – *C. flavus* and *C. luteus*. To these, Glenny adds the cloth of gold (*C. susianus*) and says that "varieties of distinct colours are sold in the seed-shops, without reference to the species". Tyas reports that the golden crocus (*C. aureus*) is to be found in "the park of Sir. H. Bunbury, at Barton Hall, Suffolk".

The crocus was known in England in the 16th century, and Gerard recorded that this "pleasant plant that bringeth forth yellow flowers was sent unto me from Robinus of Paris."

Phillips complains that the yellow crocus "is generally too sparingly planted, or placed in rows on each side the walk, reminding us of street lamps by night".

Tyas bemoans the fact that "This beautiful though common flower has perhaps been too much neglected by the professional and amateur florist". Many species of crocus, he says, are native, "while foreign species soon become naturalized". However, "It loves the pure air of the country . . . but it pines, and droops, and dies in the crowded town or its suburbs, and still more quickly is its existence brought to a close when subjected to the smoke-filled air of a manufacturing town".

The generic and English names come from a Greek myth in which a young man named Crocus pined away for love of a young woman and was turned into a plant.

CROW-FOOT

Yellow – **Ungrateful for favour**

There is a lot of crossover here with BUTTERCUP and RANUNCULUS, since buttercups are part of the *Ranunculus* genus, and many buttercups are also known as crowfoots.

The common crowfoots, says Mrs. Loudon, are weeds "but there are several border flowers belonging to this family which are well deserving of cultivation". Among these are the double-flowered yellow BACHELOR'S BUTTON (*R. acris flore pleno*) as well as the double-flowered creeping buttercup (*R. repens flore pleno*) and the double bulbous buttercup (*R. bulbosus flore pleno*).

Don writes about the water crowfoot (*R. aquatilis*) which is to be found growing wild in stagnant water and which "sometimes produces very large flowers, and makes a handsome show in ponds and ditches". And Barton describes the meadow crowfoot (*R. acris*) as "This well known plant [which] bespangles our meadows and pastures with its golden-yellow blossoms".

Many species of *Ranunculus* are acrid and poisonous, but Don writes that "on the borders of the Avon, some of the cottagers support their cows, and even horses" almost entirely on water crowfoot and also use it to fatten their hogs.

The English name, says Don, is an allusion to the shape of the leaves.

CROWN IMPERIAL

Red & yellow – **Power, majesty**

Crown imperial (*Fritillaria imperialis*) was first seen in Europe around 1576, when it was said to be a native of Persia. By the end of that century, Gerard was growing it in his garden at Holborn, but he described it as a rare and strange plant.

Phillips tells us that numerous varieties were raised from seed by Dutch florists and comments that "it possesses so strong a scent of the fox, combined with that of the garlic, as to ensure its protection from meddling fingers, and its safety from the saloon vase".

CUCKOO FLOWER

White – **Paternal error**

Several British spring-flowering plants are called cuckoo flower, says Mrs. Loudon, but the one that most often bears this name is *Cardamine pratensis*. Barton tells us that it grows "in moist meadows, marshes and the sides of ditches in humid meadows", while Phillips describes the flowers as being nearly pure white "whilst others have that purple cast so peculiar to highly-polished silver".

It has, in the past, been used as a diuretic and for the treatment of 'nervous diseases' including epilepsy, hysteria and chorea. Don says that the flowers and leaves "are agreeably pungent, and may be eaten with other herbs in a salad". According to Phillips, the juice of the plant is used "in northern countries, where salt-fish and meats are much eaten" as a remedy for scorbutic diseases, obstructions of the liver and jaundice.

The generic name, says Phillips, came about "from its having the taste of Cardamum", while the English name refers to its coming at the same time as the cuckoo. Gerard refers to it by the Latin name *flos cuculi* because "it flowers when the cuckowe doth begin to sing her pleasant notes without stammering". Other names are lady's smock, meadow lady's-smock, meadow cress, bitter cress, and bread and milk. Barton says that the first of these is "in honour of the Virgin Mary, as it first comes into flower about Lady-day".

CUCKOO PINT

White – **Warm affection**
Wake robin, scarlet – **Fervent, eager**

Once again, AMC has given two different meanings to one plant, under different names. Cuckoo pint is a native woodland plant (*Arum maculatum*) which, Phillips says, "frequently finds its way into the banks of our orchards and shrubberies, although it is seldom, if ever cultivated". Its small flowers are either yellow or purple and, in the autumn, it is instantly recognisable from its bright red berries. So while these will account for the colour AMC attributes to wake robin, it is hard to know why she has labelled cuckoo pint as 'white'.

According to Wilkinson, it is quite rare in Scotland but "abounds in England in moist hedgerows, and open, yet shady woods, as well as in . . . the dry and sunburnt soils of the [islands] in the Bristol Channel, and Portland Isle".

The acrid juice of the root has been used in medicine as a stimulant, and the powdered root was used in France as a wash for the skin which, says Phillips, "is esteemed a good and innocent cosmetic, and which sells for a high price, under the name of Cypress powder".

At one time cuckoo pint was used as a cure for rheumatism but, says Wilkinson, it "lost much of its fame through the incalculable harm done by the once much vaunted 'Portland powder'[5] a so-called specific for gout, of which this plant formed the basis".

The leaves were used in ancient times to cover cheese in order to preserve it and, in more recent times, the powdered root was used to adulterate arrow-root.

In the 16th century, a starch derived from the roots was used to stiffen ruffs, giving rise to the popular name of starch wort. "The most pure and white starch," writes Gerard "is made of the rootes of Cuckoo Pint; but most hurtfull for the hands of the laundresse that hath the handling of it, for it choppeth, blistereth, and maketh the hands rough and rugged, and withall smarting." The roots have also been used as a substitute for soap.

Other names for this plant are wild turnip, Jack in the pulpit, lords and ladies and, in Worcestershire (according to Phillips) bloody men's fingers.

---

5. Portland powder contained aristolochic acid which is now known to cause kidney damage and cancer

CUCUMBER

Yellow – **Cold, unfeeling, indifferent**

George W. Johnson's *Gardener's Monthly Volume: the Cucumber and the Gooseberry* (1847) gives us a wealth of information on the history of the cucumber. It is, says Johnson, one of the earliest mentioned kitchen garden plants and was probably introduced into western Europe by the Romans.

It was certainly well known in the 16th century. Thomas Hill mentioned it in his *Profitable Art of Gardening* (1563) and again in *The Gardener's Labyrinth*, published under the pseudonym of Didymus Mountain in 1577. In the latter, he gave directions for the cultivation of cucumbers but Johnson comments that "all his directions are mingled with many absurdities borrowed from classic authorities".

In 1597, Gerard, wrote specific directions for the cultivation of cucumbers. A hundred and twenty years later, Samuel Collins of Archester, in Northamptonshire published his *Paradise Retrieved* which contained, says Johnson, "the first separate treatise on the growth of the cucumber, with which I am acquainted". Collins described three varieties: "the long smooth, the short prickly, and a particular kind, 15 inches long, scarce amongst us."

Four years after this, Mr. Fowler, gardener to Sir Nathaniel Gould, at Stoke Newington, the first person to grow cucumbers in the autumn, presented King George I with two full grown cucumbers on New Year's Day, 1721.

Although there are varieties of cucumber that are yellow, it seems probable that AMC's colour refers to the flower.

CURRANTS (a bunch of)

Red or white – **You please all**

Don lists eight varieties of red currants and four of white. Mrs. Loudon believes that "The ornamental kinds of *Ribes* which have been introduced into British gardens since the commencement of the present century, are now some of our most beautiful shrubs".

"The red currant has been long cultivated in Britain," says Don, "and very much improved in the size of the bunch and berry." He mentions some native English species including the rock currant (*R. petraeum*) which has large, deep red berries, the common redcurrant (*R. rubrum*) which has red berries in the wild state, but cultivated varieties with white berries, and the downy currant (*R. spicatum*), All three of these species could be found growing wild in the north of England.

Currants, says Don, are "much used for jellies, jams, and wines" and have been used therapeutically to allay thirst, reduce bile secretion and correct a "putrid and scorbutic state of the fluids". That they were a popular fruit in the first half of the 19th century is indicated by the fact that the 1833 edition of Dolby's *Cook's Dictionary* has 65 recipes for using them, including ice cream (sieved currants, mixed with powdered sugar and cream, then frozen) and a sauce for venison (dried currants boiled in water, then mixed with bread crumbs, cloves, a glass of port and some butter).

The name currant, according to Don, derives from "the similitude of the fruit to that of the Corinth grape".

CYCLAMEN

White edged with violet – **Anxious to please**

Glenny describes the Persian cyclamen (*C. persicum*) as "white with a violet shade" and it may well be this species that AMC is describing. Glenny tells us that the flowers are profuse, it has a beautiful fragrance and "from seed there have been raised some very pretty varieties". Introduced into England in 1731, Don considers it "by far the most desirable species for the house". However, Phillips notes that, while all cyclamen can be raised from seed, "they require five years' attention before they will flower, [and so] they are but seldom raised in this country".

Gerard had cyclamen growing in his garden but, in common with others in the 16th century, believed that "It is not good for women with childe to touch or rake this herbe, or to come neere unto it, or stride over the same where it groweth. For the naturall attractive virtue therein contained is such, that . . . they that attempt it in manner aforesaid, shall be delivered before their time". Such was his anxiety about the dangers, that he built a cage of sticks over the cyclamen "least any woman should by lamentable experiment finde my words to be true, by their stepping over the same."

Both Glenny and Phillips give the plant the old name of sow-bread which, says Phillips, came about "because the swine eat it greedily in countries where it is plentiful".

CYPRESS

Dark green – **Despair, misfortune**

Many people are familiar with the phrase "sad cypress", both from the title of an Agatha Christie novel and from the lines in Shakespeare's *Twelfth Night* from which that title was taken: "Come away, come away, death, And in sad cypress let me be laid". Cypress has always been associated with death and mourning.

Loudon in his *Arboretum et Fruticetum Britannicum* (1838), gives us a lot of information about the cypress and its history. It is, he says, an evergreen tree remarkable for the fine grain and durability of its wood, the most common species being the common, or evergreen, cypress (*Cupressus sempervirens*). A native of Greece, Cyprus, Turkey, Persia and Asia Minor, it was introduced into Italy from Greece before the time of Christ.

The ancient Egyptians made their mummy-cases of cypress, and ancient Greeks who died for their country had their ashes preserved in boxes of the wood. It was customary to wrap a dead body in a branch of cypress when burying it, possibly because the tree was dedicated to Pluto, god of the underworld, or possibly because it was thought that the scent of the leaves would neutralise "the infectious exhalations proceeding from the corpse".

The dedication of the tree to Pluto and to death was associated with its use as an emblem of immortality, probably deriving from the extraordinary durability of the wood. According to Pliny, a statue of Jupiter, carved in cypress, lasted over 600 years with no signs of decay, while the cypress-wood doors of the temple of Diana at Ephesus looked perfectly new even when they were 400 years old. It is said that Plato had his code of laws engraved on cypress wood, rather than brass, because it would last longer. The wood was in great demand in Roman times and a plantation of cypress was considered to be a good dowry.

The Romans, says Mrs. Loudon "made verdant walls of cypress in their gardens; and . . . [clipped the] trees into a variety of forms, so as to represent a chase, a fleet of ships, and numerous other fancies. [Plato says] that, in his time, there were standing at Rome some cypresses that were more ancient than the city itself".

Even as late as the Middle Ages, Popes were buried in cypress wood coffins, since they believed that it would never decay.

Exactly when the cypress was introduced into England is unclear but Gerard, writing in 1597, mentions that cypresses were to be found at "Syon, a place neere London . . . at Greenwich . . . and likewise at Hampstead, in the garden of Mr. Wade, one of the clerkes of Her Majesties prive councell."

At the time Mrs. Loudon was writing, the Syon cypresses had become the largest, and possibly the oldest, evergreen cypresses in the London area, while one at Ditton, near Windsor, which was said to have been planted by Cardinal Wolsey, although now in a state of some decay, had a trunk that was eight feet in circumference. "The tree has long been plentiful in British nurseries . . ." says Mrs. Loudon and "there is scarcely a suburban villa or a country seat in which it is not to be found".

D

DAFFODIL

Bright yellow – **Chivalry, honour**
Wild, yellow – **Respect**

Phillips notes that there are many varieties of our native daffodil, *Narcissus pseudonarcissus*, which, he says, was "considered a kind of Lily by early writers".

Wilkinson comments that, although the root of the daffodil is poisonous, a "useful spirit" is distilled from the plant and, in 1855, "a decree was published ... whereby alcohols distilled in Algeria from the daffodil are ordered to be admitted duty free into France".

Phillips believes that "the name is a corruption of Dis's lily, as it is supposed to be the flower dropped from the chariot of that god in his flight with Proserpine".[1] However, Wilkinson believes that the name is derived from "the old English word

---

1. A Roman goddess, daughter of Jupiter and Ceres, who was abducted by Dis, king of the Underworld.

affodyle, which signified 'that which cometh early'".

Gerard referred to them as daffodowndillies. Other names that have been used are chalice flowers, and Lent lilies.

DAHLIA

Yellow – **Honour, regard**
White – **Thine for ever**
Purple – **Greatness**
Scarlet – **Magnificence**
Purple tinged with white – **Variety**

"This splendid addition to our autumnal parterres," says Phillips "was unknown to the Old World until the year 1789, when it was first sent to Spain from Mexico . . . It was introduced to this country by the late Lady Bute, who procured it from Madrid . . . but these plants were entirely lost to our gardens until seeds were re-introduced by Lady Holland, in the year 1804".

The first dahlia to arrive in Europe, *D. pinnata*, was discovered in Mexico by Baron Humboldt who sent it to Professor Cavanilles of the Botanical Garden in Madrid. It was the Professor who named the genus *Dahlia*, in honour of the Swedish botanist, Anders Dahl (1751-1789), so, as Glenny points out, it should actually be pronounced with a long 'a' – that is, dah-lia, not day-lia.

Mrs. Loudon tells us that it was from *D. pinnata* that nearly all the garden varieties were raised. "It produces flowers", she says, "in many different colours, including crimson, purple, white, yellow, orange, and scarlet, but comparatively few of a pure white". By the time she was writing, more species had been introduced from Mexico and "there are now ten or twelve distinct species, besides innumerable varieties [of *D. pinnata*], to be procured in England". Phillips notes that "these flowers have had their petals doubled and quadrupled ... whilst their colours have even been more increased than their petals".

Phillips is pessimistic about the continuing popularity of the plant because it is "better calculated to ornament large grounds than to embellish small gardens ... [while its] great size and want of perfume are objections to its admission into the small garden ... [So] notwithstanding the vivid colours which these flowers present, and the high estimation they are now held in, we do not consider it a flower that is likely to hold a long reign in the realms of fashion".

The German botanist, Carl Ludwig Willdenow (1765-1812) changed the name of the dahlia to *Georgina* (in honour of the German botanist, Georgi) because he thought *Dahlia* was too like *Dalea*, the name given by the Swedish naturalist Carl Peter Thunberg (1743-1828) to a small genus of plants in the pea family. However, the Swiss botanist Augustin Pyramus de Candolle (1778-1841) pointed out that the words were not only spelled differently but also pronounced differently (*Dalea* having a short 'a'), and he recommended that *Dahlia* be retained, a suggestion that was followed by most 19th century botanists.

DAISY

Field, white with yellow centre – **Innocence & childhood**
Garden, white – **Children, youth**
Garden, red – **Beauty without pride**
Hen & chicken – **Large family**

The common daisy (*Bellis perennis*) has been in cultivation in British gardens from time immemorial, says Mrs. Loudon. The most beautiful varieties, she believes, are the large double, the large quilled, and the hen-and-chickens.

Glenny, too, believes that the most striking are the double "and a curious sort vulgarly called the Hen and Chicken daisy, from the fact of small flower heads coming all round the large ones". Phillips gives its alternative names of proliferous daisy or childing.

Phillips reveals his snobbishness by declaring a preference for the use of the double daisy rather than box for edging borders in "the gardens of the cottagers" but going on to say that "an edging of any description to the parterre of Flora shows a want of taste in the planter".

Barton tells us that the leaves of the plant, "though somewhat acrid, have been eaten as a spring salad, or boiled like spinach". However, Phillips notes a rather stranger use: "The roots of Daisies boiled in milk was frequently given to little puppies to keep them of a diminutive size; but what effect this food would have on the growth of the canine species, we must leave to those who are curious in little dogs to discover".

Phillips tells us that the daisy was "formerly esteemed an excellent traumatic plant" and Wilkinson notes that it used to be known as bruise-wort "and the Northumbrian name of ban-wort appears to point to the same thing". In the extreme north of the country it was known as gowan which, Wilkinson believes, was derived, from the Celtic *guen* meaning fair or white.

The English name of daisy, says Phillips, is derived from "Day's eye, in which way it is written by Ben Johnson, and Chaucer calls it the 'ee of the daie'" a name that came from "the nature of its blossom, which expands at the opening of day and closes at sunset".

DANDELION

Yellow – **Coquetry, tell me if I am wanted**

We are so used to thinking of the dandelion (*Taraxacum officinale*) as a weed that it is possible to lose sight of the fact that it is actually a useful plant. In the past, it has been used therapeutically, and Wilkinson says that "it is one of those very few medicines which . . . leaves no injurious after-effects; so that as a gentle and strengthening aperient, we have no more valuable medicine". It used to be sold in "the druggist's shop" under the name of taraxacum.

It also has many culinary uses. Wilkinson tells us that "the young leaves blanched make an agreeable and wholesome early salad; and they may be boiled like cabbages, with salt meat. The French . . . [eat] the roots . . . as well as the leaves, with bread and butter; and tradition says that the inhabitants of Minorca once subsisted for weeks on this plant, when their harvest had been entirely destroyed by insects . . . On the banks of the Rhine the plant is cultivated as a substitute for coffee . . . [and] in some parts of Canada they make an excellent beer of the leaves".

The English name is a corruption of the French *dent de lion*, lion's tooth. Barton notes that "The vulgar name by which it is familiar to children, the French *pissenlit*[2], and equivalent synonymes in other languages, indicate the long and general acquaintance of the people with its diuretic qualities".

---

2. Wet the bed

DARNEL (rye grass)

Bluish green – **Wickedness**

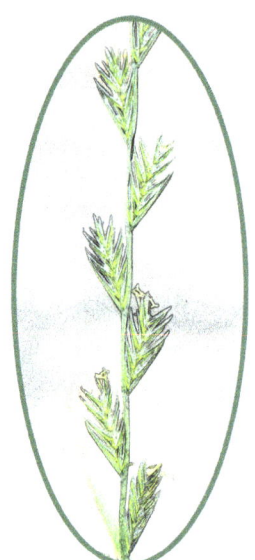

Prior states that darnel should be called 'ray grass', not 'rie-grass' which is the name given to meadow barley (*Hordeum secalinum*). Barton identifies ray-grass as *Lolium*, and mentions the perennial darnel (*L. perenne*) "which is often used as animal fodder" and the bearded darnel (*L. temulentum*) which "is a common weed in many parts of England, growing in fields among wheat, barley and flax".

The generic name, says Barton, may have been derived from the Greek *laion olein*, to ruin the corn, or from *dolios*, counterfeit. This latter refers to an old belief that the plant is wheat or another grain in a degenerate state: "it was believed that circumstances being unfavourable, wheat would change into rye, rye into barley, barley into darnel, darnel into brome-grass, brome-grass into oats, and so on; and that in favourable soils and situations these transmutations would be reversed".

DEAD LEAVES

Olive brown – **Sadness, death to hope**

It is, perhaps, a little strange that, whereas most people would describe dead leaves as brown (or possibly yellow), AMC specifies 'olive brown'. Was she, perhaps, thinking of the dead leaves of a particular plant? Or – given that some of her other colours do not fit with the true colour of the plant in question – should it be put down to a somewhat fanciful tendency in the author?

DITTANY

White & pale violet – **Humble birth**

Mrs. Loudon identifies dittany as *Origanum dictamnus*, a species of oregano or marjoram which has pink flowers. Prior suggests that dittany is *Lepidium latifolium*, a perennial which is part of the mustard and cabbage family, and whose flowers are white.

However, Don offers us a plant, *Dictamnus albus*, that tallies better with AMC's description. Called bastard or false dittany by Gerard and false white dittany by Parkinson, it has two varieties – *purpurea*, which is pale purple, striped with deeper veins, and *alba*, which is white.

D. albus, says Don, "when gently rubbed, emits an odour like that of lemon-peel, but when bruised it has something of a balsamic scent". He believes that, for its beauty and fine scent, it deserves a place in every plant collection.

DODDER OF THYME

Green - **Employment, business**

Don identifies this as *Cuscuta epithymum*, a parasitic plant, common in Britain, in cultivated fields, and "on furze, flax, thyme, nettles, heath, lavender, spurge, hops, [and] grass".

Samuel Frederic Gray, in *A Natural Arrangement of British Plants* (1821) tells us that the plant has purgative qualities "but is believed to partake, in some measure, of the virtues of the plants on which it grows".

The specific name comes from the Greek *epi*, upon, and *thymus*, thyme. The flowers are red and white, so presumably, by calling it green, AMC is referring to the plant when not in bloom.

DOG'S BANE

Green – **Deception**

Dog's bane (or dogbane) is the name given to various species of *Apocynum*. According to Mrs. Loudon, both its English and its generic name (which comes from the Greek *apókunon,* meaning 'dog away') reflect the fact that it is "peculiarly injurious to dogs". And it is not just dogs that should beware of this plant. Mrs. Loudon tells us that the flowers of flytrap dogbane (*A.*

androsaemifolium) "have a sweet, honey-like fragrance, which perfumes the air to a considerable distance, and which probably operates in attracting insects; as, when the flowers of this plant are fully blown, flies are generally found attached to them, some dead, and others alive and struggling to disentangle themselves". The plant was introduced to England from North America in 1688.

Since the flowers of dogbane tend to be pink or white, I assume that AMC's 'green' refers to the plant when not in bloom.

DOGWOOD BLOSSOM

Pale violet – **I am quite indifferent to you**

In *On Planting and Rural Ornament* (1803), William Marshall tells us that there are two species of *Cornus* that are known as dogwood – the common dogwood (*C. sanguinea*) and the flowering dogwood (*C. florida*).

Mrs. Loudon describes dogwood as "well-known shrubs, with whitish or yellowish flowers . . . [which are] generally ornamental, from the shining red bark of their branches in winter, and the intensely dark purplish red of their leaves in autumn".

William Cobbett in *The Woodlands* (1825) tells us that "Till very lately, I always looked upon this as a perfectly insignificant, or, rather, mischievous plant". But he has now discovered that it makes "the very best of charcoal for using in the manufacturing of gunpowder . . . for I have seen great quantities of it in Sussex, stripped of its bark even up to the ends of the small shoots, and tied up in bundles to be sent to the powder-mills".

No dogwood seems to have pale violet flowers, but AMC may have been thinking of the flowering dogwood, which was introduced into Britain during the 18th century and whose flowers range from white to pink. Daniel Jay Browne in *The Sylva Americana* (1832) describes it as "one of the fairest ornaments of the American forests". Its wood, he says, is "hard, compact, heavy and fine-grained, and is susceptible of a brilliant polish. The sap is perfectly white, and the heart is of a chocolate color". The wood "is used for the handles of light tools . . . It is employed by engravers for cuts used in printing. Some farmers select it for harrow teeth . . . [and] for lining the runners of sledges but . . . being liable to split it should never be wrought till it is perfectly seasoned".

The common dogwood is sometimes known as bloody twig because of the redness of its young shoots.

DRAGON WORT

Light blue – **Horror, dreadful**

There are several candidates for this plant. James Lee in his *Introduction to the Science of Botany* (1810) identifies it as *Artemisia dracunculus* (or tarragon). John Mason Good in the *New Cyclopaedia* (1813) declares it to be the Swiss cheese plant (*Monstera adansonii*). And Robert Hooper in *A New Medical Dictionary* (1817) says it is the dragon arum (*Dracunculus vulgaris*). However, none of these has light blue flowers, the first-named having yellow flowers, the second whitish-yellow and the third deep purple.

But there is another possibility. AMC may have been thinking of dragon's head (*Dracocephalum*) while giving it the meaning that other floral dictionaries have for dragon wort. Mrs. Loudon tells us that "some of the perennial species, such as *D. canescens**, *D. grandiflorum* . . . and *D. austriacum*, have large and splendid blue flowers".

Maund tells us that all species of *Dracocephalum* are very ornamental, while Robert Sweet in his *British Flower Garden* (c. 1823) mentions *D. argunense*, a "new and beautiful plant", native to Siberia and *D. canescens**, which has bright violet blue flowers and is native to the Levant.

E

EGLANTINE (sweet briar)

Pale rose – **An offer of marriage**

Eglantine (*Rosa rubiginosa*) is the traditional name for the wild rose. Loudon describes it as a rambling shrub, found in hedges and thickets, and plentiful in Britain.

Maund relates that "*Rosa rubiginosa*, in its natural form, as the wild Eglantine, with pale single flowers, is indigenous to every part of Europe; but cultivation has stepped in and produced rich-coloured double varieties".

Richard Folkard, in his *Plant Lore, Legends and Lyrics* (1884), relates a popular myth about the eglantine. It is said that when Satan rebelled against God and was cast out of heaven, he tried to climb back by making a ladder out of the thorns of the eglantine. God, however, put a stop to this by decreeing that the eglantine could grow only outwards and not upwards.

ELDER

White – **Comfort, tenderness**

The common elder (*Sambucus nigra*) is, says Mrs. Loudon, "a low tree having the character of a shrub". Don and Barton speak of elder growing wild in hedges, coppices and woods, with cream-coloured flowers and "a sweet but faint smell".

Don describes the tree as "a whole magazine of physic to rustic practitioners". The berries have been used to treat catarrh and sore throats, while an ointment made from the inner bark was considered helpful in treating burns. The dried flowers make a tea that is "useful perhaps in acute inflammations, but not to be persisted in habitually", while an infusion of the leaves acts as an insecticide and the young leaf-buds are a purgative so powerful "as to be accounted unsafe". According to Barton, the leaves are also said to drive away moles, while the berries can be used to dye linen brown.

The wood, says Barton, is hard and tough and "is made into skewers, tops for angling rods, and needles for weaving nets; it is also employed by turners and cabinet-makers" while the "light pith" contained within the branches "is much used in electrical experiments, and for fancy ornaments".

The generic name comes from the Greek *sambuke*, a musical instrument which was probably traditionally made from elder wood.

ELECAMPANE

Blue – **Call me to you**

Although known in Britain since the 16th century, and probably even before then, elecampane (*Inula helenium*) tended to be used as a therapeutic herb rather than as a garden flower. John Hill, in his *Virtues of British Herbs* (1771) describes it as "a robust and stately Plant . . . with a firm and handsome appearance . . . a fragrant, very agreeable smell, and a spicy, sharp, and somewhat bitterish taste". John Stephenson and James Morss Churchill, in their *Medical Botany* (1831), describe it as an indigenous perennial plant "occasionally met with in moist meadows, and pastures, in many parts of the south and west of England". It is, they say, one of our tallest herbaceous plants, with flowers of a golden yellow colour. Since AMC gives a different meaning from that in other floral dictionaries (which mostly list it under its alternative name, helenium, and give its meaning as 'tears') it is difficult to know whether, by describing it as blue, she was thinking of another plant or whether, as elsewhere in this book, she has just got the colour wrong.

In ancient times elecampane was used to treat a wide variety of complaints. Hill tells us that "It has long been famouse for the cure of all diseases of the Breast; and it has also great virtues in malignant fevers". But he warns that, in its dried state it has little use: "The garden must supply it fresh to those who would know its real value".

However, by Stephenson and Churchill's time elecampane was no longer used therapeutically "unless it be by cow-doctors, who are ignorant of its properties, or by dishonest druggists, who add a small quantity of tartar-emetic to it, and sell the mixture for powdered ipecacuanha". Genuine ipecacuanha could cost as much as thirty shillings a pound, whereas the elecampane mixture cost only two shillings but had "a nauseating and depressing effect, that genuine ipecacuanha would not".

ENCHANTER'S NIGHTSHADE

Purple & yellow – **Witchcraft**

Sir William Jackson Hooker in his *British Flora* (1830) writes of two species of enchanter's nightshade – common (*Circaea lutetiana*) and alpine (*Circaea alpina*). Both, he says, are to be found in woods and coppices in shady situations, while the latter can also be found "in stony places, especially by the sides of lakes in the north of England and Scotland". However, both are described as having white or rose-coloured flowers. AMC seems to have confused this plant with the NIGHTSHADES of the *Solanaceae* family, such as BITTERSWEET whose flowers are purple and yellow.

Elizabeth Kent, in an article published in the September 1828 issue of *The Magazine of Natural History*, says that enchanter's nightshade was "formerly believed to be a preservative against every species of magical incantation; alike defying the power of sorcerers, witches, demons, and evil spirits, of every denomination" and is worth looking for "for its delicate and elegant appearance".

The generic name comes from that of the Greek goddess of magic, Circe.

ENDIVE

Garden - **Frugality at all times**

Endive (*Cichorium endivia*) is a hardy annual of the chicory family, and was introduced into England in the mid 16th century. The author of *The Domestic Gardener's Manual* (1830) tells us that "Of the cultivated endive there are three varieties – green curled Endive... White curled Endive... and Batavian Endive". The last of these, which resembles a cos (or romaine) lettuce "is more esteemed for culinary uses than salads; but is excellent both ways when blanched in the heart; and is proper to cultivate chiefly for autumn use."

The 1816 edition of *Culpeper's Complete Herbal* refers to endive as "a fine cooling, cleansing, jovial plant". The leaves and juice can be used to treat inflammations of various sorts, including "heat and sharpness of the urine, and excoriation in the urinary parts". The seeds "are available for fainting, swoonings, and passions of the heart" and, applied directly, can "temper the sharp humours of fretting ulcers, hot tumours, swellings, and pestilential sores". In addition, the seeds "wonderfully help... redness and inflammations of the eyes... [and] dimness of the sight... [and are] used to allay the pains of the gout". Reassuringly, we are told "You cannot use it amiss".

ERINGO (sea holly)

Blue – News from sea, or afar

The eryngo (*Eryngium maritimum*), as its English name suggests, grows most readily on the sea shore. A concise description appears in *Letters on the Elements of Botany*, by the 18th century French philosopher Jean Jacques Rousseau (translated from the French by Thomas Martyn): "If you were by the sea side, you would easily know it by the bluish colour of the leaves, by their prickliness, and by the smooth membranous consistence of them like parchment". However, Rousseau is not enamoured of this plant, describing it as "ill-humoured" and commenting that it "has not beauty enough to make you amends for the wounds it will give you in examining it". AMC may be referring to the colour of the leaves or the flowers.

The young flowering shoots, says Don, have been "eaten like asparagus [and] are very nourishing". The roots were also candied and sold as an aphrodisiac. The first person to do this was a Colchester apothecary, Robert Burton (or Buxton) at the beginning of the 17th century. His apprentice, Samuel Great, continued the business, and this was still going strong in the early 19th century.

The generic name comes from the Greek *ereugo*, to belch, because, says Don, the plant was thought to be an appropriate treatment for "all complaints arising from flatulence". Other names for it include sea hulver, and sea holme.

EVENING PRIMROSE

Yellow – Sighs, an appointment for the evening

Mrs. Loudon lists several species of evening primrose (*Oenothera*) that have yellow flowers, including the "very beautiful" *Oe. Drummondii* and the "tall, handsome" *Oe. elata*, introduced from Mexico in 1824. The latter, she says, "may be considered as a true evening primrose, as the flowers expand only at night, and shrivel up before morning".

The common evening primrose (*Oe. biennis*) was brought to England from North America in 1614, and, according to Don, is now found growing wild particularly "on the coast of Lancashire, [and] . . . near Woodbridge, Suffolk. [It] is common in gardens, and often escapes from thence into rich waste ground".

Of the large-flowered evening primrose (*Oe. grandiflora*) Phillips writes that it was brought to England from North America in 1778 by John Fothergill, M.D. and that it "possesses an agreeable fragrance, and hence . . . is more esteemed than the *Biennis*". Another species with a "delightful fragrance", *Oe. odorata*, was introduced into Europe in 1790 by Sir Joseph Banks who bought the seeds from "the surgeon of a merchant-ship . . . on the coast of Patagonia".

The English name of the plant arose, says Mrs. Loudon, because *Oe. biennis* "has the habit of closing its flowers during sunshine, and not opening them till evening, or during cloudy weather, and this is the case with several other species". The generic name comes from the Greek *oinos*, wine and *theras*, seeker and, according to Mrs. Loudon, refers to the fact that, when *Oe. biennis* was first introduced, "its roots were eaten like olives, to give a relish to wine".

EVERLASTING FLOWER

Yellow – **Never forget, immortal**

There are two plants to which AMC may be referring here. The first is *Xerochrysum bracteatum* which was introduced from Australia in 1799. Its flowers, says Glenny, "are preserved, dyed of various colours, and sold in the shops as a component of 'winter nosegays'". Mrs. Loudon describes it as very handsome, "with bright yellow golden-looking scales, which have quite a metallic lustre in the sun".

The other possibility is *Gnaphalium*, or cudweed. Phillips says there are five species of *Gnaphalium* that are native to Britain but although it is "a plant of long standing in our gardens, its cultivation has never been attempted on a large scale for the market". As a result, large quantities were imported. "We frequently meet with it," Phillips tells us, "ornamenting the vase of the saloon ... [and] decorating the head-dresses of our belles".

Gnaphalium, says Phillips, is "frequently used on the continent to decorate the monuments and graves of departed friends" and, in Paris, "numerous families are regularly occupied, and entirely supported by forming these flowers into garlands and crosses". In Portugal, it was customary to decorate churches with it during the winter months.

Alternative names include chafe-weed, cotton-weed, and live-long or live-for-ever. In ancient times, images of the gods were crowned with garlands of *Gnaphalium*, and for this reason they were also called god's flowers.

EVERLASTING PEA

Pink – **Continued pleasure**

The everlasting pea (*Lathyrus latifolius*), says Don, has large, rose-coloured flowers and is found in woods near Cambridge, and in Cumberland, Worcestershire and Bedfordshire. Gerard (who called it 'tare everlasting' and 'pease everlasting and chickling') reported it growing "in shadowie woods, and among bushes . . . in Kent . . . and in divers other places".

An article in *Vick's Monthly Magazine* for August 1878 explains that "the Everlasting Pea is so called not because it is everlasting in the sense that the *Gomphrena* and *Helichrysum* are everlastings, because the flowers are dry and do not fade, but on account of its perennial character and in contradistinction to the Sweet Pea which is an annual".

EYEBRIGHT, or wake robin

Scarlet – **Joyful tidings**

This is a puzzle because eyebright is the English name for *Euphrasia officinalis*, which has flowers that are white, yellow or purple. Wake robin, on the other hand, is *Arum maculatum* which is known for its scarlet berries. In addition, AMC has already included *A. maculatum*, under its alternate name, CUCKOO PINT.

Eyebright's generic name is said to relate to the belief that the plant can cure blindness and comes from the Greek *euphraino*, to delight, which fits well with AMC's meaning of 'joyful tidings' and suggests that this is, indeed, the plant to which she is referring.

In *A Catalogue of Rare or Remarkable Phaenogamous Plants Collected in South Kent* (1829), Gerard Edwards Smith tells us that *Euphrasia* is "plentiful upon the chalk turf... its whiteness... tastefully varied with purple and pale yellow". No gems, he says "can equal this brilliant and lasting ornament of the turf. When summer, with her gay companions, has deserted the woods and fields, when the completion of the harvest has robbed the landscape of its richer features, the grassy downs are still glowing with the tufted *Euphrasia*".

Barton tells us that the first people to write about the medicinal properties of eyebright were the Spanish physician Arnoldus de Villa Nova (c. 1240–1311)) and the French physician Bernard de Gordon (fl.1270-1330). It is a remedy that has stood the test of time, since it is still used by herbalists and (in great dilution) by homoeopaths to treat eye conditions.

F

FAIR MAID OF FRANCE, the white bachelor's button, applicable to ladies only

With leaves, white – **Single from choice**
Without leaves, white – **Single from necessity**

Ranunculus aconitifolius is a species of white buttercup that is also known as fair maid of France and BACHELORS' BUTTON.

A native of Germany, northern Italy and Switzerland, it was introduced to Britain before 1596. Mrs. Loudon comments that it flourishes in moist soil under trees but it is not tolerant of the London smoke.

FENNEL

Yellow – **Strength of mind**

The common fennel (*Foeniculum vulgare*) has yellow flowers and, says Barton, grows "on chalky cliffs in England near the sea, and near towns at a short distance from the coast, and is very common in gardens".

In the 19th century, as now, it was used for culinary purposes. "The tender stalks are used in salads" says Barton, "the leaves boiled enter into many fish sauces and are served up with mackarel in many parts of England. The blanched stalks of the Sweet Fennel . . . are eaten with vinegar, oil and pepper as a cold salad, and much esteemed by the Italians, who likewise use them in soups. In Germany, the seeds are used as a condiment in bread and various dishes".

Wilkinson reports that large quantities of the seed are imported to be used in the manufacture of gin, and of medicine "as a harmless carminative". An infusion of the seed, known as dill-water, "is greatly prized . . . as a 'baby-medicine' [and is also] given to sickly lambs". She tells us that Gerard "attributes to the boiled roots an efficacy in dropsy . . . [and] recommends that the powdered seed be drunk 'for certaine daies together fasting,' in order to preserve the eyesight".

The French pharmacist, Pierre Pomet, in his *History of Drugs* (1694) writes of sugar-covered green fennel seeds being sold by confectioners to sweeten the breath, and a distillation of green fennel being "esteemed excellent for taking away Inflammations of the eyes".

The Arabs, says Wilkinson, stew minced meat in fennel leaves, and use the stalks as a vegetable, while the Kurdish inhabitants of Chaldea use dried fennel as "the principal winter provender of their cattle" and its stems as food for the villagers. They also soak chopped fennel in sour milk to make "a wholesome drink which they highly value for its fine aromatic flavour".

In the south of France, fennel was placed over doors, strewn around beds, and laid under pillows, especially on St. John's Eve, because, according to Wilkinson, it was said to have the power "to keep off evil spirits, and other such 'bugges'".

The generic name is derived from the Latin *foenum*, meaning hay, which is said to have a similar smell.

FIG

Green – I do not care for you
Ripe, purple green – Argument

John Stephenson and James Morss Churchill write extensively about the fig (*Ficus carica*) in their *Medical Botany* (1831). The tree, they say, is considered to be a native of Asia "but has been cultivated in the south of Europe from the most remote antiquity". In Greece it was considered a staple food, so much so that its export was prohibited. In Rome it was "carried next to the wine in the processions in honour of Bacchus[1] ... [who] was supposed to have derived his corpulency and vigour, not from the wine, but from the fig".

The fig was introduced into England from Italy in 1525 by Cardinal Pole and two of those trees "are still in the Archbishop's garden at Lambeth ... [bearing] excellent fruit". The authors go on to say that, in this country, fig trees need "good walls ... but in some parts of England, as about Worthing in Sussex, they are trained as standard trees, and produce abundance of fruit". Stephenson and

---

1. The Roman god of wine

Churchill mention several species 'esteemed' by Philip Miller, including the black ischia, the black Genoa, the Brunswick, the brown Italian and the common blue.

In the early part of the 19th century, 900 tons of dried figs "subject to a duty of £1 1s" (presumably per ton) were being imported into Britain every year, mostly from Turkey. In northern France, we are told, "there are many fig-gardens, particularly at Argenteuil near Paris, where the culture of the fig-trees is one of the chief employments of the people".

The fruit of the fig is described by Stephenson and Churchill as "soft, and succulent, and, eaten with moderation, . . . digestible, wholesome, and very delicious . . . [however] if too many be partaken of, they occasion flatulency, and sometimes diarrhoea, attended with pain".

Therapeutically, roasted figs have been used as hot applications for gum-boils.

FILBERT

Green & bright brown – **Reconciliation**

Filbert is another name for hazel nut. Loudon describes the hazel tree (*Corylus avellana*) as being a large-sized shrub . . . very common in most woods, and extensively cultivated about Maidstone, in Kent. According to A.J. Downing of the Botanic Garden in Newburgh, New York, writing in *The Magazine of Horticulture* (1841), "Kent is the most celebrated nut-growing district, and the average crop there is about 800 weight per acre, although, in good soils and favorable seasons, 3000 weight[2] has been raised on an acre of ground".

---

2. 800wt is about 400kg; 3000wt is about 1500 kg. or one and a half tons

According to the *Library of Agricultural and Horticultural Knowledge* (1830) the reason for the large numbers of hazel trees in Kent was the soil which was "congenial both to the filbert and the hop", with the same type of manure – including old woollen rags – suiting both crops.

Mrs. Loudon tells us that "As a table nut it is in universal esteem", and she lists several varieties: "The red-filbert is accounted to have a finer flavour than the white. The cob-nut is large . . . [and] the kernel is considerable in size, and sweet. The Barcelona, a good large nut, with a thin shell, is well known. The cossford is very sweet, kernels well, and the tree is a great bearer".

The wood from the wild varieties of hazel has been used for making stakes, pegs and other gardening equipment.

FIR TREE

Green – **Prosperity, elevation**

In his *Gardener's Dictionary* of 1759, Philip Miller writes extensively about the fir tree (*Abies*) and lists nine species "which are at present to be found in the English Gardens". Two, the silver fir and the common (or Norway) fir are natives of Europe. Four are native to America – the Virginian fir, the black and white Newfoundland spruce firs, and the BALM OF GILEAD fir. The eastern fir tree, came to Europe from the Levant by way of the Royal Gardens in Paris. And the great fir tree and the China fir tree, both very common in China, are "at present, very rare in England".

Silver firs, says Miller, are to be found in Strasbourg and parts of Germany, and the turpentine yielded by them is imported into England. "But the most beautiful of these Trees are growing upon Mount Olympus, from whence I have received Cones, which were upwards of a Foot in Length".

The Virginian, said by Miller to be less beautiful than the other firs, "was formerly growing in the Bishop of London's Garden at Fulham" and has leaves with "so much the Resemblance of those of the Yew, that at a small Distance they are not easily distinguished from that Tree, even by Persons of Skill". Miller tells us that the finest Newfoundland firs he has ever seen are "those in the elegant Gardens of His Grace the Duke of Argyle, at Whitton near Hounslow". In America, he says, the leaves of these firs are used "for the making of Spruce Beer".

Both types of Newfoundland fir produced turpentine "which the Native Indians[3] use to cure green Wounds, and also for some internal Disorders: And of late Years the English Physicians in North America, have likewise adopted it into their Practice". Miller tells us that balm of Gilead, frequently sold in England, is the turpentine from the fir of that name which, when young, is "the most beautiful of any of the Kinds yet known; but in almost all the Places where these Trees have been planted, they have not continued fair above ten or twelve Years; . . . This sudden Decay of the Trees has brought them into Disrepute, so that few Persons at present care to plant them . . . nor have I seen any free from this Accident, except at his Grace the Duke of Bedford's at Woburn Abbey; where . . . are Numbers of this Sort of considerable Growth, which yet remain in good Health".

The generic name, according to Miller, is said to come either from the Latin *abeo*, to extend, "because it advances much in Height . . . [or] from *A-beo*, to go away, because the Bark splits, and, as it were, falls away, or is broken off easily".

---

3. ie Native Americans

FLAX

Blue – **Domestic industry**

The common flax (*Linum usitatissimum*), says Mrs. Loudon, "has large clear blue flowers; and where it is allowed room to spread, it makes a handsome plant". Although now naturalised, flax was thought originally to have been introduced from Egypt "and it has been in cultivation for its fibre from almost the earliest period of civilisation". Mrs. Loudon describes another species – the whorled flax (*L. verticillatum*) – as a pretty delicate little plant with very pale blue flowers which is "more common than those of any other in the seed-shops".

Glenny and Don list several species, including the English perennial flax (*L. perenne subsp. anglicum*) found on chalky hills in Cambridgeshire, Northamptonshire, Westmoreland and Norfolk, while Wilkinson tells us that "at least twenty-six species . . . are in cultivation in our gardens".

According to Barton, very little flax "is grown in England, as it exhausts the soil more than any other crop, and wheat is much more profitable", although Don tells us that "the legislature of the country . . . has paid more attention to framing laws regarding the husbandry of flax than to any other branch of rural economy". Wilkinson says that in Ireland in mediaeval times, flax became so important to the economy of the country that every farmer was required by law "to acquire a full acquaintance with the best mode of dressing and working it".

While flax has mostly been grown to be made into linen, Barton tells us that the seeds, bruised and mixed with honey, have been used as food in parts of Asia and, in times of scarcity, in Holland "but they afford little nourishment, and are very difficult of digestion". The seeds also provide linseed oil.

The first step in linen-making is to break the plant down by soaking it in water but, says Barton, this makes the water "of so poisonous a nature to animals, that the practice of macerating or steeping flax in any pond or running stream is prohibited[4] under severe penalties". However, Don tells us that a new method that doesn't require soaking, was invented in 1810 and was later improved upon "by the new patent machines of Messrs. Hill and Bunby, which are portable, and ... [suitable] for parish workhouses and charitable institutions; a great part of the work being so light, that it may be done by children and infirm persons".

The manufacture of linen uses only the long fibres produced from flax. Short or broken fibres, known as tow, were used to make a much coarser cloth, giving rise to the phrase 'tow rag' to describe something (or someone) of little worth. The generic name of the plant and the word 'linen' are both derived from the Celtic *lin*, meaning thread. The common flax was also known as lint or lyne.

FLAX-LEAVED GOLDEN LOCKS

Yellow – **Laziness, idle**

Flax-leaved golden locks (*Galatella linosyris*) is also known as goldilocks aster and is described by Mrs. Loudon as "low soft-wooded shrubs from the Cape, with yellow flowers". However, Maund tells us that golden locks is native to Britain "but of rare occurrence. We find its only acknowledged habitat to be the rocky cliffs of Berryhead, Devonshire . . . Its growth is neat and upright; but its terminal yellow blossoms are only showy through their numbers".

According to the 1633 edition of *Gerard's Herbal* the specific name was given

---

4. By an Act of Henry VIII

because the plant was "stalked and leaved like common flax, (*Linum*)".

FLOS AERIS

***Blue & pale pink* – Lightness**

Flos aeris or 'air plant' is a name that seems to have been given to a number of plants in the *Aerides* genus of orchids. I have been unable to identify a particular species with blue and pale pink flowers. However, I found the following reference to *Flos aeris* in Maria Edgeworth's *Harry and Lucy*, a book of 'early lessons' for young people, published in 1814: "There is one species of the *epidendrum* family, the *flos aeris*, a native of India, that deserves to be particularly distinguished. It is so called, because it grows and blossoms when suspended in the air; and we are assured, that hanging from the ceiling of a room, it will vegetate for years; it is likewise said to be remarkably reviving to the inhabitants, by the fine odour of its blossoms."

See also Orchis

FLY ORCHIS

Blue – Mistake, error

The fly ORCHIS (*Ophrys insectifera*) acquired its name because its flowers look exactly like flies. Their colour varies from a dark brown-purple to a dark red (and there is a rare yellow variety) but none could truly be described as blue. Whether AMC has just got the colour of the fly orchis wrong, or whether she was thinking of another flower entirely it is impossible to know.

FORGET-ME-NOT, MOUSE EAR

Cerulean blue – Forget me not
Blue – Ingenuous simplicity

Forget-me-not and mouse ear are names given to a number of species in the *Myosotis* genus. AMC lists it under both names but, since most species produce blue flowers it is impossible to say to which she is referring.

Don lists 51 species of *Myosotis* with blue flowers, including the tufted forget-me-not (*M. laxa subsp. caespitosa*) which is found "in boggy places . . . [and is] common about ponds", and the creeping forget-me-not (*M. secunda*) which is a native of Scotland, Yorkshire, Kent and Sussex, and is found on open heaths and in forests. He also mentions the water forget-me-not (*M. scorpioides*) which can be found growing wild "in humid meadows, bogs, banks of rivers, rivulets, and ditches . . . [and] is now a general favourite, and deservedly so."

Wilkinson, probably referring to the common forget-me-not (*M. arvensis*) believes that "there can be few more beautiful plants for 'bedding'" and she recommends it for "window gardening". Phillips, too, is a fan: "For some years past this little flower has been cultivated in France with the greatest care, and when sent to the Parisian markets it finds a more ready sale than any exotic plant . . . We earnestly recommend the cultivation of this rustic little beauty, and particularly so to those cottagers who live near towns, as . . . they would find it a profitable employ to send them to market, for few people would withstand the temptation of purchasing these alluring flowers".

Phillips has been told that "if edged tools [of steel] be made red-hot and then quenched in the juice [of the plant] and this be repeated several times . . . the steel will become so hard as to cut iron, or even stone, without turning the edge".

The ancient Egyptians, according to Pliny, had another use for the forget-me-not, believing that if the plant was picked on the 27th day of the month of Thoth and the juice was used to anoint the eyes of someone before he spoke in the morning, his eyes would remain strong for a year.

The generic name of this plant comes from the Greek *myos*, a mouse, and *otos*, an ear, as the leaves were thought to resemble mouse ears. Another name is scorpion grass.

FOX GLOVE

White or pink – **Falsehood**

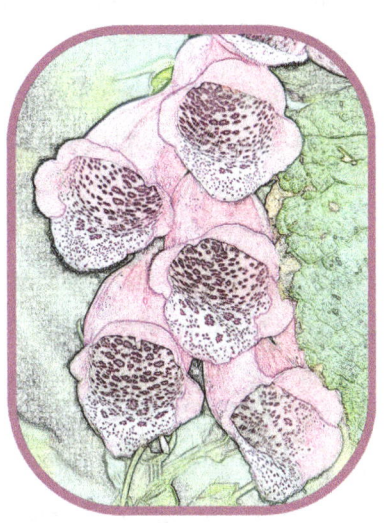

"If this plant were not a common British weed," comments Mrs. Loudon, "it would be thought very ornamental". Barton, writing about the purple foxglove (*Digitalis purpurea*), calls it a "beautiful and stately plant . . . [that] flourishes on dry banks, hilly pastures, and the borders of woods . . . [but] is almost unknown in the extreme eastern counties of England". This however, contradicts Turner whose *New Herball* (1568) states that it grew "very much in Englande, and specially in Norfolke". Maybe Barton was thinking of more northerly eastern counties or, perhaps more likely, the flora had changed considerably in the three hundred or so years since Turner's time.

Extracts of the foxglove have been used therapeutically for centuries and the drug digoxin (a synthetic version of the digitalis produced by the plant) has long been used by doctors to treat a variety of heart conditions. Don gives a list of conditions that digitalis has been used for, but points out that "in excessive doses it produces vomiting, dimness of sight, vertigo, delirium, hiccough, convulsions, collapse, and death". Ingesting any part of the plant can result in an excessive dose.

Phillips mentions that "within these last few years [digitalis] has come into such high repute with the Parisian apothecaries, that they frequently ornament the outside of their houses with paintings of this flower". However, it is interesting to note that, as late as 1845, Barton could relate that while some writers believed it exerted "a peculiar power over the heart" others still strongly denied this.

Wilkinson quotes Gerard's comment that digitalis is "good for them that have fallen from high places," but points out that "the old herbalist . . . does not explain whether the healing to which he alludes is for cases of a moral or a physical character". In Gerard's time, she says it was "highly esteemed for coughs, as well as for all maladies of the spleen and liver . . . [and was] employed by the country people of Somersetshire, in fevers . . . [while] others mingling them with lard, put them underground for forty days, and then apply them as an ointment in cases of the king's evil". Another use for the foxglove, says Wilkinson, was found by Welsh peasant dyers who used an infusion of the root to treat woollen yarn, in order to make it more receptive to dyeing.

Perhaps one of the most intriguing things about the foxglove is its name. The generic name is straightforward, being derived from *digitale* (finger-like) and relating to the shape of the flowers. This name was first applied to the plant by Fuchs in his *Plantarum Omnium Nomenclaturae* (1541), and he was the first person to write about its medical properties. However, when we come to the English name, things are not so clear cut.

Phillips, who always seems to have an opinion on everything, somewhat surprisingly writes "we are at a loss to account for the origin of the name of Fox-glove". Don quotes the great 17th century botanist, John Parkinson, as saying "some thinking Foxglove to be a foolish name, do call them finger flowers, because they are like unto the fingers of a glove, the ends cut off". Barton puts forward the suggestion of "Sir J. Smith" – presumably the botanist and founder of the Linnean Society, Sir James Smith (1759-1828) – that the original name was Fuchs'-glove.

Wilkinson maintains that there are many superstitions associated with the foxglove "which the peasant declares to be a favourite lurking-place of the fairies" and therefore that the derivation is from folk's-glove ('folk' referring to fairies).

"In the south of Scotland," says Wilkinson, "it is called 'bloody-fingers', more northward, 'deadmen's bells'; . . . amongst the Welsh . . . it bears names [including] 'elves-gloves'". Turner adds the name of Thimble-wurt, saying that the many flowers hang down "like belles or thumbles."

FRENCH HONEYSUCKLE

Red – **Rustic beauty**

Phillips tells us that French honeysuckle (*Hedysarum coronarium*), which he describes as large and straggling, was known in Britain "previous to the year 1596". And, never one to mince his words, he observes that "this species of *Hedysarum*, which we have so improperly named after a country that it does not belong to, and after a flower to which it has no resemblance, is a native of Spain, and also of some parts of Italy". Its flowers are either deep red or white.

The generic name comes from the Greek *hedysma*, sweetness, and *aron*, ointment. Phillips comments that cows fed on French honeysuckle "produce abundance of milk, and the butter made from it [is] good flavoured".

FRENCH MARYGOLD

Gold colour – **Doubt, jealousy**

Phillips describes French marigolds (*Tagetes patula*) as autumnal flowers that "have only their gaiety to recommend them, since their odour is more offensive than agreeable". Mrs. Loudon believes that "The commonness of this flower prevents its exciting the admiration that its brilliant colours could not fail to obtain, if the plant they belong to were either new or rare". She comments that Curtis, in his *Botanical Magazine*, mentions a "common dwarf sort, with a very strong disagreeable smell, and a larger kind, usually called the sweet-scented, [whose only claim] to that title [was] being rather less disagreeable than the other".

The history of the French marigold is obscure, says Mrs. Loudon, "as the early writers on plants appear to have confounded it with the upright or African marigold". However, Phillips states that "The *Tagetes* appears to have been introduced into this country as long back as the year 1573, and we conclude that they were called French Marygolds from our having first received the seed from France", although they probably originated in Mexico.

Phillips remarks that the generic name is said to have been derived from that of Tages, a grandson of the Roman god Jupiter, "who first taught the science of augury and divination to the twelve nations of the Etrurians, who from hence became so celebrated for their pretended knowledge of omens and incantations. But as Tages could not have taught the use of plants peculiar to lands which the gods themselves had not visited, we think the name badly adapted". He goes on to pour scorn on the legend that "French Marygolds became first stained and marked with a dark red, by the blood of the unhappy Mexicans whom the insatiable Spaniards slew in their own peaceful fields". More likely, says Phillips, is the suggestion "that these flowers were called *Tagetes*, from the Greek *tage*, meaning principality, which shows the rank these plants held in the parterre".

FRENCH WILLOW

Pink – **Courage, bravery, humility**

French willow or willow herb (*Chamaenerion angustifolium*) is perhaps best known as a wild flower. Phillips describes it as a beautiful rustic plant with tall spikes of showy flowers, which is "admirably adapted to embellish the banks of our streams, the foreground of our woods, and wilderness scenery in general".

Gerard, writing in 1596, refers to it as a "goodly and stately plant ... garnished with brave flowers of greate beautie ... it groweth in Yorkshire ... from whence I had these plants, which do grow in my garden". But in the 1762 edition of his *Gardener's and Florist's Dictionary*, Philip Miller notes that the plant is losing some of its earlier popularity as a garden flower.

Phillips states that the English name comes from "the resemblance which its leaves bear to those of the *Salix* or willow, and French willow, we presume, from its being originally brought from that country".

FUCHSIA

Crimson & purple – **Accepted love**

Following their introduction in 1788, from their native South America to the Royal Garden at Kew, fuchsias were mostly treated as greenhouse plants. However, Mrs. Loudon tells her readers that "many very beautiful varieties and hybrids have been raised in this country", and that these grow freely in the open air and "enliven our flower-gardens . . . with their beautiful crimson flowers".

Phillips comments that he has "seen it in conservatories from ten to fifteen feet, having all the lower branches pruned off, and thus forming a tree of the most enchanting appearance". However, Glenny grumbles that "Very few people grow these plants as they ought to be grown; and they are rarely seen at the exhibitions in a state that is any credit to the gardener".

Don lists several species that match AMC's crimson and purple flowers, including the hardy fuchsia (*F. magellanica*), the small-flowered fuchsia (*F. parviflora*) and the scarlet fuchsia (*F. coccinea*).

Phillips records that the first fuchsias available to the public were sold by Mr. Lee, who had a nursery in Hammersmith, and because of "its great beauty, [it] brought a high price for several years, until its easy propagation became generally known". Mrs. Loudon comments that the best fuchsias to be found in the neighbourhood of London at the time she was writing were "those of Mr. Standish at Bagshot, but some very handsome varieties have been raised by Mr. Groom of Walworth".

The generic name was given in honour of Leonard [Leonhart] Fuchs, a celebrated 16th century German botanist.

G

GERANIUM

Scarlet – **Home, a place of rest**
Oak, pink – **Lady deign to smile**
Silver-leaved, pink – **Come back again**
Nutmeg, pink – **An expected meeting**
Large, pink – **I prefer you**
Ivy, violet – **I engage you for the next dance**

Mrs. Loudon believes that "There are few plants more easily grown . . . than Geraniums, or, as they are more properly called, Pelargoniums". Don recommends them for indoors, since they tolerate "the confined air of a sitting room better than most plants". The colours given by AMC for the oak leaved, the silver-leaved and the ivy-leaved geraniums are all correct but the flowers of the nutmeg geranium are white.

The name geranium comes from the Greek *geranos*, a crane (because, says Don "the long beak which terminates the carpels resembles the bill of the crane"). Wild geraniums are generally known as CRANE'S BILL.

GILLY FLOWER

Red – **Unfading beauty**

Gilly flower, or gilliflower, is a name that has been given to STOCKS, WALLFLOWERS, PINKS and CARNATIONS, all of which have red species or varieties, and all of which are listed elsewhere in the book.

GLOBE AMARANTH

Purple – **True to eternity**

The globe amaranth (*Gomphrena globosa*) has, says Phillips, flowers "of a fine shining purple, [which] will retain their beauty and freshness for several years if gathered before they are too far advanced", but Mrs. Loudon is unimpressed, writing that the plant "has but little beauty to recommend it". Introduced into Holland from the East Indies around 1670, it was brought to England in 1714 by the Duchess of Beaufort.

The globe amaranth is associated with death and funerals and, says Mrs. Loudon, "In the churches on the Continent, the Globe Amaranth is generally used, as a symbol of eternity, to deck the shrines on fete days; and it is sold in Paris … woven into wreaths, to hang on the tombs in the cemetery of Pere la Chaise". Phillips adds that it is "much cultivated in Portugal and other warm Catholic countries, for the purpose of adorning the churches in the winter".

GOATS' RUE

Violet – **Reason**

Goats' rue (*Galega*) is described by Mrs. Loudon as "weedy-looking . . . with small purple or white flowers". However, Don considers all the species of the genus to be "very elegant". It may be that these two writers are describing different species, since Maund differentiates between the more common *G. officinalis* and the more ornamental *G. orientalis*, which was introduced from the Levant in 1801.

The generic name comes from the Greek *gala*, meaning milk, because the plant was said to increase the milk yield of the animals that ate it.

GOLDEN ROD

Deep yellow – **Encouragement**

Glenny describes golden rod (*Solidago*) as a large family of herbaceous perennials, all with yellow flowers. Phillips says that Canada golden rod (*S. Canadensis*) which was introduced into England in 1648, "seldom exceeds more than two feet in height [and so] is not so much sought after as the taller kinds". Barton mentions the common golden rod

(*S. virgaurea*) which "is frequent in woods and thickets, on heaths and among furze in the British islands" and which was said to have been imported "by the Christians who returned from the Saracen wars". Its flowers and leaves produce "a yellow dye superior to that obtained from . . . dyer's-weed (*Reseda luteola*)".

In the 16th century, according to Phillips, *Solidago* was so highly esteemed for its therapeutic properties that "it ranked amongst the most expensive drugs". The imported dried herb was, according to Gerard "solde . . . in London, for halfe a crowne[1] an ounce [until]. . . it was founde in Hampsteed-wood, . . . [since when] no man will give halfe a crowne for an hundred weight of it".

The generic name, says Phillips, comes from the Latin *solidare*, to consolidate, because of "its supposed efficacy in healing wounds", while the specific name of the common golden rod is derived from the Latin *virga*, a rod, and *aurum*, gold. Other English names are woundwort and Aaron's rod.

GOOSEBERRY

Red or green – **Anticipation**

The gooseberry (*Ribes uva-crispa*), which Don describes as a "wholesome and useful fruit" is, he says, "plentiful in some parts of Britain, in hedges, thickets, and waste ground." However, the climate of Lancashire and the Lothians seem to suit it best and "it is cultivated in greater perfection in Lancashire than

---

1. Approximately four days' wages for a skilled craftsman

in any other part of Britain". In Lancashire, and parts of the adjoining counties "almost every cottager, who has a garden, cultivates the gooseberry, with a view to prizes, given at what are called Gooseberry-prize Meetings, of which there is annually published an account . . . in what is called the Manchester Gooseberry Book".

The gooseberry was cultivated in England as early as 1573. By the time Don was writing, some of the Lancashire growers were listing over 300 varieties. Don himself lists 55 green varieties and 87 red.

The English name was said by some to come from gorseberry, because the bush resembled gorse. Others, however, thought it related to the use of the berry as a sauce for geese. According to Gerard, it was called feaberry (or feverberry) in Cheshire, Lancashire and Yorkshire. In Norfolk, this was shortened to feabes, or fapes. Another English name was carberry.

GORSE

Yellow – **Displeasure**

"A very showy plant when in flower," says Don, "being profusely clothed with elegant double yellow flowers. Also known as furze or whin, its botanical name is *Ulex Europaeus*.

Gorse was at one time used for fences against cattle but, as Don relates, although it grew quickly, within a few years "these hedges become naked". In Scotland it was sometimes used for animal fodder and "in some parts of Britain it is cultivated for fuel, where peat or coals are dear".

The generic name is said to be derived from the Celtic word *ac*, meaning a point, and referring to the spiny branches.

GOURD

***Yellow* – Bulk**

There are numerous types of gourd. Mrs. Loudon mentions the bottle gourd (*Lagenaria siceraria*), a native of the East Indies, which was sometimes grown because of its "curious shape". Don describes the common yellow gourd (*Cucurbita maxima*) whose fruit could be yellow, red or green. However, perhaps the most likely candidate for AMC's gourd is the vegetable marrow (*Cucurbita pepo*).

This plant was still something of a novelty in Don's time. "The first kind of vegetable marrow was introduced to Britain from Persia within the last few years", he writes. "The fruit . . . is of a uniform pale yellow or light sulphur colour when very young [and] is good if fried with butter". When larger, he recommends it "either plain boiled or stewed with rich sauce". He tells us that there are "several kinds of vegetable marrow in cultivation" and points out that "the tender tops of all the edible species of *Cucurbitaceae*, boiled as greens or spinage [sic], are a fully more delicate vegetable than the fruit".

The generic name comes from the Latin *curvitas*, meaning crookedness.

GRAPE

Purple – **Rural joy, gladness**

Grapes, says Don, "appear to have been in demand for the table as early as the 16th century . . . Parkinson, in 1627, enumerates 23 varieties". Don lists 64 British grapes being cultivated in nurseries. And, in *A Practical Treatise on the Cultivation of the Grape Vine on Open Walls* (1841), Clement Hoare list twelve varieties including the black Hamburgh ("a splendid table fruit"), the white sweetwater ("very juicy and luscious") and three – the black Frontignan, grizzly Frontignan, and white Frontignan – that the author declares to be "so extremely delicious, that no good vine wall should be without them".

SEE ALSO VINE

GRASS

Green – **Submission, utility**

We may assume that AMC is referring here to grass in general, such as would be found in any lawn or field. Prior, however, lists 38 distinct types including

RAY GRASS, KNOT GRASS, five finger grass, hair grass, pudding grass, ribband grass, sparrow grass, squirrel tail grass and worm grass.

Simeon Shaw in *Nature Displayed* (1823) lists 16 varieties of British grasses, including silver hair grass and fine bent grass "found on the best pastures", sheep's fescue grass, "much esteemed as the sweetest feed for sheep", purple fescue grass and mountain hair grass, both found on sheep pastures, and crested dog's-tail grass, which "is proper for deer in parks, and for sheep". Others on the list are annual meadow grass (also known as Suffolk grass) "which makes the finest turf, [and] grows everywhere by way-sides, and on rich sound commons", great meadow grass which "makes both good pasture and hay", sweet scented VERNAL GRASS and the curiously named bulbous foxtail grass.

GROUND IVY

Purple – **Domestic comfort**

Ground ivy (*Glechoma hederacea*) is described by Don as growing "in hedges, ditches, woods and waste places".

Before hops were introduced into the beer-making process, ground ivy leaves were put into ale to clarify it, preserve it and give it flavour.

Infusions were used to treat headaches and, Don says, "In obstinate coughs it is still a favourite remedy with the common people".

Alternative names are ale-hoof and tun-hoof, gill-go-by-the-ground and cat's-foot.

GUELDER ROSE

White – **Age with friendship**

"An interesting small tree" is how Mrs. Loudon describes the wild Guelder rose or wayfaring tree (*Viburnum lantana*). But the kind "grown in small gardens" is a different species, *V. opulus*. Loudon says that the latter, in its wild state, "is not remarkable for the beauty of its flowers; but its bright red berries, which . . . towards the middle of October, assume a beautiful pink, almost compensate for the inferiority of the . . . flowers". Mrs. Loudon comments that, when cultivated, *V. opulus* has flowers that are so compact and so snowy white "as amply to justify its popular name of the snowball tree".

Loudon suggests that the berries of the Guelder rose "might be cultivated in our kitchen-gardens and orchards for the same purpose as the common cranberry[2] . . . [and] a crop of fruit might be depended on with greater certainty. At all events, this and similar experiments offer interesting and useful employment to the amateur who has nothing better to do".

The English name, Guelder rose, relates to Guelderland (in the Netherlands), from where the double-flowered variety originally came.

---

2. Although Guelder rose berries are only safe to eat once they have been cooked

H

HARE BELL

Blue – **Retirement**

Regarding the harebell, I can do no better than quote Mrs. Loudon, who writes "It is rather curious, that though few poets can write a sonnet without mentioning the Harebell, and though it is sure to be introduced in every eloquent prose description of country scenery, botanists cannot exactly decide what plant is meant by the name – some supposing it to be the beautiful little blue *Campanula rotundifolia*, and others, the wild Hyacinth, *Scilla non-scripta**. The fact is, that both plants are now known by the name in different parts of Britain".

Both plants are also known as BLUEBELLS.

HAWTHORN

White – **Hope**
Pink – **Rural beauty**

The common hawthorn (*Crataegus monogyna*) is said by Don to be found in thickets, hedges, copses, and high open fields and to have flowers that are white, or occasionally pink, and sweet-scented.

The hawthorn (also known as the may tree) was used to create "impenetrable, close, durable, and easily raised fences, called quickset hedges". The timber "of such plants as grow singly and attain a tolerable size" was used by millwrights and turners, while the roots were used by cabinet makers.

HAWKWEED

Pink – **Clear sightedness**
Yellow – **Support me or I fall**

"The plants properly called Hawkweed," says Mrs. Loudon "belong to the genus *Hieracium*; they have generally yellow flowers". Phillips tells us that there are 18 native species and another 37 exotic species, but most are regarded as weeds.

The species "generally cultivated in the English parterre," is, according to Phillips, the orange hawkweed (*H. auranticum*). Phillips says of it "This species sports considerably in colour, some plants producing red, and others a bright orange or pale yellow flowers". There seem to be no other candidates for AMC's pink hawkweed, so it is probably this species to which she is referring.

The English name, says Mrs. Loudon, "is said to be derived from the juice of these plants being formerly given to hawks, to clear and improve their sight; and it is still used for bathing the eyes in ophthalmic disorders".

HEARTSEASE or PANSY

Purple yellow – Thoughts
Wild, purple yellow – A kiss at the garden gate
Purple – I think on you
Purple edged with yellow – Heartsease, happiness
Love in idleness, red – You doat on a fool

Heartsease (*Viola tricolor*) is nowadays more commonly known as the pansy. Don describes it as growing in cultivated fields and gardens throughout Europe. Mrs. Loudon tells us that cultivation of the plants from seed has resulted in there being over a thousand varieties.

Although a favourite garden flower for a long time, it was only in the early 19th century that it achieved recognition from florists. According to Mrs. Loudon, Lady Mary Bennet, daughter of the Earl of Tankerville, had a small garden in her father's grounds at Walton-upon-Thames. She had a particular liking for pansies and, with the help of the Earl's gardener, Mr. Richardson, "several pretty varieties were raised". Within a few years, some of Mr. Richardson's work was noticed by Mr. Lee, of the Hammersmith nursery and from this "may be traced the rage which has since prevailed for cultivating this flower".

According to legend, the heartsease played an unusual and significant role in the development of botanical sciences in America. John Bartram (1699–1777), known as the 'father of American botany' was a farmer who one day, so it is said, while standing at the edge of one of his fields talking to his farm hands, idly picked a heartsease and started to pull off its petals. The construction of the flower caught his attention and he took it home to examine it more carefully, eventually becoming, in the words of Linnaeus, "the greatest natural botanist in the world".

Don mentions that "Heart's-ease was represented by old writers . . . as a powerful medicine in epilepsy, ulcers, scabies and cutaneous complaints".

The plant has acquired numerous names over the centuries. Don relates that "In days of superstition it was called Herb Trinity . . . Heart's-ease is the general name by which it is now known; its more elegant name, Pansies, is from the French *pensée*[1] ". Phillips adds others to the list: "Three faces under a hood, Flame Flower, Jump up and kiss Me, Flower of Jove, Pink of my John, and others equally whimsical and unappropriate". And Mrs. Loudon has still more: love and idleness, love in idleness, live in idleness, kiss behind the garden gate, Kit run in the streets, call me to you, and look up and kiss me.

---

1. Meaning thought

HEATH

White or pink – **Solitude**
Purple – **Liberty**

The words heath and heather are often used interchangeably to describe two closely related genera, *Erica* and *Calluna*. Wilkinson tells us that "In Great Britain we have seven species of heather, including six Ericas and one ling . . . *C. vulgaris*", while Tyas observes that "Our native Heaths, though few in number, are rich in beauty . . . Some are almost purple, while others are roseate, and others are nearly white".

Many of the cultivated species came originally from the Cape of Good Hope. Tyas says they were hardly known in Britain until the end of the 18th century and Wilkinson confirms that "we have received nearly four hundred species, now in cultivation in this country; the whole of which were introduced . . . subsequently to the claim made on Cape Colony by the British Government in the year 1795".

Wilkinson tells us that the Danes who invaded Britain made a "much celebrated heather-ale; . . . [but] the secret of brewing this liquor perished, and was never imparted to Saxon or to Briton . . . . [although] the inhabitants of the Isle of Skye still do brew an ale of two parts of heather-tops to one part of malt".

Heather was once a valuable component of house-building. According to Wilkinson it was used to make not only the thatch, but the ropes that bound down the thatch, and was incorporated into the mortar of straw and black earth used to build the walls. Another use was as fuel, while *Erica cinerea*, and *Calluna vulgaris* make "the best of brooms"

HELIOTROPE, CHERRY-PIE PLANT

Violet – **Devoted attachment**

The common heliotrope (*Heliotropium arborescens*) is known as cherry-pie plant because its scent is reminiscent of cherries and vanilla. Lizzie Deas in her *Flower Favourites* (1898) writes "This little 'bride of the sun' is a native of South America and was brought from Peru to Paris by the famous botanist Jussieu,[2] where it at once became popular with the Parisians, more especially the women . . . naming it 'la herbe d'amour'[3] and receiving with indifference all bouquets in which their favourite found no place. From France . . . [it] quickly passed to other European countries, in all of which it is a frequent and always valued plant." 'father of American botany'

The generic name is derived from the Greek *helios*, the sun. and *trope*, turning. An alternative name for heliotrope is turnsole.

---

2. Antoine Laurent de Jussieu (1748-1836)

3. Herb of love

HELLEBORE (Christmas rose)

White – **Calumny, inconstancy**

The Christmas rose or black hellebore[4] (*Helleborus niger*) is a hardy perennial and, in the words of Glenny, "a dwarf, tufted species, which flowers all through the winter, having large white blossoms". A native of Austria and Italy, it was introduced into Britain some time before 1597, when Gerard reports having it in his garden. In the early 19th century, it was a popular plant, although Phillips points out that "it loves a pure air, and will not therefore flourish within the precincts of London".

Most of those who write about hellebore, however, concentrate on its therapeutic properties. Phillips tells us that "few plants have been more celebrated by the physicians of antiquity", while Don comments on its "drastic purgative" and diuretic properties and its past use in "cases of mania, melancholy, coma, dropsy, worms, and psora". At the time Phillips was writing, powdered hellebore was still being used to treat worms by "many country people". However, it is a dangerous plant. Don says "its use requires very great caution, for its effects are very uncertain" and Phillips seems uneasy about it being used at all.

Phillips tells us that "the ancients" used hellebore "to purify their houses . . . and they had a belief that by strewing . . . their apartments with this plant, they drove away evil spirits . . . In the same manner they blessed their cattle with the Hellebore, to keep them free from the spells of the wicked". The powdered root has been used as snuff, and it is said that the Greek philosopher Carneades (214-c.129 BCE) "sharpened his wit and quickened his spirit, by purging his

---

4. So called because of the colour of its roots

head with powdered Hellebore". The Gauls, says Phillips, "never went to the chase without rubbing the points of their arrows with this herb, believing that it rendered all the game killed with them the more tender".

The generic name is said to come from the Greek *helein*, to cause death or destroy, and *bora*, food or pasture.

HEMLOCK

Purple – **You will cause my death**

Hemlock (*Conium maculatum*), says Don, is found throughout Europe "in cultivated ground, among rubbish, and on dung hills". It is reputed to be the plant whose poisonous juice was taken by the Greek philosopher, Socrates (470-399 BCE) when he was ordered to kill himself. It has many 'lookalikes' (such as cow parsley and wild carrot) and, like them, has white flowers. However, the *Apiaceae* family, to which all these plants belong, is huge and does contain some species with purple flowers. But these purple varieties are uncommon and I have been unable to identify any British plants that are likely candidates for AMC's description. It is possible, however, that she was thinking of the purple blotches found on the stems of hemlock, which is one way of distinguishing it from its non-toxic relatives.

Although it is a poison, Don mentions that hemlock has been used therapeutically. "The first physician who endeavoured to bring hemlock into repute as a medicine," he says, "was Baron Stoerck, of Vienna, who announced its extraordinary effects in the most inveterate chronic disorders in 1760".

The Baron, it seems, found that small doses were perfectly safe although, in overdose, "it produces vertigo, dimness of sight, difficulty of speech, nausea, fetid eructations, anxiety, tremors, and paralysis of the limbs".

"The tranquillity maintained by Socrates after swallowing the deadly potion" comments Barton, "will scarcely accord with the known effects of Hemlock-juice", suggesting that it was just one ingredient "in the fatal cup".

The generic name, says Don (who, in turn, is quoting Linnaeus), comes from the Greek *konis*, meaning dust or powder. However, Barton says the word is not *konis* but *konos*, meaning a top "whose whirling motion resembles the giddiness produced in the human brain by a poisonous dose of the juice of this plant."

HEMP

Purple – **Doom, fate**

Cannabis sativa, or hemp, is a close relative of *C. Indica* from which marijuana is derived. Hemp is valued for its seed and oil, as well as its fibre which can be used in the manufacture of rope, cloth and paper.

Glenny describes it as "insignificant in its flowers . . . [and] somewhat coarse, but a stately plant" which can grow to a height of six or eight feet.

The flowers which, as Glenny says, are insignificant, cannot be described as purple so it is hard to know why AMC has described the plant as being this colour.

HENBANE

Dark blue – **Not harmless**

Despite AMC's assertion, there are no blue henbanes. Typically, the flowers are a creamy yellow with purple veins. In England, according to Mrs. Loudon, henbane (*Hyoscyamus*) is usually found "on old dunghills or heaps of mould from decayed vegetables". She comments that the leaves of the common or black henbane (*H. niger*) "have a very strong and disagreeable smell" but that the plant is handsome in appearance, something she considers to be "very unsuitable to so poisonous a plant".

Henbane, says Mrs. Loudon, yields a narcotic drug which can be used in the same way as opium. The seeds, however, are perfectly safe to eat, and "oculists employ extract of henbane to dilate the pupils of the eyes, when they want to perform any operation of peculiar delicacy". A synthetic version of the active element in the plant is still used by doctors in the treatment of some eye conditions.

The generic name comes from the Greek *hyos*, a hog and *kyamos*, a bean. Don says this is because hogs can be poisoned by it, whereas Barton says it is because they can eat it with impunity.

HEPATICA

Blue – **Depend on my fidelity**

Glenny describes *Hepatica* as "a pretty genus of very dwarf, hardy, herbaceous perennials". The common hepatica (*H. nobilis*) can be single or double, pink, blue or white. Don says these plants "are great favourites for the flower-border, both as being evergreen in their foliage, and for their abundant early blossoms".

Phillips believes that hepatica came originally "from the woods and shady mountains of Italy, Germany and Sweden", although a single variety "was cultivated in our gardens previous to the time of Gerard, who . . . [described the double varieties as] strangers to England".

Like the hydrangea, hepatica seems to change its colour according to the soil in which it is growing. Richard Bradley in his *Philosophical Account of the Works of Nature* (1721) tells the following story: "Some Roots of the Double Blue Hepatica . . . were sent to Mr Harrison of Henley upon Thames from Mr Keys's Garden in Tuttle-fields, whose Soil was so different from the Ground they were planted in at Henley, that when they came to blossom there they produced White Flowers, and were therefore returned back to their first Station, where they retook the Blue Colour they had at first."

The generic name comes from the Greek *hepaticos*, meaning relating to the liver and thought to refer to the leaves which, in form, resemble the three lobes of the liver. The form of the leaf was probably the reason why the plant has also been known as trinity herb.

HOLLY

Red berry – **Am I remembered? Forethought**

Holly (*Ilex*) forms a genus of evergreen shrubs or low trees. Don lists 47 species, most of which have red berries. However, it is likely that AMC is thinking of the common holly (*I. aquifolium*) which is, says Mrs. Loudon, "among the most ornamental of British shrubs" with many varieties.

Barton remarks that "if not truly indigenous, it has been naturalized from time immemorial. There are some fine specimens of the tree in Needwood Forest, Staffordshire, and the woods of Dumbartonshire". Mrs. Loudon comments that a holly hedge is very useful in shutting out "unpleasant objects . . . [and] is also well adapted for a street or roadside garden; as, while it serves as a screen, it has a cheerful look".

However, Barton points out that, while holly is "much prized for making hedges, as it forms a most impenetrable and durable fence", it is rarely used because it grows so slowly. Despite this, the 17th century diarist, John Evelyn had a holly hedge that, according to Barton, was four hundred feet long, nine feet high, and five feet broad.

Don tells us that holly yields "the whitest of all hard woods" which, according to Barton, is "susceptible of a fine polish, [and] much used by turners, especially in the manufacture of Tonbridge ware[5]; it is also used in veneering, and is sometimes

---

5. Small wooden items, such as boxes, inlaid with a mosaic of woods, manufactured, from the late 18th century, in and around Tonbridge in Kent

stained black, to imitate ebony". The branches have been used to make walking sticks and knife handles.

The generic name may be derived from the Celtic *ac*, a point (referring to the spiny leaves). Similarly, the specific name of the common holly comes from the Latin *acus*, a point, and *folium*, a leaf. In England, holly has also been known as hulver and holme.

HOLLYHOCK

White, rose, purple – **Ambition, desirous of praise**

The hollyhock (*Alcea rosea*) is, says Glenny, "a noble flower, and the varieties are becoming so numerous and so much improved that it is an established favourite". Phillips agrees that "We have but few flowers that contribute more to the embellishment of large gardens... [with colours] from the palest blush to the deepest carmine... [and] a pale reddish purple running up to a black".

Once again, Phillips displays his snobbishness, issuing lengthy instructions on how he thinks hollyhocks should be used in the garden, insisting that "they must not be planted too near each other" and must never be planted in rows, as is done by "the vulgar planter, who has no idea of the beauty of perspective gardening". He would like to see hollyhocks planted in the hedges bordering fields but says that this cannot happen until "the children of the lower classes of society are become more civilized, and their parents sufficiently enlightened to instruct them in their duty, so that their amusement may not consist in idly destroying what cannot benefit them, but materially injures their more polished neighbours".

Although the hollyhock was well known by the late 16th century, Tyas comments that "A few short years ago we spoke of the hollyhock and the general neglect of its beauties". However, since then it had started to get "great attention from those who are well able to improve its character and multiply its varieties".

Phillips tells us that "a good strong cloth" can be made from the fibrous bark of the flower stalks and that, in 1821, hollyhocks were being grown in Wales "with the view of converting the fibres of this plant into thread similar to that of hemp or flax". It was then discovered that the plant could also be used to make a blue dye "equal in beauty and permanence to the best indigo".

The English name is thought to have come from the Anglo Saxon *holi hoc* meaning holy mallow.

HONESTY

Pink – Sincerity

Honesty (*Lunaria annua*), says Phillips, "is now solely cultivated for the beauty of its lilac corollas and the singularity of its seed vessels", the plants often growing to a height of three to five feet. He goes on to tell us that it "was held in high repute among the credulous of former ages, being considered a charming, enchanting, and bewitching herb".

The generic name comes from the Latin *luna*, the moon, in reference to the round silvery seed-pods. Similarly, the English name probably relates to the transparent nature of the pod, which allows the observer to see which pods contain seeds and which do not.

Other, earlier, names include pennie flower, money flower, silver plate, pricksong wort, and white satin.

HONEY FLOWER

White – **Love, secret and sincere**

William Curtis in *The Botanical Magazine* (1795), tells us that there are two species of honey flower (*Melianthus*) – *M. major* and *M. minor*. Both, he says, "are cultivated in our nurseries; the major is by far the most common, the most hardy, and the most ornamental plant; its foliage indeed is peculiarly elegant". *M. minor* can grow to a height of five feet. Both came from the Cape of Good Hope and *M. minor* was said to have been cultivated by the Duchess of Beaufort in 1708.

Don describes the flowers of *M. major* and *M. minor* as dark brown, and mentions a third species, the tufted honey flower (*M. comosus*) whose flowers can be orange or red. I have been unable to find any reference to a white honey flower.

Sydenham Edwards, in *The Botanical Register* (1815), tells us that *M. major* was imported into Holland in 1673 "and thence to England by Mr. Bentinck, afterwards Lord Portland". He describes it as a perennial plant which can grow to a height of ten feet or more, "spreading itself in all directions by suckers". He describes the flowers as purple-chocolate colour and mentions the "unpleasant narcotic smell" emitted by leaves if they are bruised. If the flowers are shaken, they drop "a sweet brownish liquid". In South Africa, "this juice is a well-known dainty, and when the plant is in bloom the flower is unfailingly plucked by the first of them that descries it."

The generic name is derived from the Greek *meli*, honey and *anthos*, a flower.

HONEYSUCKLE

Red and yellow – **Bond of love**
Monthly or woodbine, red and straw
– **Domestic happiness, contentment**
Wild, yellow – **Inconstancy in love**

All species of honeysuckle (*Lonicera*), says Don, are "truly ornamental". Two candidates for AMC's red and yellow version are the Japanese honeysuckle (*L. Japonica*), described by Glenny as "robust, nearly evergreen, [and flowering] for several months in succession" and the trumpet honeysuckle (*L. sempervirens*) which Don tells us has "flowers of a beautiful scarlet outside and yellow inside". However, these two species may also qualify as "monthly honeysuckle", since this seems to be an epithet given to a number of species which flower throughout the summer months.

AMC's wild honeysuckle with yellow flowers is probably the common honeysuckle or woodbine (*L. periclymenum*) which, says Don, is frequently found in hedges, groves, and thickets. However, "the beauty and exquisite fragrance of the flowers make it a favourite plant in gardens and shrubberies" as well.

Glenny believes that if we consider "the exquisite fragrance of this family, its abundant bloom [and] its pretty bushy and climbing habit . . . we can hardly admit that it has a superior among all the hardy trees and shrubs".

Barton tells us that a blue dye can be manufactured from the honeysuckle root and that the branches are made into "teeth for rakes, weavers' stays, and tubes for tobacco-pipes".

The generic name was given to the plant in honour of the 16th century German botanist, Adam Lonicer.

HOP

Green – **Bitterness**

The common hop (*Humulus lupulus*) is, says Barton, "completely naturalized, if not truly indigenous", and is found growing in thickets and hedges. Mrs. Loudon describes it as "a very ornamental climber". Barton lists several varieties in cultivation, including the garlic, the long white, the Flemish and the Canterbury.

According to Barton, hops were introduced into the breweries of the Netherlands in the 12th century but were only imported into England some 400 years later. The first English author to write about hop cultivation was probably Reginald Scott whose book *Perfect Platforme of a Hoppe Garden, Necessarie Instructions for the Makinge and Maintenance Thereof* was published in 1578.

Barton records that "In 1830, the number of acres cultivated with Hops in Great Britain were 46,727; and the average quantity of Hops grown annually has been computed at 20,000,000 of pounds". He goes on to say "The Hops are plucked by women and children, and after being carefully separated from the leaves and stalks, are put into large sacks and carried away to be dried".

Before the 16th century, ale had been made in England using just malt, with GROUND IVY being added to clarify it. The introduction of hops met with considerable hostility and Henry VIII issued an injunction forbidding brewers from putting them into ale. In the following century, Walter Blith, in his *Improver Improved* (1649) wrote that the City of London had recently petitioned Parliament against hops "in regard they would spoyl the taste of drink, and endanger the people." However, by the early 19th century, all this had changed and heavy penalties were inflicted on brewers who used anything other than hops to preserve their beer.

In addition to its use in brewing, Barton tells us that the young shoots or stems of the hop, gathered in spring, can be boiled and eaten like asparagus, and are "sometimes sold in the markets by the name of hop-tops". The stems can be processed to make "excellent cloth and cordage, and strong paper" while the leaves and dried flowers produce "a fine cinnamon brown dye". Wilkinson adds that "its flowers are occasionally made into a pillow to procure sleep", but she quotes Gerard as saying that they "hurte the head with their strong smelling". However, Gerard believes that hops taken internally are good for the liver, cure agues and purify the blood, and by their "manifest virtues do argue wholesomenesse".

The generic name, says Barton, comes from the Latin *humus*, meaning soil, since hops grow best in rich damp soil. The specific name is derived from the Latin *lupus*, a wolf because "according to Pliny, the plants suffered to grow among osiers[6], strangle and destroy them, as wolves the shepherd's flock".

The English name comes from the Anglo-Saxon, *hoppan*, meaning to climb.

---

6. Willow

HOREHOUND

White – **Brightness, fine**

Don lists 21 species of horehound (*Marrubium*), several of which have white flowers, but AMC is probably referring to the white horehound (*Marrubium vulgare*) which, Barton tells us, "is rather a common plant in England, on rubble and in waste places, particularly in warm dry situations".

Don comments that the common horehound "has a strong penetrating smell, not altogether unpleasant" and, although it is plentiful in parts of Britain, it is probably not indigenous.

Linnaeus believed that the generic name was derived from Maria-Urbs, a town in Italy, but an older tradition says that it comes from the Hebrew *marrob* meaning bitter because the plant produces a very bitter juice.

HORSE CHESTNUT

Pink and white – **Splendour, luxury**

The horse chestnut (*Aesculus hippocastanum*), Don tells us, was first imported into Europe from Asia around 1550. Gerard describes it in his *Herbal* (first published in 1597) as a foreign tree. However, in the 1633 edition, this has been amended to read "the horse-chesnut groweth in Italy, and in sundry places of the East countries; it is now growing with Mr. Tradescant at South Lambeth". But it was many years before it became a common sight in Britain.

Barton describes the timber of the horse chestnut as "white and soft, but not durable; it is consequently very little used in building". But, according to Don, it was used by turners. Its main use, however, was for fuel. The nuts were used to feed horses and other animals. Barton notes that "the milk of cows that feed on them is said to be very rich". The nuts were also a source of a soap-like substance "which may be substituted for common soap, and used in bleaching flax, hemp, and wool". The husks, too, were of value, both in tanning leather and, when burnt, to produce a black watercolour paint.

The generic name is derived from the Latin *esca*, food, while the specific name comes from the Greek *hippos*, a horse, and *kastanon*, a chestnut, because it is said to have been used to cure horses of coughs and lung disorders.

HOUSELEEK

Pink and white – **Domestic comfort**

The houseleeks (*Sempervivum*) are succulents and, here, AMC is probably referring to the common houseleek (*S. tectorum*). This, says Don, is found growing on walls and cottage roofs in many parts of Britain although it is probably not indigenous. Barton describes it as being "remarkable for the beauty and singularity of its flowers".

The juice of the common houseleek has been used as a remedy for burns and skin irritations and, mixed with honey, to treat thrush. According to Don, "it is also said to cure corns... Boerhaave[7] found... the juice beneficial in dysenteries, and others have found it useful in gonorrhoeas; but it is not admitted into modern practice".

Barton tells us that, in some countries, "the simple and credulous inhabitants" attribute to the houseleek "the power of defending them from enchantments, and the malevolence of pretended sorcerers". In Sweden it used to be planted on the roofs of houses to protect them from decay.

The generic name comes from the Latin *semper vivo*, I live for ever, reflecting the robust nature of the plant. Over the centuries, it has had a number of English names, including sengreen, aygreen, Jupiter's eye, bullock's eye, and Jupiter's beard.

---

7. Herman Boerhaave (1668-1738) Dutch plant biologist and chemist

HOUSTONIA (stone crop)

White and yellow – **Contentment**

As with the entry on cedar, which AMC bracketed with fennel, this entry brackets together two quite different plants although, in this case, it is very hard to see why. *Houstonia* is a genus of plants native to North America. Stonecrop is a succulent plant, some species of which are native to the British Isles. Both have species with white flowers.

A 1797 issue of *Curtis's Botanical Magazine* contains an entry on the blue-flowered houstonia (*Houstonia caerulea*) which tells the reader that "Of this genus, two species only have been discovered, both natives of Virginia, the *caerulea* and *purpurea*; the former is the only one that has been introduced to this country, and that by Mr. Archibald Menzies, in 1785".

However, in an 1828 issue of the same work, there is a description of a third species, the thyme-leaf houstonia (*Houstonia serpyllifolia*), which the illustration shows to have white flowers. The author tells us that "This plant flowered in June 1827, in the nursery grounds of Mr. Cunningham ... near Edinburgh ... [It was] brought from North America by Mr. Blair, and ... was found by him, on the tops of the mountains of New Hampshire".

In the earlier volume, Curtis admits that "We scarcely know a plant that has afforded us more pleasure in the cultivation than this ... though a native of the warmer parts of North-America, it bears our ordinary winters uninjured ... [and] flowers perpetually, spring, summer, and autumn".

Curtis tells us that this genus was given its generic name by the Dutch writer,

Gronovius, in honour of Dr. William Houston[8] "a name that must be familiar to all who have read the *Gardener's Dictionary* of Mr. Philip Miller, as there is scarcely a page in that book in which the writer does not record the obligations he is under [to Dr. Houston]".

HYACINTH

Blue – **Playful, sportive**
Rose – **Enchantment**
Purple – **Improvement by education**
Yellow – **Jealousy**

According to Mrs. Loudon one of the best places to see hyacinths in the early 19th century was the garden of the Zoological Society in Regent's Park, where they were "planted in the sloping borders . . . and flower vigorously every spring". As indoor plants, she recommends the red and blue varieties since she believes that the white and yellow varieties have "a fragrance too powerful for rooms".

Glenny comments that hyacinth bulbs are imported "in immense quantities from Holland", while Phillips tells us that it is calculated that more than a hundred acres is set aside for raising bulbs, "principally Hyacinths, near the village of Overveen, in the neighbourhood of Haarlem, where the best growers keep

---

8. William Houstoun (c. 1695–1733) Scottish surgeon and botanist. While working as a ship's surgeon for the South Sea Company, he collected plants in Jamaica, Cuba, Venezuela, and Mexico and sent seeds and plants to Philip Miller.

about 50,000 bulbs as breeders, and these florists now enumerate upwards of 2000 varieties of the Hyacinth".

Hyacinths were being grown in British gardens by the end of the 16th century. According to Phillips, one of the earliest cultivators of the double variety (at the start of the 18th century) was a man called Peter Voerhelm. He was responsible for a variety called King of Great Britain, "a single bulb of which used to bring the price of . . . one hundred pounds sterling, and about seventy years back, two hundred pounds[9] was no uncommon price for a single bulb of a favourite Hyacinth". After that, prices gradually came down and, by the early 19th century ten pounds was "the general price given for the finest bulbs, and from one to ten shillings for the varied sorts . . . the common mixtures are sold from two to three pounds a hundred".

In Greek legend, the hyacinth was said to have sprung from the blood of a young man called Hyacinthus who was killed when the god Apollo threw a quoit which Zephyr, god of the west wind, then blew off course.

HYDRANGEA

Pink or violet – **Ostentation, falsehood**

Mrs. Loudon tells us that most hydrangeas are American shrubs but *Hydrangea macrophylla*, which comes from China, has become very common despite only having arrived in Britain in

---

9. In 1750 a skilled tradesman would earn £200 in about six and a half years

1790. Indeed, Glenny says it is "one of the commonest of the market plants which sell annually by thousands in all large towns".

H. Hortensia, whose flowers are naturally pale pink but will change to blue in certain soils, was named, according to Mrs. Loudon, after Mme. Hortense Lapeaute, a friend of the naturalist Sir Joseph Banks who brought the plant from China and gave it to the Royal Gardens at Kew. However, other theories say that it is named after the French astronomer and mathematician Nicole-Reine Hortense Lepaute, or that it is derived from the Latin word *hortus*, meaning 'garden'.

Phillips recalls that "few flowers ever excited greater interest than the Hydrangea produced on its first introduction into Europe, nor do we remember an instance of any tender plant's having become common in so short a period. When it first became known in Paris, it was so eagerly sought after, and bore so high a price, as to make the fortune of the florist who had procured the first plants from England".

The generic name, according to Phillips, was coined by Gronovius, a Dutch writer, "who derived the appellation from the Greek … in allusion to the quantity of water that these plants require".

HYSOP

White – **Purity, cleanliness**

Don lists four species of hyssop with flowers that are white, "whitish" or white tinged with purple: the hedge hyssop (*Gratiola officinalis*), the narrow-leaved hedge hyssop (*G. linifolia*), the shaggy hedge hyssop (*G. pilosa*), and the four-sided hedge hyssop

(*G. tetragona*). The first of these, he tells us, "is much recommended by several eminent medical writers in cases of dropsy . . . but is said generally to occasion vomiting".

Barton says that the common hyssop is probably of Asiatic origin but "was first cultivated in this country about the year 1548, and is now well known in gardens, being valued not less for its beauty and fragrance when in flower, than for its medicinal qualities".

The generic name is derived from the Latin *gratia*, grace, because of its supposed therapeutic qualities.

I

ICE PLANT

Pale pink – **I refuse you, winter**

The ice plant (*Mesembryanthemum crystallinum*) was introduced to England in 1775. Its English name relates to the little papulae (or blisters) on the leaves which are filled with a watery substance and glisten so the whole plant looks as though it is covered in ice.

The generic name comes from the Greek *mesembria*, midday, and *anthos*, a flower, because the plants tend only to open their flowers in bright sunshine.

INDIAN PINK

Dark pink – **Always lovely**

The Indian pink (*Spigelia Marilandica*) is a native of the eastern states of the USA. Don says all the species in the genus have flowers that are rose coloured or purple and are "very showy".

The root was first used therapeutically by the Cherokee Indians and, in Britain, was sold as a treatment for worms under the name of Indian pink, worm-grass or pink-root. However, it was not without its dangers, with side effects including headache, flushing and even stupor.

The generic name was given in honour of Adrian Spigelius, a Flemish Professor of Anatomy and Surgery in the early 17th century.

IRIS

Blue-white – **I have a message to you**
Yellow – **I am jealous**
Pencilled, blue-white – **Hope**

AMC's readers would have had a wide choice of flowers here, since Mrs. Loudon tells us that there are innumerable species, hybrids, and varieties of iris and Glenny notes that the varieties "are extensively cultivated as florists'

flowers". Wilkinson comments that there are two native species of iris, one of which is the yellow flag iris (*I. pseudacorus*).

According to Phillips, a beautiful watercolour paint can be obtained from the bearded iris (*I. germanica*). Wilkinson, however, concentrates on its therapeutic uses. It was used, she says, to cure "coughs, bruises, 'evil spleens', convulsions, dropsies and serpent-bites, and... was even employed as a cosmetic, and still finds favour for this purpose in the eyes of our rustic maidens". However, she quotes Gerard's note of caution that "it dothe in two daies, at the most, take awaie the blacknesse and blewnesse of any stroke or bruse; so that if the skinne... be very tender and delicate, it shall be needful that ye laye a piece of silk... between the plaistre and the skinne, for otherwise... it often causeth hete and inflammation".

Wilkinson relates a case recorded by the botanist and physician William Withering (1741-1799) in which the fresh root of the flag iris was "given to some swine bitten by a mad dog, [and] they entirely escaped the disease; while some others bitten at the same time, having been kept without it, died with all the symptoms of confirmed hydrophobia".

The English and generic name comes from Greek mythology, Iris being the embodiment of the rainbow and the messenger of the gods.

IVY

Green – **Attachment, I cling to you**

The common ivy (*Hedera helix*), says Mrs. Loudon, "will bear the smoke and want of pure air in cities better than most other plants". Don recommends it for "training into fanciful shapes".

Barton notes that about fifty species of *Hedera* have been described. This includes "the Irish Ivy of the gardens,[1] distinguished by its rapid growth, luxuriant foliage and red berries".

Ivy was greatly esteemed in ancient times, says Don, and "Bacchus is represented crowned with it to prevent intoxication". Barton adds that "opinion, early and for a long period entertained, [was] that this plant was an antidote to the effects of the juice of the grape; and, even in the present day, we find that in some parts of the south of Europe, Ivy is suspended at the entrance of taverns".

Don goes on to report that "Common people apply [the leaves] to issues and corns... [and] the roots are used by leather-cutters to whet their knives upon". A wide range of other uses is recorded by Barton: "The wood is sometimes employed by turners; it is soft and porous, and vessels made of it may be turned so thin as to transmit liquors... the leaves and branches are useful in tanning. A decoction of the leaves has been used to dye the hair, and to remove stains caused by ink or fruit. The resin which exudes from the old branches is employed... in the composition of certain varnishes, and is said to attract fish".

There are a number of explanations of the generic name. Don believes that the most likely is that it came from the Celtic *hedra*, cord. The specific name of the common ivy is derived from the Greek *eileo*, to turn around. And the English name comes from the Celtic *iw*, green.

---

1. *H. hibernica*

J

JASMINE

White – **Amiable and sincere**
Yellow – **Elegance and grace**
Cape, blue – **Transport of joy**

The jasmines, says Mrs. Loudon, "are shrubs remarkable for their fragrant flowers; and the common species, *Jasminum officinale*, is one of our most vigorous-growing wall-evergreens". However, she points out that it is evergreen not because of its leaves but, rather, because of the deep green colour of its long, graceful shoots.

Don comments that the common jasmine has been "a favourite wall shrub from time immemorial . . . Gerarde, in 1597, says it was in common use for covering arbours". He identifies 72 species of jasmine, all with white or yellow flowers.

Cape jasmine is the name usually associated with a gardenia, *G. jasminoides,* but this has white flowers. AMC's specification of blue suggests that she is thinking of *Plumbago auriculata* which is known as blue jasmine or Cape leadwort and was introduced into Britain from the Cape of Good Hope in 1818.

The generic name was derived by Linnaeus from the Greek *ia*, a violet and *osme*, smell, although, in fact, jasmine smells nothing like a violet.

JONQUIL

Yellow – **Desire, I desire a return of love**

The jonquil (*N. jonquilla*) is a species of NARCISSUS. Phillips tells us that it is distinguished from other species of narcissus by its rush-like foliage, "and hence the name, which is derived from *juncus*, rushy. Gerard, and other old writers, call it the rush Daffodill and *Narcissus Juncifolius*". It has, says Phillips, flowers of the brightest yellow and is "the most fragrant of all the species of the Narcissus, and is often found too powerful for small rooms".

JUNIPER

Yellow – **Help or protection**

The junipers form a genus of evergreen shrubs and trees. According to Mrs. Loudon, the common juniper (*Juniperus communis*) makes excellent garden hedges "and was formerly cut into a great variety of shapes".

Mrs. Loudon comments that Himalayan juniper (*J. recurva*), a "very elegant" plant native to Nepal, is suitable for cemeteries, being one of the hardiest of the species, thriving "even in the smoke of London". Another species, the savin juniper (*J. sabina*), has a long history in cultivation, "being almost the only coniferous evergreen planted in the time of Queen Elizabeth".

Juniper has a variety of uses. The wood, says Mrs. Loudon, "is burned in ovens or kilns to flavour dried beef, hams, or fish", while the fruit of the common juniper "is used throughout Europe to flavor ardent spirits[1]". It is still used in the manufacture of gin in the 2 century.

Barton tells us that the wood is both hard and very durable and is used for turning, cabinet making and veneering, while the bark can be made into rope. In addition, the wood makes an excellent charcoal. A resinous gum secreted by the old stems used to be powdered to make pounce "which is used to give consistence to paper, and to prevent the ink from sinking in parts which have been erased". Pounce could also be dissolved in pure alcohol to make a brilliant varnish.

The berries were used in Germany to give flavour to sauerkraut. In alcohol, says Barton, "they form an excellent ratafia[2], and they enter into several liqueurs and confections".

The generic and English names probably come from the Celtic *jeneprus*, meaning rough.

---

1. Strong alcoholic liquors

2. A sweet wine or liqueur

K

KING CUP

Bright yellow – **Youthful days, joy**

Although AMC has, earlier in the book, equated the BUTTERCUP to Shakespeare's kingcup, the former is more likely to be *Ranunculus acris*, *R. repens* or *R. bulbosus*, while the term kingcup may relate to another member of the *Ranunculaceae* family, *Caltha palustris* or marsh marigold.

C. palustris, says Don, is to be found throughout Europe on the margins of ponds, rivers and brooks. The large golden coloured flowers, if picked when they are still buds, "are said to be a good substitute for capers". It is, he continues, "a vulgar notion wholly unfounded" that the yellowness of butter in spring is caused by cows eating this plant, since they will not eat it unless compelled to do so by extreme hunger.

KNOT GRASS

Yellow – **I can't tell what to do**

Books written in the early to mid 19th century show that the term 'knotgrass' could be applied to at least five different genera. The *Encyclopaedia Londinensis* (1811) lists five species of *Illecebrum*, including the white flowered verticillate knot-grass, found mainly in Devon and Cornwall, as well as shrubby knot-grass, flat knot-grass, mountain knot-grass and hooded knot-grass, all of which are native to other parts of Europe, although the last of these was recorded as being cultivated in Britain in 1640.

In *Welsh Botanology* (1813), Hugh Davies mentions the common knot-grass (*Polygonum aviculare*) and five species of *Persicaria* – water knot-grass (*P. amphibia*), spotted knot-grass (*P. maculosa*), pale-flowered knot-grass (*P. lapathifolia*), biting knot-grass (*P. hydropiper*), and small creeping knot-grass (*P. minor*), all of which have pink flowers.

In 1842, Cuthbert William Johnson in his *Farmer's Encyclopaedia* tells us that the common oat-like soft-grass (*Arrhenatherum elatius*) is often called knot-grass by farmers, and he goes on to mention the powdery sea-heath (*Frankenia pulverulenta*) which was known as Valentia knot-grass in some districts, and the whorled knot-grass (*Illecebrum verticillatum*), a dwarf perennial plant, "not uncommon in marshy boggy ground in Cornwall and Devonshire" and having small, white or reddish flowers.

It may be that AMC is referring to the colour of the foliage rather than the flowers but, even so, I am unable to identify exactly which plant she means. (The illustration shows *Polygonum aviculare*, the common knot-grass.)

L

LABURNUM

Yellow – **Pensive beauty, sorrow**

The common laburnum (*Laburnum anagyroides*) "would be thought extremely beautiful", says Mrs. Loudon, "if it were less common". However, she considers the Scotch laburnum (*L. alpinum*) to be much more beautiful. Nearly all species of *Laburnum* have yellow flowers.

Laburnum wood, says Don "is much used by cabinet-makers and turners, for its hardness, beauty of grain, and durability". But, he says, the plant has other uses, too. In plantations of trees, sowing laburnum seeds can protect other trees from hares and rabbits "who will touch no other tree as long as a twig of Laburnum remains. Though eaten to the ground every season, it rises again in the spring, thus affording a constant supply for these animals, so as to save the other trees till of a size to resist their attacks".

LADIES' (or LADY'S) SLIPPER

Blue – **Coquetry, fickleness**

"A great many varieties of this curious and beautiful orchid are found wild in America", says Ildrewe of lady's slipper (*Cypripedium calceolus*). "Some are yellow, some white, some purple". Since none is described as blue, we have to assume that AMC is referring to a purple variety.

Glenny describes the lady's slipper as "remarkable as well as beautiful". And the editor of an American edition of one of Mrs. Loudon's books adds that "These plants, frequently called Moccasin flowers in the USA, are among the most beautiful and curious of all our native plants".

LADIES' BEDSTRAW

Yellow – **Domestic carefulness**

Galium verum – known as ladies' bedstraw, lady's bedstraw, or Our Lady's bedstraw – has yellow flowers and is to be found, says Don, "in meadows, way sides, margins of fields and woods, and among bushes".

Don goes on to say that "boiled in alum-water[1] the flowering stems dye a good yellow colour. The roots dye a very fine red". The plant used to be put into milk, supposedly to curdle it (the generic name comes from the Greek *gala*, milk), although Don suggests that it was less to curdle the milk than to flavour the cheese being made from it.

The term 'bedstraw', says Don, "is from the verb to strew, anciently written straw. Before the invention of feather-beds a variety of herbs were used to strew beds with".

LARKSPUR

Blue – **Giddiness, levity**
Double, pink – **Stateliness, pride**
White – **I cannot depend on you**

Possibly better known nowadays as delphiniums, larkspurs make up a genus of hardy annuals, biennials and perennials with flowers that can be white, red, pink, blue or purple. "They are mostly plants of considerable beauty" says Glenny.

Mrs. Loudon likes the branching or wild larkspur (*Delphinium consolida*) which is usually very dark blue but can be "red, pale-reddish, lilac, pinkish, [or] white". Usually found in cornfields "it abounds in the open chalky or sandy fields in some parts of Cambridgeshire,

---

1. Water in which aluminium sulphate has been dissolved

Suffolk, and Kent."

The upright or rocket larkspur (*Consolida ajacis*), introduced into England towards the end of the 16th century, is described by Mrs. Loudon as having white, blue, rose, flesh-coloured, dark purple and variegated varieties "all of which kinds are very ornamental". It is, she says, a great favourite in the flower garden, on account of its dense mass of blossom.

Don mentions the stavesacre or lousewort larkspur (*D. staphisagria*) which is found in cornfields throughout Europe and has white, blue, red or purple flowers. It was, he says "employed by the ancients as a cathartic, but it operates with so much violence both upwards and downwards, that its internal use has been for some time almost laid aside. It is chiefly employed in external applications for some kinds of cutaneous eruptions, and for destroying lice and other insects". A native of southern Europe, Gerard was growing it in England at the end of the 16th century.

Phillips describes two blue species: the palmated bee larkspur, (*D. elatum*), a native of Silesia and "a perennial plant of great beauty", and the great-flowered larkspur, (*D. grandiflorum*), a Siberian perennial. The latter was first grown in England in 1758 by Philip Miller at the Chelsea Physic Garden. By the 19th century it was being "propagated in a double state, and forms one of the most splendid ornaments of the garden".

The larkspur was popular not only in gardens but also as a cut flower. Philip Miller, writing in his *Gardener's Dictionary*, says "to make flower-pots to adorn rooms, there is scarcely any so proper", while Phillips comments that "the Siberian and the Silesian Larkspurs have a fine effect in the vase of the saloon, where they retain their beauty longer in water than flowers in general".

The generic name comes from the Greek *delphinion*, a dolphin, because, says Phillips, "the flower-buds before they are expanded are thought to resemble that fish". The English name, says Mrs. Loudon, arises from "the horned sepal being something like the hind claw of the foot of the lark.

LAUREL

Dark green – **Glory**

The common laurel (*Prunus laurocerasus*) and the Portuguese laurel (*Prunus lusitanica*) deserve to be cultivated, says Mrs. Loudon, on account of their showy spikes of flowers and shining evergreen leaves.

Glenny comments that "The Portuguese laurel, besides its ordinary use in shrubberies, is sometimes trained up formally, with a straight bare stem, and a thick round head of branches like the orange tree, which it pretty well resembles." And the editor of the American edition of one of Mrs. Loudon's books remarks that the common laurel and the Portuguese laurel, together with the hollies "are the pride and glory of the English gardens and shrubberies in autumn and winter".

In the Victorian era collectors would kill butterflies by putting them into a box containing laurel leaves which had been bruised in order to release the poisonous hydrocyanic acid that they contain. A different use of the leaves was made by young girls who believed that if they wrote the name of a young man they loved on a laurel leaf, the writing would turn red if the love was reciprocated. But if the writing turned black, it meant that the young man was not interested.

LAURUSTINUS

Pink – **I die if forsaken**

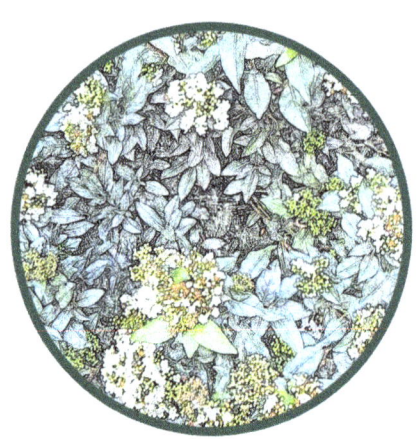

Glenny describes the laurustinus or laurestine (*Viburnum tinus*) as "one of the best of cultivated garden shrubs, being evergreen, free-growing, free blooming, of handsome appearance at all times, and flowering in winter".

Don tells us that the flowers are white "but rose-coloured before expansion, and sometimes afterwards for a little time". It was given its English name "by old authors, they supposing it to be a kind of bay or laurel". The generic name is said to have been derived from the Latin *vico*, to tie, because of the pliable nature of the branches of some species.

LAVENDER

Blue – **Doubt, distrust**

Common lavender (*Lavandula angustifolia*) has, says Barton, been cultivated in English gardens since 1568. Mrs. Loudon believes that French lavender (*L. stoechas*) is a more ornamental plant but warns that it is somewhat tender.

"The essential oil" says Don, "has been used for stimulating paralytic limbs

... but it is only now used as a perfume ... distilled from the flowers, for which purpose the plant is cultivated extensively in different places, but more especially at Mitcham in Surrey, and Maidenhead in Berkshire". Another centre of large scale cultivation was Henley on Thames.

Barton tells us that lavender "has the reputation of preventing the depredations of moths and other insects. The distilled water is a well-known cosmetic; and the oil obtained from the flowers ... is employed ... as a varnish, also for preserving stuffs, books, &c., and for destroying insects".

The generic name is derived from the Latin *lavare*, to wash, because, says Barton, "the ancients used it as a perfume when they took the bath".

LEMON

Yellow – **A love-test**
Flower, white – **Faithful in love, discreet**

Don comments that the flowers of the lemon (*Citrus limon*) are white and exquisitely fragrant, and he lists 15 varieties being grown in English gardens.

John Stephenson, in the 1834 edition of his *Medical Botany*, tells us that, although the lemon tree has for a long time been cultivated in the West Indies and southern Europe, it is a native of Asia, from where it was brought to Greece and thence to Italy. It is, he says, "a beautiful evergreen, attaining, in warm countries, the height of twenty feet or more, but in our hothouses seldom exceeding the size of a large shrub".

According to Stephenson, the lemon was first cultivated in England in the

Botanic Garden, Oxford, in 1648. By the time he was writing it had become a common greenhouse plant "where, under proper management, it produces large and ripe fruit". In plant catalogues, lemons "are usually reduced to two classes: 1. The egg-shaped lemons, with blunt nipples; and, 2. The oblong lemons, with large nipples; to which must be added the monstrous fingered lemon – the *phat-thu*[2] of the Chinese". Stephenson goes on to list what he describes as "the most remarkable sub-varieties". These include "the sweet-lemon ... the pear-shaped ... the lemon called Adam's Apple ... the furrowed fruited ... the wax ... and the lemon with double flowers".

Lemons were commonly imported into England from Spain and Portugal, "packed in chests, each lemon being separately rolled in paper".

That lemons were a popular culinary ingredient in the 19th century can be demonstrated by the fact that Dolby gives around 60 recipes for using them, including lemon bonbons, lemon brandy, lemon honeycomb, lemon pickle and lemon cheesecake which consists of a pastry case filled with a mixture of sugar, butter, eggs, lemon rind and juice, a Savoy biscuit[3], almonds and brandy.

Stephenson describes lemonade at length: "Properly diluted with water, and rendered palatable by the addition of sugar, [lemon juice] forms one of perhaps the most agreeable and refreshing beverages that can be employed to quench thirst and diminish heat in febrile and inflammatory diseases". He goes on to report claims that lemon juice is an effective treatment for hysteria, palpitations of the heart and bites of poisonous animals. It is "also given as a means of counteracting the fatal effects of narcotic poisons, especially opium". Large quantities of concentrated lemon juice are "taken on board ships destined for long voyages" to combat scurvy. In addition, "Lemon-juice is given in combination with camphor mixture, cinchona, and aromatic confection, as a useful cordial and antiseptic in gangrenous affections, putrid sore throat, and low fevers", while

---

2. Now known as the fingered CITRON.

3. A very light sponge cake

the essential oil found in the rind is used as perfume.

LETTUCE

Yellow – **Cold of heart, over careful**

Barton comments that the garden lettuce (*Lactuca sativa*) "with its numberless varieties, is familiar to every one; but it has been so metamorphosed by the skill and industry of man, that its origin is unknown". There are, he says, three species that are native to Britain: the strong-scented lettuce (*L. virosa*) which grows "on banks, and by way-sides, in a chalky soil", the prickly lettuce (*L. serriola*) and the least lettuce (*L. saligna*) which is found "in chalky waste ground, near salt marshes, in the south-east of England". I imagine that it is to the flower of the plant that AMC is referring when she describes it as yellow.

Lettuce was eaten, as far back as Roman times, as a salad vegetable and also, according to Barton "after vinous liquors, to correct their effects, and at night to procure sleep"

In Greek myth, it is said that Venus, to assuage her grief after the death of Adonis, threw herself onto a bed of lettuces!

The generic name comes from the Latin *lac*, meaning milk, because of the milky fluid that flows from the stem when it is cut.

LICHEN

Purple – **Attachment**

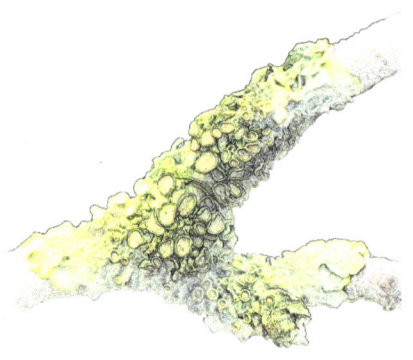

Mrs. Loudon describes lichen as "moss-like plants, generally found on old walls, desert heaths, or the bark of old trees [and] on dead wood" but nowadays it is known that lichen is not a MOSS or even a plant in its own right but a complex symbiotic relationship of a fungus with an alga.

There are numerous forms of lichen. In his *History of the County of Derby* (1829), Stephen Glover lists 45 species found in that county alone. Some lichens are purple, but it is possible that AMC believed all lichens were this colour because of their importance as a source of purple dye, particularly between the 15th and 17th centuries. The dye was extracted from a number of imported lichens and also from the *Ochrolechia* species in Britain. The British dye was known as cudbear.

LILAC

Garden, white – **Modesty, youth**
Garden, purple – **First love**
Persian, lilac – **Majesty**
Wild, purple – **Humbleness**

Loudon tells us that the common lilac (*Syringa vulgaris*) is native to Persia and Hungary and was introduced into England in 1597. According to Phillips, not long after this, a marble fountain "set round with six lilac trees" could be seen in the gardens of Nonsuch palace in Surrey. William Marshall, in the 1803 edition of his *On Planting and Rural Ornament*, describes the common lilac as having purple, blue and white varieties, of which the purple is the tallest, growing up to 20 feet in height. This variety, he says, is not just beautiful in the spring: "All winter the plant has a bold and healthy look, occasioned by the large and turgid purplish buds, which will have begun to swell early the preceding summer, and which will burst forth into leaf soon in the spring following".

Loudon describes more varieties than Marshall, listing blue, white, double, red, and purple, the last of which is known as Scotch lilac "because it was first recorded in Sutherland's *Catalogue of the Edinburgh Botanic Garden*". Phillips describes Scotch lilac as "The most beautiful variety of the common purple lilac" with flowers "of a much richer colour than those of the blue lilac, the buds and under side of the petals being of a hue between purple and carmine".

Loudon says of the purple Persian lilac (*S. Persica*), which was introduced in the first half of the 17th century, that "it is frequently planted in pots, and forced so as to come into flower at Christmas". Phillips comments on its "loose branches of delicate flowers, which are of a more agreeable, though less powerful odour, than those of the common lilac". Wild lilac is a term used to refer to a different genus – *Ceanothus* – whose flowers bear a resemblance to those of the common lilac and can be white, blue, purple or pink.

The generic name comes from the Greek *syrinx*, a pipe. Loudon tells us that "The tubes of the finest Turkish pipes are manufactured from the wood of this shrub; and also from that of the *Philadelphus coronarius*, to which the name was originally given. Hence the old English name of Pipe Tree, which was applied both to the *Philadelphus* and the *SYRINGA*". Gerard believed the lilac to be a species of privet and it was sometimes known as the pipe privet. The English name is derived from *lilag*, the Persian word for flower.

LILY (GARDEN)

Yellow – **Playful, mischief**

There is a wide range of yellow lilies, including the DAY LILY. The species to which AMC is referring could be one of many. Some floral dictionaries which list a yellow lily identify it as *Lilium lutea* but this just translates to 'yellow lily' and is not a recognised botanical name.

LILY (DAY)

Yellow – **Coquetry, pride**

The yellow day lily (*Hemerocallis lilioasphodelus*) is, according to Phillips, a native of Hungary, Siberia, and the northern parts of China. Parkinson, writing in the 17th century, says that it grows in moist places in Germany, and he calls it *Liliasphodelus*, because its root resembles that of the asphodel.

Mrs. Loudon tells us that the day lily, which has flowers that are "delightfully fragrant", was the first of the *Hemerocallis* genus to be introduced into England, some time before the end of the 16th century. Phillips considers it to be "an admirable flower for the vase of the saloon, as its graceful corollas being supported on an erect stem show to peculiar advantage when towering above roses or lilacs".

The generic name is derived from the Greek *hemera*, day, and *kallos*, beauty and, like the English name, refers to the fact that the flowers are short-lived.

See also amaryllis

LILY (JERUSALEM)

White – **Purity and sweetness**

The term 'Jerusalem lily' has sometimes been used to refer to montbretia (*Crocosmia*) which has lily-like flowers but, since these flowers are brightly coloured, this cannot be what AMC is thinking of here. It seems most likely that she is referring to the common white lily (*Lilium candidum*) which is also known as the Madonna lily.

The common white lily, says Phillips, is a native of the Holy Land, and was probably introduced into Britain by the returning Crusaders. He tells us that it was a favourite flower of the ancient Greeks, and, in the 19th century, still played a role in Greek wedding ceremonies, with a garland of lilies and ears of corn being placed on the heads of the bride and groom to represent purity and abundance.

Greek legend says that Jupiter, wishing to make the infant Hercules immortal, put him to the breast of Juno, Queen of the Gods. As the greedy child sucked faster than he could swallow, a few drops of milk fell onto some yellow lilies, changing them to white.

A preparation of lily flowers was for many years used as a cosmetic and was said to preserve the freshness of the skin, and to clear both pimples and freckles.

LILY, WATER

White – Eloquence

"A family of the most beautiful of water plants" is how Glenny describes the water lily (*Nymphaea*), commenting that nearly all the hardy sorts (including the commonest, *N. alba*) have white flowers. Don lists a number of cultivated species and mentions that *N. alba* is common in Britain "in ditches, lakes and rivers". He tells us that its roots were used in Ireland, the Scottish highlands and the island of Jura to make a dark brown dye and that "it was reputed by the ancients as an antiphrodisiac, and as a remedy in dysentery".

The generic name comes from the Greek *nymphe*, referring to the water nymphs of Greek legend.

LILY OF THE VALLEY

White – Return of happiness, delicacy

Glenny describes lily of the valley (*Convallaria majalis*) as "white, bell-shaped flowers of delicious fragrance", while Phillips calls it an "elegantly modest plant". There was a time when it grew profusely in the wild. In the late 16th century, Gerard reported an abundance of it on Hampstead Heath, on "Bushie Heath", and in Essex. However, Phillips tells us that "the increase in the number of our gardens, and the high state of cultivation of the country in general, have rendered the plant rare in its natural state, but it is cherished in the garden by all the admirers of good flowers".

The roots used to be eaten in Turkey, like asparagus, and the leaves, if treated with lime, would produce a green dye. Wilkinson writes about a distilled extract called *Aqua aurea* "which was anciently held in such high repute, as a preventative of infection from plague. It is esteemed, though apparently without good reason, in nervous disorders, being for this purpose, made into a conserve".

The generic name comes from the Latin *convallis*, meaning a valley. In England it has also been called conval lily, May lily, liriconfancie, lily convalley, May-blossom, and ladder to heaven.

LIME TREE

Green – **Conjugal love**

Don describes the lime or linden (*Tilia*) as a genus of "handsome trees, with yellowish, fragrant flowers . . . continually haunted by bees". He lists the species found in Britain, including the small-leaved lime tree (*T. Americana*), which was found especially in Essex and Sussex, the common lime tree (*T. Europaea*), found all over England and in parts of Scotland "in woods and hedges, or upon grassy declivities", and the broad leaved lime tree (*T. platyphyllos*), found "in woods and hedges, particularly in Surrey about Dorking and Streatham".

Don records that the broad leaved lime can grow to a very large size, as apparent at Waltham Abbey, where the plantation is "of very ancient date". Some old trees of this species in the churchyard at Sedlitz in Germany became famous, he says, because they were "reported to have miraculously borne hooded leaves ever since the monks of the neighbouring convent were all hanged upon them". In France, *T. Europaea* was adopted "for ornamental plantations in the time of Louis XIV.[4] It generally composes the avenues about the residences of the French as well as the English gentry of that date".

The inner bark of the common lime was used to make "the Russia mats used by gardeners", while "the smooth, light, delicately white, and uniform wood is used . . . by the carver, turner, and musical-instrument maker". It was also used extensively by Grinling Gibbons (1648-1721), the master wood-sculptor, whose work can be seen in some of the finest English historic houses. Don tells us that the wood also makes "an excellent charcoal for gunpowder".

Robert Hogg in his *Vegetable Kingdom* (1858) notes that "At Kowno, in Lithuania, there are immense forests of this tree . . . [from which] the celebrated Kowno Honey is gathered, and which is sold at more than double the price of any other, it being used extensively in medicine, and for mixing in liqueurs".

Barton lists other uses to which the tree was put. A coarse but smooth paper was made from the bark, baskets and cradles were made from the twigs, and the wood was used by shoemakers in cutting leather, because it didn't blunt their knives. In addition, the 17th century German naturalist Georg Marcgrave found that he could distil a "fine flavoured brandy" from the flowers.

The origin of the generic name is obscure. One suggestion is that it comes from the Greek *ptelia*, an elm, in reference to the shape of the leaves, while another is that it comes from the Latin *telum*, a dart, since these could be made from the wood. The English name, and the alternative name linden, come from the Old English *lind*, meaning flexible. The Swedish name for the lime is *linn*, and it is said that the family name of the great Swedish botanist Linnaeus originated as a reference to an ancient lime-tree which grew near his ancestral home.

---

4. 1643-1715

LIQUORICE

Purple – **I declare against you**

Several other floral dictionaries give this meaning specifically for wild liquorice (*Abrus precatorius*) rather than the common liquorice (*Glycyrrhiza glabra*) so it seems likely that AMC is also referring to wild liquorice.

Mrs. Loudon describes wild liquorice as "a pretty climbing stove plant, which requires a strong heat to throw it into flower" and whose scarlet and black seeds are sometimes made into necklaces for children. However, a modern source, the *Western Journal of Emergency Medicine* tells us that its seeds "contain one of the most potent toxins known to man".

LOBELIA

Lilac – **Malevolence**

Mrs. Loudon believes that nothing can exceed the beauty of the plants in this genus. However "they are all dangerous in their qualities, on account of an acrid milk, in which they abound".

She mentions two species which may match the 'lilac' flowers described by AMC. These are *L. erinus*, which was introduced into England in 1828, and the stinging lobelia, *L. urens*, a native of England, both of which have 'purplish' flowers. In addition, there are numerous species with blue flowers.

Lobelia was given its name by Charles Plumier, an eminent 17th century French botanist, in honour of Matthias Lobel (1538-1616), who superintended Lord Zouch's botanical garden at Hackney in the latter part of Queen Elizabeth's reign, and subsequently was appointed botanist and physician to James I. This, says Mrs. Loudon, was one of the first times a plant was named after someone with whom it had no direct connection.

LOCUST PLANT

Green – **Affection beyond the grave**

A number of species are known as locust plants. The first of these is *Robinia pseudo-acacia*, which we have already met under its other English name of false ACACIA. Mrs. Loudon comments that the name locust (which originated in America) "appears to have no definite meaning, unless it alludes to the leaves, which bear a very slight resemblance to those of *Ceratonia Siliqua*, the Locust Tree of Holy Writ". This latter tree is more commonly known as the carob. 'Locust' can also refer to the African locust bean tree (*Parkia biglobosa*).

However, it seems most likely that AMC is referring to the honey locust (*Gleditsia triacanthos*), also known as the thorny locust, which was introduced into Britain around 1700. These trees can grow to a height of 80 feet and frequently have sharp thorns. If AMC's description of 'green' refers to the colour of the flowers, this is the only one that fits, having small greenish-white flowers.

The honey locust is a native of North America and appears in some Native American myths. The Cherokee tribe has a legend in which Thunder's son, Lightning, needs to prove to his father that he is, indeed, his child. James Mooney in *Myths of the Cherokee* (1902) tells the story: "Thunder showed him a seat and told him to sit down. Under the blanket on the seat were long, sharp thorns of the honey locust, with the points all sticking up, but when the boy sat down they did not hurt him, and then Thunder knew that it was his son." Mooney suggests that the story "may indicate that in Indian[5] as in Aryan thought there was an occult connection between the pinnated leaves and the lightning, as we know to be the case with regard to the European rowan or mountain ash".

LONDON PRIDE (saxafrage)

Pink and white – **Pleasure, amusement**

London pride (*Saxifraga umbrosa*), says Glenny, is a valuable plant in town gardens since "it thrives anywhere, as well in the midst of smoke and shade as in the pure air". It has pink flowers that are "prettily spotted". Phillips tells us that "it was in cultivation for many ages before it had been noticed as an indigenous plant of these islands".

The generic name comes from the Latin *saxum*, a stone, and *frango*, to break, since it

---

5. Native American

was believed that the plant could be used therapeutically to break and dissolve stones in the bladder. Gerard records that it was also used to treat a whitlows.

Other English names include prince's feather, none so pretty, shady saxifrage, St. Patrick's cabbage, breakstone and nailwort.

LOTUS FLOWER

White – **Estranged love**
Yellow – **Eloquence**
Leaf, green – **Recantation**

'Lotus' and 'WATER LILY' are sometimes used interchangeably, but in fact the former refers to the genus *Nelumbo* and the latter to the genus *Nymphaea*. However, in the 19th century, even the botanists got confused and sometimes referred to the lotus (incorrectly) as *Nymphaea nelumbo*.

Mrs. Loudon says that, while the lotus usually has white or pale pink flowers, there is a West Indian *Nelumbo* that is pale yellow, and Don mentions the species *N. lutea*, which has yellow flowers.

The seeds and sliced root of the lotus were, says Don, frequently served, with walnuts and apricot kernels, at breakfasts given by Chinese mandarins to the British ambassador in China. And the roots "are laid up by the Chinese in salt and vinegar for the winter".

The lotus forms an important part of both Hindu and Buddhist iconography, representing purity and spiritual awakening.

LOVE IN A MIST

Blue – **Embarrassment**

Love in a mist (*Nigella Damascena*) can have blue or white flowers. It is, says Mrs. Loudon, a very common flower in English gardens and has probably been so since the 16th century. *The London Gardener* (1760) expresses the opinion that it is grown "for the sake of its strange appearance", while Don describes it as "curious and ornamental".

Gerard praises the therapeutic uses of *Nigella*, and both Hippocrates and Galen mention it as being a stimulant. The seeds, which are aromatic, can be used as a substitute for pepper.

Mrs. Loudon tells us that it is known as *N. Damascena* because it was said to have been imported into England from Damascus in 1570. However, she believes that it was introduced before that, since Thomas Tusser in his *Five Hundred Pointes of Good Husbandry*, published in 1572, writes about it as though it is already a common plant.

The generic name is derived from the Latin *niger*, meaning black, and alludes to the colour of the seeds. Mrs. Loudon relates the legend of a wicked nymph "who was changed into this plant, which was afterwards called Nigella, to commemorate the blackness of her heart".

Other English names are fennel-flower (because the leaves resemble those of fennel), devil in a bush (alluding, Mrs. Loudon says, to the "horned carpels peeping through its bushy leaves"), St. Katherine's wheel, melanthium (from the Greek *melania*, meaning blackness), love in a puzzle, Bishop's wort, and gith (the Saxon name for a weed that grows among corn).

LUCERNE

Crimson – **Joyful life**

Lucerne (*Medicago sativa*) is probably better known nowadays as alfalfa. Its main use is as an animal feed and it has been used as such since Roman times. According to Philip Miller, it was introduced into England from Spain in 1657. But Don notes that "though it was so much esteemed by the ancients, and has been long cultivated to advantage in France and Switzerland, it has yet found no great reception in this country . . . [and] it is not likely that the plant will ever come into general culture in this country". This prediction was correct – nowadays some 13 million hectares of alfalfa are grown worldwide, but very little is grown in Britain.

Lucius Junius Moderatus Columella, the foremost writer on agriculture during the Roman empire, believed lucerne to be the choicest of all fodders because it lasted many years and could be cut four or five times a year. Don comments that "It is said to be much superior to clover, both in increasing milk and butter, and improving their flavour".

Don describes the flowers of lucerne as large and violet. Whether AMC was thinking of another plant or whether she just made a mistake in the colour, having never seen it, is impossible to say.

LUPINE (MUTABILIS)

Yellow – Imagination
Blue – I shall conquer
White and blue – Uncertain, changeful

Mrs. Loudon describes lupines (or lupins) as "A genus of herbaceous annuals and perennials, which contain some of our most beautiful border flowers: yellow, blue, white, and pink". She mentions, in particular, the sky lupin (*Lupinus nanus*) and the broad leaf lupin (*L. latifolius*), both of which are natives of California and have blue flowers, the yellow lupin (*L. luteus*), which was imported from Spain around 1590, the blue narrow leaf lupin (*L. angustifolius*), which was introduced in 1696, and the dwarf pearl lupin (*L. mutabilis*) which was "found by Alexander Cruckshanks, Esq., growing upon the Andes of Peru . . . [and] was introduced in 1829". The last of these, which she describes as "magnificent", has flowers of "almost every possible shade, between purple, blue, pink, yellow, and white". Glenny's favourites include the blue garden lupin (*L. polyphyllus*) and its white variety (*L. p. albus*).

Phillips is less enthusiastic than the other authors, saying that while lupins "appear to have been common in the time of Gerard . . . they scarcely deserve a situation amongst choice flowers . . . [although] the Yellow Lupine, *Luteus*, is acceptable, on account of its fragrance".

The Romans, says Phillips, grew lupins as food both for their cattle and for themselves, as they were "thought to brighten the mind, and quicken the imagination". He goes on to tell the story of Protogenes, a celebrated painter who lived in Rhodes some 300 years before Christ and who, for seven years, "lived entirely upon Lupines and water, with an idea that this aliment would give him greater flights of fancy".

Because lupins grow readily in poor soil, they have been grown since Roman times as 'green manure', being dug into the ground just as they start to flower. In the early 19th century, this was still the practice in the Naples region of Italy and in the south of France.

The generic and English names come from the Latin *lupinus*, a wolf which, says Phillips is "on account of its voracious nature".

M

MAGNOLIA

White – **Truth, perseverance, constant**

Magnolias, says Glenny, are "among the handsomest of hardy evergreens" and all are beautiful as flowering plants. He believes that a place should be found for *Magnolia grandiflora*, with its "large white fragrant cup-shaped blossoms" in every garden. Mrs. Loudon, echoes his opinion and adds a further two species – the Yulan magnolia (*M. denudata*) and the saucer magnolia (*M. soulangeana*) – that "ought never to be omitted in any garden, whether small or large". The saucer magnolia, according to Don, has been cultivated in China since the early seventh century.

Don mentions the deciduous swamp magnolia (*M. virginiana*), a native of North America, which is also known as the beaver tree "because the root is eaten as a great dainty by beavers". Various parts of it are said to have medicinal properties and it has been used in the treatment of chronic rheumatism and of fever. The berries put in brandy are considered to be a cough cure, and the wood has been used to make joiners' planes.

Don also mentions the temple magnolia (*M. doltsopa*) whose wood is "at first greenish but changing to a fine yellow colour, with a very fine grain" and which is greatly prized in its native Nepal.

The magnolia was named after the French botanist Pierre Magnol (1638-1715).

MAIDEN HAIR

White – Secret, discreet

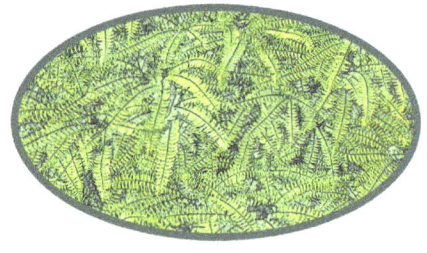

The maidenhair fern (*Adiantum*) is a genus of ferns, some of which says Glenny "are very beautiful, and possess in their fronds the remarkable property of repelling water".

The true maidenhair (*A. capillus-veneris*) is described by Barton as a "delicate and graceful fern . . . very common in the south of Europe, in stony, moist, and shady places, especially by the sides of springs and the inside of wells". It is rarer in Britain, occurring mostly in Scotland, Wales and Ireland. Barton notes that eighty species of *Adiantum* have been identified and that the northern maidenhair (*A. pedatum*) "is said to be so abundant in some parts of Canada, that it is used for packing merchandize instead of hay".

The generic name is derived from the Greek *adiantos*, meaning dry because the plant is not affected by water being poured onto it. The specific name, (which means 'hair of Venus') was said by Pliny to refer to the supposed ability of the plant to strengthen and beautify the hair, but others believe that it alludes to the form of the plant itself.

MAID WORT

White – **Single**

Since I can find no reference to a 'maidwort', it seems likely that this is a mis-spelling of 'madwort', although AMC's meaning of 'single' suggests she thought that 'maidwort' was correct.

The name madwort has been applied to several different plants. Chandler identifies it as *Asperugo procumbens*, while Don lists the large calyxed madwort (*Alyssum alyssoides*) and the dense flowered madwort (*Achyrospermum densiflorum*). But, of these, only the last two have white flowers. Since, in a letter published in the February 1840 issue of *The Magazine of Natural History*, Daniel Cooper, the curator for the Botanical Society of London, describes the large calyxed madwort as "as one of our rarest British plants", it seems likely that AMC is referring to the dense flowered madwort.

MALLOW

White – **Mildness**
Marsh, yellow – **Benevolent, useful**
Garden, pink – **Live for me, persuasion**

AMC lists the mallow in two places. The first is under 'Althaea' which she describes as 'garden, deep pink' and gives a meaning of 'persuasion' and the second is under

'Mallow'. However, the garden mallow is a member of the *Malva* genus, whereas it is the marsh mallow (which is pale pink, not yellow) that is *Althaea officinalis*.

Mallows have been popular for centuries – the herbalist John Parkinson, writing in 1620, tells us that they are "in every country-woman's garden". Don lists a number of mallows with white flowers, including the common mallow (*M. sylvestris*), and several with pink flowers. Phillips describes the common mallow as "a plant which we see bordering the road sides in most parts of Europe . . . their petals being of delicate reddish-purple, sometimes varying to a white". He comments that "we have now more than sixty species, some of which are only humble herbs, whilst others are tall shrubs, and some . . . reach the size of large trees . . . Several beautiful species . . . have lately been brought from the Cape of Good Hope, but these at present are confined to the green-house".

The Greeks and Romans, says Phillips, ate the mallow "both boiled, and raw in salads" and both the Chinese and the Egyptians included mallow in their diet. It was also common in ancient times to plant mallows around graves.

MALOPE

Grandiflora, crimson – **Consumed by love**

Mrs. Loudon describes the *Malope* genus as "annual plants with very handsome flowers" and comments that *M. trifida* has "very large and showy brilliant crimson flowers".

"In the summer and autumn of 1838", she tells us, "an immense quantity of *Malope trifida* was growing in the nursery of Mr. Forrest, at Kensington, where its magnificent flowers produced an effect quite dazzling to the eye".

Don says that the generic name comes from the Greek *malos*, meaning tender.

MARIGOLD

Bright yellow – The French call it sans souci (devoid of care). Shakspeare calls it "a flower of mature age" and signifies welcome

There are several handsome species of marigold, says Mrs. Loudon. However, she considers the Sicilian marigold (*Calendula stellata*) and the common marigold (*C. officinalis*) to be the handsomest of the annual species.

She tells us that, in the early 18th century the common marigold was "a common flower in every garden; and it is only since so many finer flowers have been introduced, that it may be said to have gone out of fashion. The double variety is still, however, very generally grown".

The English name seems to derive from 'Mary's gold' and, it is said "to allude to the great use made of this plant as a pot-herb, by the wives of cottagers". The generic name is from the Latin *calends* (meaning the first day of the month) "because, from the great length of time the plant continues in flower, it may be said to bloom every month".

MARJORAM

Violet – **Blushes, welcome**

Wild marjoram (*Origanum vulgare*) is, says Barton, native to Europe "and occurs not unfrequently in Britain, in dry hilly and bushy places". Mrs. Loudon comments on "the fragrance of the flowers, and the delight which the bees appear to have in them". The sweet marjoram (*O. majorana*) is, she says, a native of Portugal, but is cultivated in England as a pot herb. However, Don tells us that the seed is usually brought over from France as it "seldom ripens in this country". Sweet marjoram is used, he says, like other culinary species of marjoram "as a relishing herb in soups, broths, stuffings, &c".

Sweet marjoram has white flowers but wild marjoram has purplish flowers that might, at a stretch, be described as violet.

Barton tells us that dried leaves of the sweet marjoram can be substituted for tea and that "the country people use the flowering tops to dye linen cloth purple. The herb also imparts a bright reddish brown colour to wool. The dried plant suspended in a cask of beer is said to prevent or correct the acidity of that liquor."

The generic name comes from the Greek *oros*, a mountain, and *ganos*, joy.

MARVEL OF PERU

Red or yellow – Evening, timidity

Opinions on this plant, *Mirabilis jalapa*, differ quite dramatically. Gerard thinks it should be called "rather the Marvell of the World than of Peru alone" but Mrs. Loudon believes "there is nothing very remarkable about it". However, she acknowledges that, when it was introduced, very soon after the discovery of Peru, "everything belonging to the new world was thought strange and wonderful, and being found to bear flowers of several different shades of colour at the same time, it received this name". It can, she observes, have both red and yellow flowers on the same plant. Marvel of Peru was, says Glenny, a great favourite at one time but, since the introduction of the dahlia has been greatly neglected.

Phillips comments that the plants "retain their beauty for a great length of time . . . [and] have a most cheerful appearance . . . [but] seldom expand in warm weather before four o'clock in the afternoon, on which account it is sometimes called Four o'Clock Flower . . . [appearing] awake and gay when most other blossoms sleep".

MEADOW LYCHNIS or RAGGED ROBIN

Pink – **Vivacity, wit**

Dixon identifies this plant as *Silene flos-cuculi*, which Phillips declares to be a native species "which has been taken from our meadows into the garden". Don describes it as growing in moist meadows and bogs and having scentless, rose-coloured flowers.

Phillips gives its alternative names of cuckoo flower and meadow pink, and says that the name ragged robin comes from "the finely-cut or ragged appearance of its petals", while cuckoo flower relates to the fact that it blooms "about the time this . . . messenger of spring begins its monotonous song".

MEADOW SWEET

White – **Useless, though pretty**

Don lists ten species of meadow-sweet, several of which have white flowers. One of these is *Filipendula ulmaria* which, he says "abounds in moist meadows, about the banks of rivers, brooks, and ditches, perfuming the air with the sweet hawthorn-like scent of its numerous blossoms".

Barton gives the alternative English names of mead-sweet and queen of the meadows, and comments that, if the flowers are infused in ale or wine, they "impart a very agreeable flavour". The roots, however, are very astringent and have been used for tanning leather. In Russia, "a kind of granulated flour ... possessing nutritious qualities" was prepared from the roots and "the Icelanders obtain a durable black colour from a decoction of the whole plant".

The specific name comes from the Latin *ulmus*, an elm, and relates to the appearance of the leaves.

MEZEREON

Red – I wish to please

Mezereon or *Daphne* is a genus of "some of the prettiest and most fragrant ornaments" of the shrubbery, according to Glenny. Mrs. Loudon calls it "a genus of beautiful low shrubs ... [with] elegant and often fragrant flowers, and ... bright red, poisonous berries".

The common mezereon (*D. mezereum*) is, says Mrs. Loudon, "so general a favourite that it has pet names in almost every language. The French call it genteel wood, and pretty wood; the Italians, the fair plant; the Germans, silky bark; and even the grave Spaniards term it the lady laurel". It has two varieties, "one with white, and the other with dark-red flowers".

Barton tells us that the common mezereon has been found growing wild in Hampshire, Suffolk, Buckinghamshire, Berkshire,

Oxfordshire, Worcestershire and Staffordshire.

The branches of the plant, says Barton, yield a fine yellow dye, while the bark can be "made into a kind of greyish paper, [and] also into thread and cordage". A red-lake colour used by painters can be prepared from the ripe berries. Peter Simon Pallas (1741–1811), a German botanist who worked in Russia, recorded that Russian women used mezereon berries as a form of rouge to rub onto their cheeks, a practice that was also observed among Tartar women by the Swedish botanist, Johan Peter Falk (1732–1774).

In some respects, the mezereon was thought to resemble the laurel, and its generic name is that of the nymph Daphne, who in Greek myth was turned into a laurel.

MICHAELMAS DAISY

Violet yellow – **Cheerful old age**
White and red – **Late blossoms**

Although, nowadays, the term 'Michaelmas daisy' tends to be used specifically to refer to *Aster amellus*, in the 19th century it was common to use it for any late flowering asters or STARWORTS. In *The English Flower Garden* (1893), William Robinson describes them as hardy flowers which "during the last days of autumn when our gardens are nearly bare of bright colour and when hardy flowers of nearly all kinds are at their lowest ebb . . . bloom bravely having all the soft delicate tints between white rose and purple while their bright yellow disc gives them an additional charm".

MIGNONETTE

Green & speckled with red – **Sweetness, your virtues surpass your beauty**

The mignonette (*Reseda odorata*), says Mrs. Loudon, is a shrub which, after two or three years, will become what is referred to as a tree mignonette. The individual flowers are very small and have reddish stamens, giving the impression that the flower head is green, speckled with red.

Mignonette was very popular in the early 19th century, mainly because of its scent. Phillips waxes lyrical about "the fragrance which it throws from the balconies into the streets of London" and comments that "it must be a luxurious treat to catch a few ambrosial gales on a summer's evening from the heated pavement, where offensive odours are but too frequently met with . . . We have frequently found the perfume of the Mignonette so powerful in some of the better streets of London, that we have considered it sufficient to protect the inhabitants from those effluvias which bring disorders in the air". However, he cautions that some people find the scent too strong to have inside the house.

"This fragrant weed of Egypt" says Phillips, "first found its way to the south of France, where it was welcomed by the name of Mignonette, Little-darling". In 1742, the seed was sent "from the Royal Garden at Paris, to Mr. Richard Bateman, at Old Windsor". However, it was only after the Dutch botanist Adrian van Royen sent some seed to Philip Miller, who grew it in the Physic Garden at Chelsea in 1752, that it started to become popular.

The generic name is derived from the Latin *resedo*, I calm, or appease, referring to the healing properties that the plant is said to have.

MILFOIL or YARROW

Yellow – **Discord, war**
Garden yarrow, dark pink – **I shall quarrel**

Glenny describes milfoil or yarrow (*Achillea*) as "An extensive family of hardy herbaceous composite flowered plants, of which many of the kinds are weedy, but some very pretty". Mrs. Loudon agrees that "most of them have no great beauty" but points out that they grow vigorously and will thrive anywhere, even in smoke or the cold.

Mrs. Loudon mentions golden yarrow (*A. tomentosa*) which has a profusion of rich yellow flowers, and the tansy leafed yarrow (*A. distans subsp, tanacetifolia*) whose flowers are red (and might possibly be what AMC is referring to as 'dark pink').

An alternative candidate for the pink variety is the common milfoil (*A. millefolium*) which, Barton notes, is one of three indigenous British species and is commonly seen "in pastures and by way-sides".

According to Barton, the leaves and flowers have been used to increase the intoxicating effects of fermenting beer, and extracts of the plant have also been used in tanning. Gerard tells us that if the leaves are inserted into someone's nostrils, their hairy surface will precipitate a nose bleed, and this used to be recommended for the treatment of 'megrim' (low spirits or migraine). The plant was therefore sometimes known as nose-bleed.

The generic name comes from that of the Greek warrior Achilles. The English name derives from the Latin *millefolium*, meaning thousand leaves, and refers to the shape of the leaves which are almost fern-like.

MILK VETCH

White – **Your presence softens my pain**

The milk vetches belong to the genus *Astragalus*. In *The Wild Garden* (1881), William Robinson describes them as a "numerous family of beautiful hardy plants represented to but a very slight extent in our gardens though hundreds of them are hardy and many of them among the most pleasing of the many Pea flowers which adorn the hills and mountains of the northern world in Asia, Europe and America".

Of the species listed in gardening books of the time, most are purple, but the Sainfoin milk vetch (*A. onobrychis*) and the purple milk vetch (*A. hypoglottis*) are mentioned as having white varieties.

The generic name may come from the Greek *aster*, a star, and *gala*, milk.

MIMOSA (sensitive plant)

Pale yellow – Sensitiveness, touch me not
Green – Susceptibility

This is a confusing entry. Mrs. Loudon comments that "many species formerly included under the genus Mimosa are now removed to ACACIA" whose flowers are mostly yellow and which AMC has already listed. And in addition to listing 'Mimosa (sensitive plant)', describing it as pale yellow, AMC also lists 'Sensitive plant' separately, describing it as green. Presumably the first refers to the flowers and the second to the leaves. However, most mimosa flowers are a shade of pink or purple.

Glenny describes mimosa leaves as very elegant and remarks that "the peculiarity which obtains for them both their name and popularity is the shrinking of the branches and folding up of the leaves at the slightest touch of the finger, or even a puff from the mouth. If a limb be touched it falls down, and the leaflets close; but if the whole plant be shook or jerked, all the leaves close and hang down directly".

The generic name comes from the Greek *mimos*, a mimic, referring to the fact that the plants mimic animal movement.

MINT

Green – **Virtue**

Writing of mint, Don comments, seemingly with some exasperation, that "the repeated attempts by different authors in different countries to reduce these inconstant and ephemeral variations to so many species, have thrown so much confusion into this difficult genus that it is now almost impossible to clear up the chaos thus produced".

Barton tells us that "there are thirteen species of Mint indigenous to Britain". Don lists the round leaved or apple mint (*Mentha suaveolens*) which grows "among rubbish by way sides, and in ditches", the meadow mint (*M. pratensis*), found "in ditches and watery places", and the bergamot or eau de cologne mint (*M. piperita f. citrata*) which grows "in watery places in Cheshire, North Wales and near Bedford".

As to the peppermint (*M. piperita*), Barton says that it is usually acknowledged to be a native of England, is found "in moist and watery places, and is often cultivated in gardens". Don comments that it is cultivated "almost entirely for distillation", the distilled water being "a domestic remedy for flatulent colic, [while] the essential oil is often given with advantage in cramps of the stomach". Barton tells us that "for medicinal purposes, more than one hundred acres of this plant are cultivated about Mitcham in Surrey".

It seems that the primary culinary mint in Don's time was spearmint, and it was this species that was also known as green mint, so it may well be the variety to which AMC refers. Don tells us that the young leaves and tops were used in salads and soups and "to give flavour to certain dishes, as peas, &c., being boiled for a time, and then withdrawn, in the manner of garlic".

Barton records a belief that mint hinders the coagulation of milk in cheese-making and quotes Linnaeus as saying that "dairy-maids frequently complain that much less than the usual quantity of cheese is obtained from the milk of cows which, after harvest, are allowed to feed on the Corn Mint, (*M. arvensis*) but they ascribe the effect to enchantment".

The essential oil of the peppermint, says Barton "is used by perfumers, and is employed in various ways by confectioners, especially to form lozenges; the solution of it in alcohol or gin, forms the well known liqueur or dram called pepper-mint".

In Greek mythology, Minthes was a nymph who was turned into a mint plant by the goddess Proserpine, in a fit of jealousy.

MISELTOE OF THE OAK

White – **Difficulties surmounted, a kiss**

If AMC had read Mrs. Loudon's works, she would have learned that it was a "vulgar error [to suppose] that the mistletoe grows generally on the oak, as it is extremely rare on that tree in England; it is found most commonly on the apple, and next on the hawthorn; it is also found on the lime, the sycamore, the willow, the poplar, and the ash: occasionally on the cherry, and sometimes, though rarely, on pines and firs".

Mrs. Loudon is not enamoured of the plant. "This curious parasite," she says, "can hardly be called ornamental" and Don comments that the only species that can be grown in gardens is the common mistletoe (*Viscum album*). He describes its flowers as yellowish, so AMC is probably referring to its white berries.

Mrs. Loudon comments that "the wood of the mistletoe is of a very fine pale yellowish tinge, and it is as hard and of as fine a grain as box".

There are many legends surrounding mistletoe. Barton relates that in Saxon times, "when growing on the oak, it was considered the peculiar gift of the gods, and was gathered by the Druidical priest himself, clothed in a white robe, and armed with a golden sickle. This ceremony was performed annually, and was accompanied with the sacrifice of two white bulls . . . At the commencement of the new year, the plant was distributed among the people as a sacred relic, and was deemed a panacea against every disease, and a remedy for poisons".

Barton mentions that in times of scarcity, mistletoe branches and leaves have been dried, then pulverised and mixed with rye-flour to obtain "a kind of bread which was by no means unwholesome".

MOON WORT

Green and white – **Forgetfulness**

The common moonwort (*Botrychium lunaria*) is a fern. *The Visitor or Monthly Instructor* for 1849 calls it 'elegant' and comments that it "grows on open places, flourishing on hilly pastures and wide heaths, almost throughout our island". It may be distinguished from other ferns, the writer tells us "by its frond, composed of leaflets crowding on its stem, and each leaflet of a crescent shape". He goes on to say that it was,

in the past, valued by both witches and alchemists, the latter calling it martagon.

Samuel F. Gray, in his *Natural Arrangement of British Plants* (1821) says that if moonwort is "made into an ointment with butter, and rubbed in opposite to the kidneys, it is esteemed a certain remedy for a dysentery".

Culpeper, in his *Herbal*, relates yet another belief about the plant: "Moonwort . . . they say, will open locks and unshoe such horses as tread upon it: this some laugh to scorn, and those no small fools neither, but country people that I know call it unshoe the horse. Besides, I have heard commanders say that on White Down, in Devonshire, . . . there were found thirty horse-shoes, pulled off from the feet of the Earl of Essex's horses, . . . many of them being newly shod, and no reason known".

MOSS

Green – **Motherly love, retirement**

Mrs. Loudon tells us that "of terrestrial Mosses, those which are most common are the *Dicranum glaucum**, which is of a whitish green, and *Bryum hornum**, which is of a yellowish green". Both the green mosses and the yellow mosses, she says, may be readily purchased in Covent Garden market.

There seems to have been a fashion for 'moss houses' in the mid 19th century. Loudon, writing in *The Gardener's Magazine* for November 1834, describes the Moss House in the garden at Bagshot Park, where different mosses were used to great decorative effect: "The ceiling of the portico is inlaid with moss of various colours, representing a star and diamonds" while, under two stained glass Gothic windows were "four square panels with a large diamond in the centre of each, all formed with moss".

Eleven years later, in the April 1845 issue of the same magazine, there is a report of a prize being offered by the Caledonian Horticultural Society for the best model of a moss house, "with an account of the materials". And in September 1845, there is a description of a moss house that has been built at Murtle in Aberdeenshire. Moss, we are told, was "rammed in with a wedge-shaped piece of wood" between the upright slats forming the walls. The ceiling was done in the same way and had "the form of a star in the centre, pointing towards each corner: this star is made of *Cenomyce rangiferina*". Nowadays, *Cenomyce rangiferina* is known as *Cladonia ciliata*, and is identified as a LICHEN, not a moss, reminding us that the Victorians frequently had difficulty distinguishing one from the other.

MOUNTAIN LAUREL

Pale pink – **Excellent, exalted**

Don describes the mountain laurel (*Kalmia latifolia*) as "a very elegant shrub when in flower". A native of North America, most information about it is to be found in books written in the United States and Canada, although one of these points out that it was "long since introduced into Europe".

Francois Andrew Michaux, in his *North American Sylva* (1841) tells us that the scentless flowers are usually "of a beautiful rose color, and sometimes of a pure white". They grow in large numbers "and their brilliant effect is heightened by the "richness of the surrounding foliage".

A Report on the Trees and Shrubs . . . in the Forests of Massachusetts (1846) records that in mountainous country, in deep, shady ravines, the mountain laurel "sometimes attains a height of fifteen or even twenty feet . . . [but] in most other places, and especially on open ground, it rarely exceeds four or five feet in height".

The wood, according to Daniel Jay Browne's *Sylva Americana* (1832), is "compact, fine-grained and marked with red lines", is very hard when dry, and it "turns and polishes well. It is employed for the handles of light tools, for screws, boxes, etc.; it is said also to make good clarionets".

Other names for the plant are spoonwood and calico bush.

MUGWORT, WORMWOOD

Light blue & pink – **Happiness**
Green – **Absence**

The name mugwort is given to several species of *Artemisia*, or wormwood. The flowers can be pink or purplish. AMC lists mugwort and wormwood separately, giving the 'light blue and pink' description to the former and 'green' to the latter.

Barton says two species are indigenous to Britain – the sea wormwood (*A. maritima*), found on the sea shore and in salt marshes, and the common wormwood, (*A. absinthium*) – both of which have medicinal properties. The latter has been used as a treatment against worms but is probably best known for being a major constituent of the alcoholic drink, absinthe. Barton also mentions the tarragon wormwood, (*A. dracunculus*), which has been used to flavour fish sauces.

Mugwort, says Barton, is common "in waste places, the borders of fields, and under hedges", while Wilkinson tells us that "the common wormwood . . . abounds in dry waste places about houses and villages; and marks out so definitely the dwellings of man, that in the Pyrenees and other places the spots where shepherds' huts formerly stood are indicated by the occurrence of the plant, though no other trace of them remains".

The plant has long been regarded as therapeutically valuable. Wilkinson quotes Pliny as saying that "the wayfaring man that hath the herbe tied about him feeleth no wearisomenesse at all, and . . . he who hath it about him can be hurt by no poysonsome medicines, nor by any wild beast, neither yet by the sun himself".

In the East, according to Wilkinson, mugwort is used as a charm against witchcraft. She accepts Gerard's view that it is useful in the treatment of "weak stomachs and eyes, loss of appetite, fainting fits, worms, and jaundice . . . [and] for driving away gnats" and she goes on to tell us that "Dr. Home . . . gives an instance of a woman who was cured of hysteric fits of many years standing, after . . . more powerful drugs had entirely failed".

Mugwort was frequently (and, according to Wilkinson, successfully) used by the peasantry in the treatment of "pulmonary weakness, and even of consumption". She relates a "universally believed" legend of a young woman who was cured of terminal consumption after her lover was told by a mermaid to give her mugwort.

Barton tells us that "the flesh of poultry, particularly of geese, is said to be rendered more tender and savoury by being stuffed with this herb". And in Wales and Ireland, the tops of mugwort plants were used to flavour both beer and "purl" (wormwood ale). Purl was believed at one time to have therapeutic qualities, and was recommended by a 17th century broadsheet as a protection against plague, if drunk fasting, "with a slice of lemon and herb of grace".

The generic name is said to commemorate either the Greek goddess Artemis or Artemisia, wife of Mausolus (377-353 BCE), king of Caria in Asia Minor, who first discovered the virtues of the plant.

MULBERRY

Brown purple – **Wisdom**

The common mulberry tree (*Morus nigra*) has been cultivated in England since the mid 16th century, having been imported from Italy, which had received it from Persia.

The tree is usually grown for its fruit (which, presumably, is what AMC is referring to, since the flowers are white). Barton comments that the fruit can be fermented to produce "a pleasant wine, which is sometime, particularly in Devonshire, mixed with cyder".

Some of the fine mulberry trees to be found "in the old gardens near London", says Barton, probably date from the start of the 17th century, when King James I tried to establish a silk manufactory (mulberry leaves being the food of choice for silkworms).

The wood is hard, close-grained, and very durable. The inner bark, according to Barton, is tough and fibrous and "is made into baskets, mats, cordage, ropes, and brown paper".

The generic name is derived from the Greek *morea*, meaning black. Greek legend relates that the mulberry fruit was white until the tree absorbed the blood of star-crossed lovers Pyramus and Thisbe who killed themselves underneath it.

MULLEIN

Bluish red – **Good nature**

Mrs. Loudon describes mullein (*Verbascum*) as "showy herbaceous plants, generally with yellow flowers, and most of which are natives of Britain". It would seem, therefore, that AMC is thinking of *V. phoeniceum*, which Glenny calls "a beautiful perennial purple-flowered kind".

Gerard refers to mullein as "Cow's Lungwort," because it was used to treat pulmonary conditions in cattle. And Wilkinson tells us that "the Kentish, like the Norwegian, farmers consider its decoction a sovereign remedy for coughs, and winter leanness, of cows".

It has also been claimed, at various times, that mullein will prevent 'falling sickness', will preserve figs, will stupefy fish and, made into a soap, will restore grey hair to its original colour.

Wilkinson tells us that the downy covering of the plant "was formerly employed for making the wicks of tapers, on which account the plant is known in some parts of England as 'candle-wick plant'. These tapers . . . were considered as peculiarly appropriate to the service of the Church, and to this use botanical works generally attribute the origin of the names torch-blade, or torch-mullein". Other names include flannel plant, high taper, wool blade, grace of God, bullock's lungwort, St. Peter's staff, ladies' foxglove, and hare's beard.

The generic name is a corruption of *barbascum*, from the Latin *barba*, meaning a beard and referring to the woolly hairs that cover the plant. The

English name is probably derived from the French *moelleux*, meaning soft.

MUSHROOM

***Brownish white* – Suspicion**

In 1779, John Abercrombie published a 54 page booklet entitled *The Garden Mushroom*, in which he described it as "universally admired as one of the delicacies of the kitchen garden".

Seventy years later, *The Visitor or Monthly Instructor*, contained an article which showed that the mushroom had lost none of its popularity. "The common mushroom of our meadows" says the author, "is very extensively used in this country in the preparation of catsup[1], and is also frequently eaten when roasted with butter". However, he tells us that many writers believe it to be poisonous "under some circumstances, as when gathered from a river side, or any other damp situation". The author is dubious about this: "when we consider how often this mushroom is eaten in this country, and how few well-ascertained cases of its poison are recorded, it seems probable that those who have suffered from its effects have either eaten this vegetable immoderately, or have had some constitutional peculiarity which rendered the food unwholesome to them".

The meadow mushroom, continues the *Visitor* writer, "is much eaten on the continent; but its similarity to some poisonous species, as well as the damp places on which it grows, renders caution necessary with respect to its use". Another species, the tall mushroom, "a native of our hedge-banks, and . . . more spongy in

---

1. A seasoned sauce; ketchup

its substance than the common species" is, he says, sometimes sold in the London market, while the so-called twisted mushroom, although edible, "is of a leathery texture, and has, therefore, been considered indigestible, and recommended to be used in the form of powder, for which it seems well suited, as its flavour is higher than that of the common mushroom". Possibly it was the anxiety surrounding the identification of poisonous mushrooms that gave rise to the meaning of 'suspicion' found in most floral dictionaries.

MUSTARD SEED

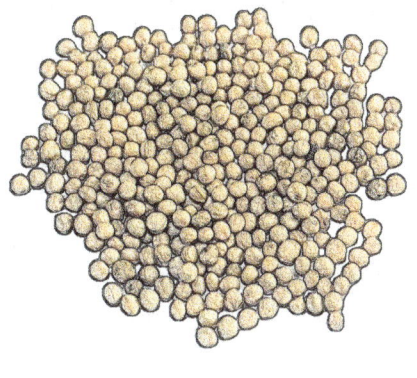

Yellow – **Want of affection**

Since AMC specifies that the seed is yellow, she must be referring to that of the white mustard (*Sinapis alba*). Don tells us that, in Britain, it is to be found both cultivated and wild, on waste ground and by road-sides. Barton notes that it is "cultivated to a great extent in Durham".

Mustard has been used in poultices to treat coughs and muscle pains. Don recommends swallowing a tablespoon of the seed to treat indigestion.

The generic name is said to be derived from the Celtic *nap*, a general name for rape-like plants. The English name is supposedly a corruption of the Latin *mustum ardens*, 'hot must' since, according to Barton "the sweet must[2] of new wine [was] formerly an ingredient in preparing mustard for dietetic purposes".

---

2. Freshly crushed grapes – juice, skins and seeds

MYRRH

Green – **Glad, joyful**

The *Penny Cyclopaedia* (1835) describes myrrh as a gum-resin secreted by the *Commiphora myrrha*, "a small scrubby tree" found in Arabia Felix (modern day Yemen) and goes on to tell us that both the wood and the bark of the tree have "a strong and remarkable odour". At first the resin is light yellow but, as it hardens on exposure to the air, it becomes a reddish brown. So it seems that AMC is referring not to the resin itself but to the plant.

The *Penny Cyclopaedia* goes on to tell us that, although it was formerly considered to be a cure for many diseases, myrrh "has now fallen into disuse".

The English name comes from the Arabic *mur*, meaning bitter.

MYRTLE

White – **Friendship and love**

Mrs. Loudon describes the myrtle (*Myrtus*) as a genus of beautiful evergreen shrubs. She is of the opinion that the varieties of the common myrtle (*M. communis*), with their pure white sweet-smelling flowers and fragrant leaves, "are not surpassed in beauty of foliage by any exotic shrub".

Mrs. Loudon comments that the common broad leaved myrtle "will stand the winter . . . in dry soil, in most parts of England, and also in Scotland, more particularly in low situations near the sea. In most parts of Ireland it is as hardy as the common Laurustinus is in the climate of London. Garden hedges are made of it at Belfast, and also at Cork".

The myrtle, says Don "was a great favourite among the ancients, and was sacred to Venus. Myrtle wreaths adorned the brows of bloodless victors, and were the symbol of authority for magistrates at Athens". The berries were used in wine and in cookery, and the myrtle was also believed to have therapeutic properties.

N

NARCISSUS

White – **You admire yourself**

The narcissus genus comprises around 150 species, and the flowers can be yellow, orange or white, says Glenny, "but the principal good ones are imported annually in great numbers". His favourites include those "known as *polyanthus narcissus** . . . because they throw up their flowers in large trusses".

Writing of the "Poetic or White Narcissus" (*N. poeticus*), Phillips tells us that he is dubious about the common assertion that this species is indigenous to Britain, and he suggests that plants found in Kent and Norfolk "are the offsets from imported plants, probably of as early a date as the time of the Romans". The narcissus has certainly been cultivated in England since the 16th century, and Gerard describes four species.

The florists of the Low Countries and France raised numerous varieties of narcissus, and Phillips comments that "their catalogues contain upwards of an hundred sub-varieties, which are distinguished by similar pompous and ridiculous names as the English florists now bestow on their Geraniums".

Maund tells us that the generic (and English) names come from the Greek word for stupor, *narke*, from which the word 'narcotic' is also derived. Pliny, he says, explained that the name was given to the plant "on account of its qualities; which he describes as hurtful to the stomach, and stupifying to the senses". Maund then pours scorn on those who "maintain that the name was first applied by the ancient poets to the fabled boy, who very stupidly fell passionately in love with his own shadow in a fountain . . . pined away . . . and by favour of the gods was changed into the flower that now bears his name".

NASTURTIUM

Yellow – **Patriotism, a trophy of victory**
Scarlet – **Splendour**
Sanguinary, dark red – **Trophy of war**

Although this genus of ornamental climbing plants (*Tropaeolum*) is commonly known as nasturtium or Indian cress, the botanical name *Nasturtium* actually applies to a different genus containing watercress and related plants.

The first *Tropaeolum* to be introduced to Europe from Peru in the 16th century was the dwarf nasturtium (*T. minus*). Mrs. Loudon tells us that the plant was first sent to Spain, from where seeds were sent to Gerard, who raised them in his garden at Holborn towards the end of the 16th century. It was given the name of *Nasturtium Indicum* because it tasted like watercress and it had come from 'the Indies' – the common name at the time for the Spanish possessions in South America.

However, by the time Mrs. Loudon was writing, the dwarf nasturtium had become relatively rare, "its modest merits having been eclipsed by its more showy rivals". Both the dwarf nasturtium and the common nasturtium (*T. majus*) have flowers that can be yellow, orange or red.

Nasturtiums are, says Mrs. Loudon, common in every garden. Indeed, they are "so much cultivated, that there is scarcely a child, who has ever seen a garden, who is not acquainted with them". The young shoots are succulent, she says, and, together with the flowers and leaves, can be used in salads, while the pickled fruit is frequently used as a substitute for capers.

Mrs. Loudon also describes a "curious discovery" made by one of Linnaeus' daughters. In 1762, she "observed the *Tropaeolum majus*, or Garden Nasturtium, emit sparks or flashes in the mornings before sunrise, during the months of June or July, and also during the twilight in the evening, but not after total darkness came on." Nowadays, this effect, which is more likely to be observed by young people, is known to be an optical illusion caused by a combination of the red petals and the red light of the sun.

The generic name is derived from the Greek *tropaio*, meaning trophy, because the leaves are said to look like shields and the flowers like helmets.

NEMOPHILLA

Cerulean blue – **Sincere and unpresuming love**

The first species of *Nemophila* to be discovered, *N. phacelioides*, was, according to Mrs. Loudon, found by the English botanist Thomas Nuttall

(1786-1859) "in shady places on the banks of the Missouri in the Arkansas territory, in North America". Although some seeds were sent to England and grown in several gardens, the plant was lost and only reintroduced in about 1837.

N. phacelioides, whose flowers are described by Mrs. Loudon as "pale lilac" was still uncommon in the 1840s, but another species, *N. menziesii* had become "an almost universal favourite" after being discovered in California in 1834 by the Scottish botanist David Douglas (1799–1834). Glenny believes that it is the best species of *Nemophila*, while Mrs. Loudon says "it is not possible to imagine a more beautiful blue than is displayed in this lovely little flower. It is like the finest ultra-marine, softened in the centre into white".

The generic name comes from the Greek *nemos*, a grove, and *phileo*, I love, since the plants prefer the shade.

NETTLE

Green – **Slander, cruelty**

Barton identifies the three nettles indigenous to Britain as the common nettle (*Urtica dioica*), the small nettle (*U. urens*) and the Roman nettle (*U. pilulifera*). The last of these "grows on waste ground near the sea, is more rare, and has more venomous stings than the common nettle", although Mrs. Loudon says that it is sometimes grown in gardens as an ornamental annual.

The nettle has had many uses over the centuries. According to Barton, it was used to feed poultry, pigs and cattle, and was said both to increase the milk of cows, and to protect horned cattle "against the contagious distemper". Barton also tells us that "the tops of the common Nettle are boiled and eaten in many places as greens, and are said to be not only nutritive, but slightly aperient". Wilkinson agrees that the young shoots are wholesome and notes that they are said to resemble asparagus in flavour, although she comments that "I will not pretend that I could ever discover the similarity". However, she points out that "during the last famine in Ireland, hundreds of the poorer people were for days – nay, perhaps for weeks – without any other sustenance".

The juice of the nettle has been used as rennet, to curdle milk for cheese making, while folklore has it that nettles will drive away frogs. Wilkinson tells us that "the great amount of heat evolved by the nettle during the process of fermentation makes it one of the best substances for the formation of 'hot-beds', for which purpose it is much prized by market-gardeners".

The plant has been used therapeutically to treat a wide range of complaints, including scurvy, gout, jaundice and nephritis. The 16th century Italian physician Gerolamo Cardano suggested it was possible to "let out melancholy" by brushing the skin with nettles. Wilkinson quotes a contemporary "authority", Dr. Thornton, as saying that nettles could be used to cure goitre and treat paralysis. Nettle tea, says Wilkinson, is "one of the most esteemed of those cooling spring medicines which our peasantry hold in such high repute".

The stems of the plant have been used to make coarse cloth, fishing lines and paper. The seeds yield an oil for lamps, while the juice of the plant will make a green dye, and the roots will make a yellow one.

The poet Thomas Campbell wrote in his *Letters From the South* (1836) "In Scotland I have eaten nettles; I have slept in nettle-sheets, and I have dined off a nettle-tablecloth . . . The stalks of the old nettle are as good as flax for making cloth. I have heard my mother say, that she thought nettle-cloth more durable than any other species of linen".

The generic name comes from the Latin *uri*, to burn. The English name is derived from the Anglo Saxon *noedl*, a needle.

NETTLE, DEAD

White – **Harmless**

Don and Barton identify the dead nettle as *Lamium purpureum* or *L. album*. Don tells us that a variety of *L. purpureum*, with white flowers, is to be found in English fields and "on road sides about Croydon". *L. album* also has white flowers and is to be found "in shady mountain places... [and] in some parts of Scotland". Another name for *L. album* is common archangel, while *L. purpureum* is also known as red archangel, purple hedge nettle, and dee nettle.

There are various opinions as to the derivation of the generic name. Some, such as Don, say it comes from the Greek *laimos*, throat, because the flower looks like an open mouth. Others say it was named after Lamia, a child-eating demon from Greek mythology.

NIGHTSHADE

Dark purple – **Witchcraft**

AMC has listed the BITTERSWEET, or woody nightshade (*Solanum dulcamara*), with the meaning of 'truth', earlier in the book. She has also listed ENCHANTER'S NIGHTSHADE (*Circaea*) with the meaning of 'witchcraft'. It seems likely, therefore, that here she is referring to deadly nightshade (*Atropa belladonna*), although she has given it the same meaning as *Circaea*.

Don describes deadly nightshade as inhabiting "church-yards, dung-hills, and gloomy lanes, and uncultivated places in England, but in other countries it is said to be common in woods and hedges".

Barton adds that "it is perhaps not truly indigenous, being generally met with near towns and the ruins of ancient buildings, particularly in places occupied by the Roman army... which encourages the supposition that it was introduced into this country by the Romans". He lists a number of places where it has been found, including Furness Abbey, where it grew "very abundantly in the vicinity of the ruins... on which account its place of growth is called the Vale of Nightshade". And he quotes the botanist William Curtis (1746–1799) who reports it growing in the chalk pits of Kent, and in Buckinghamshire, where a child told him that it was called "naughty man's cherries".

Like the foxglove (the original source of digitalis), the deadly nightshade has progressed from the herbal pharmacopoeia into modern medicine, providing the natural form of two drugs, belladonna and atropine. Despite the poisonous nature of the nightshade berries, their therapeutic value was discovered and they were used over many centuries. Don tells us that "under proper management this virulent poison may become an excellent remedy... [but it] requires the greatest caution". The leaves, he says, "have been sometimes successfully applied to cancerous tumours" and its anti-spasmodic properties have been used to treat epilepsy and convulsions, while Barton tells us that it was common practice to use "the extract of Belladonna... for the purpose of dilating the pupil prior to the operation of extraction of cataract".

Ildrewe relates that, in the 11th century, after the Danish invasion of Scotland, the Scots mixed the juice of deadly nightshade berries into the wine "which the conditions of a truce bound them to supply the Danes. They were so intoxicated by it that the Scots killed the greater part of them before they had recovered consciousness".

The generic name is that of the Greek goddess of destiny, Atropos. The specific name (meaning beautiful woman) arose because women used it to dilate their eyes and, as a wash, to clear their skin.

Other names for the plant all relate to the madness and delirium caused by an overdose – lethale, maniacum, furiosum, and dwale (this last being derived from the old provincial word *dwaule*, meaning to wander or be delirious).

O

OAK APPLE

Green – **Hospitality, safety**

Oak apples are growths produced on the young branches of the oak in response to chemicals injected by the larva of certain types of gall wasp. They can be brown, yellow, green, pink or red.

According to Barton, their juice mixed with iron sulphate and gum arabic makes a good black ink. Gerard tells us that, in the 16th century, "the expert Kentish husbandmen" would use them to foretell the future by interpreting what they found when the oak apple was broken open: "if they found an ant, they foretell plenty of graine to ensue; if a white worm or magot, murren of beasts and cattell; if a spider, then, say they, we shall have a pestilence or some such like sickness amongst men".

OAK

***Leaf, bright green* – Courage**
***Acorn, brown olive* – Future strength**

There are, says Barton, two species of oak native to Britain – the common oak (*Quercus robur*) and the sessile oak (*Q. petraea*) – and nearly 150 foreign species of which more than half are natives of America, including the live oak (*Q. virens*) and the black oak (*Q. velutina*), both of which are prized for their wood.

Oaks are very long-lived and can grow to a great size. William Gilpin, in his *Remarks on Forest Scenery* (1791) records that there are "a few venerable Oaks in the New Forest, that chronicle upon their furrowed trunks ages before the Conquest." An oak in Withy Park, Shropshire, which was cut down in 1697 was, says Barton, "nine feet in diameter [and] contained twenty-eight tons of timber in the body alone". An oak in Welbeck Park, Nottinghamshire, he goes on, "measures thirty-five feet in circumference, near the base, and is supposed to be full seven hundred years old . . . [while] in Ampthill Park, Beds., there is a fine specimen measuring forty feet in circumference at the base, [that] is supposed to be one thousand years old".

When oak forests were common in Britain, acorns formed the staple food for herds of pigs. The right to feed your pigs in the woods was, says Barton "one of the most valuable kinds of property . . . and it often constituted the dowry of the daughters of the Saxon kings". During the 11th & 12th centuries, Norman lords who wanted the forests for hunting, took these rights away from the lower classes, but they were believed to be so important that their restoration was included in Magna Carta in 1215.

The oak has had many uses, not least for ship building. Barton tells us that it has been calculated that the wood of 2000 trees, "the full produce of fifty acres", is needed to build a 74-gun ship. The quality of the wood means that it has also been used for "staves, laths, and spokes of wheels, also for mills, presses, wine-casks, and for all purposes where strength, solidity and durability, are required". Oak sawdust was used to dye a thick, hard-wearing cloth known as fustian, while the bark was used in tanning leather and to produce a purple dye.

The acorn, when pressed, dried and powdered "is pleasant and nutritious," says Barton, and has been used as a substitute for coffee. However, the French "during the great dearth which prevailed in 1709, were driven to the extremity of eating it as bread, and experienced very injurious effects, such as obstinate constipation and destructive cholera".

The generic name, according to Barton, is derived from the Celtic *quer*, beautiful, and *cuez*, a tree. The specific name of the common oak comes from the Latin *robur*, meaning strength.

OATS

Straw – **Harmony, union**

Loudon, in his *Encyclopaedia of Agriculture* (1826), writes extensively about the oat. It is, he says, a very useful grain and "more peculiarly adapted for northern climates than either wheat, rye, or barley", being cultivated mainly in "latitudes north of Paris".

Oats have been cultivated in Britain for centuries. In the north, some parts of Yorkshire and Derbyshire, and in Ireland, they are used "partly for meal and partly for horse food. In the south it is almost entirely for horse-food, poultry, and groats for gruel". The fine powder which resulted from husking the corn was used in Scotland and Ireland to make "an agreeable light and wholesome supper dish" known as sowen or flummery. Dolby's recipe for flummery, however, uses whole oats which are soaked in water for up to 20 days until sour, after which the resulting flour is sieved and washed, then boiled in milk.

The 1835 edition of Miller's *Gardener's Dictionary* tells us that oats are "esteemed the most wholesome food for horses, being sweet, and of an opening nature".

Loudon lists a number of varieties of oat including the white or common oat (the one most usually cultivated in England and Scotland), the black oat, the red oat, the Poland oat, the Dutch oat and the "potatoe oat". This last, says Loudon, "usually brings a higher price in the London market than any other variety. It was discovered growing in a field of potatoes in Cumberland, in 1788, and from the produce of the single stalk which there sprung up by accident . . . has been produced the stock now in general cultivation".

Other varieties, such as Church's oat, the Angus oat and the dun oat are, says Loudon, "either too local or obsolete to require particular notice . . . as in other plants extensively cultivated, new varieties will always be taking place of old ones".

OLEANDER (geranium)

Scarlet – **Home**

Quite why AMC has put 'geranium' after 'oleander' is unclear, since the two plants are unrelated and do not share a meaning. Glenny describes oleander (*Nerium*) as "remarkably showy" and "noble objects in the conservatory . . . [that] will grow ten or fifteen feet high into splendid trees, and be covered with rose-coloured, or white, or variegated flowers".

The Practical Florist, an American book published in 1833, calls the common oleander (*N. oleander*) "a beautiful green-house shrub" and tells us that there are three varieties, the white-flowered, double hybrid, and variegated, all of which are natives of southern Europe. However, Don says it can also have large bright red flowers, so this may be the species to which AMC is referring.

The generic name is derived from the Greek *neros*, meaning humid, and refers to the preferred habitat of the genus.

OLIVE

Dark green – **Peace**

Whether AMC is referring here to the leaves of the olive tree or to the olives themselves is not clear. Don tells us that the cultivated olive (*Olea europaea*) was said to have come from Asia but grows abundantly in Syria and Lebanon and is naturalised in the south of France, Spain and Italy. It is a tree, he says, that rivals the oak in terms of longevity, with some Italian trees being thought to date back to the first century.

Don suggests that olive trees can be grown in the latitude of London if they are protected against frost, and grown against a wall. Some trees, he tells us, have survived many winters in Devon, but their fruit doesn't ripen. Olives and olive oil come "chiefly from Languedoc, Leghorn, and Naples . . . the best oil is from Leghorn, and the best pickles from Genoa and Marseilles". Olives, says Don, "are eaten abroad as a whet before, and during the principal meals, and in this country chiefly as a dessert. They are supposed to excite appetite, and promote digestion". The description of olives as a dessert is surprising but, according to Maund, "the preserved olives which are so admired as a dessert, are the green unripe fruit deprived of part of their bitterness by soaking them in water, and then preserved in an aromatised solution of salt".

The olive has been used to treat worms and digestive problems, and the oil has been incorporated into "plasters, liniments, cerates, ointments, and enemas . . . [and] applied externally to prevent the contagious influence of the plague".

The generic name is derived from the Greek *leios*, meaning smooth.

ORANGE BLOSSOM

White – **Chastity, pure, a bride**

Glenny tells us that the common orange (*Citrus sinensis*) and its numerous varieties are "cultivated for the sake of their highly fragrant flowers [and] their richly coloured fruit".

In the 1754 edition of his *Gardener's Dictionary*, Miller lists 20 varieties of orange, including the Seville orange, the China orange, the horned orange, the nutmeg orange, the large warted orange, the starry orange and the pumpelmoes or shaddock (which was named after Captain Shaddock, who brought it from the East Indies).

He tells us that the China orange "rarely produces good Fruit in England, [and] the Leaves [are not] near so large, or beautiful, as those of the Seville Orange", while the starry orange "differs from the other Sorts, in the Fruit dividing into five

Parts, and the Rind expanding in form of a Star" and, together with the distorted orange, it is "preserved by some curious Persons for Variety; but they are not so beautiful as the common Orange".

Miller says that the flowers of the common dwarf or nutmeg orange "grow very close together, and appear like a Nosegay". When it is in flower, he says, it is "proper to place in a Room or Gallery . . . the Flowers, being very sweet, will perfume the Air of the Place; but these are seldom to be found in good Health, because they must be treated with more Care than the common Orange and Lemon-trees".

Miller also tells us that "of late Years . . . some few curious Persons have planted these Trees in the full Ground, and have erected moveable Covers over [them] in Winter, which are so contrived as to be all taken away in Summer". Where this has been done properly, the trees have produced "a much larger Quantity of Fruit, which have ripened so well, as to be extremely good for eating".

Don mentions that the orange can be used to make "various liquors and conserves" and is also used to make perfumes and pomades, while the flowers are distilled to produce orange-water.

Dolby gives nearly 90 recipes for the orange, including instructions on how to make orange fritters, orange fool, orange custard, hot buttered oranges, and orangeade pie (a pie filled with sliced apples and oranges over which has been poured some "syrup of orangeade").

ORCHIS

Purple – A belle

AMC has already listed the BUTTERFLY ORCHIS, the FLY ORCHIS and FLOS AERIS. Here she seems to be referring to the genus as a whole.

Mrs. Loudon tells us that a large number of wild orchids are to be found in Britain, and she divides them into those that grow naturally in peat or heath-mould, and those that grow in dry chalky soils. Both groups contain species with purple flowers. The early purple orchid (*O. mascula*) is, according to Barton, frequently found in meadows, pastures, and woods.

The kinds of orchids that have flowers resembling insects, says Mrs. Loudon, "are now mostly included in the genus Ophrys". Prior gives a list of 14 species which includes, as well as insect-related orchids, the frog orchid, the green man orchid and the lizard orchid.

The generic name comes from the Greek *orchis*, meaning a testicle and referring to the shape of the tuber.

ORIENTAL PERSICARIA

Crimson – **Restoration**

Mrs. Loudon describes the oriental persicaria (*Persicaria orientalis*) as a very showy plant with deep rose-coloured flowers, and she recommends it for London gardens "as it is not in the least degree injured by smoke".

Phillips tells us that the plant was introduced into Europe by the French botanist Joseph Pitton de Tournefort (1656–1708) who procured the seeds from the garden of the monks who lived near Mount Ararat (in modern day Turkey). It was brought to England in 1707 by the Duchess of Beaufort.

Linnaeus stated that oriental persicaria, if picked when in full bloom and preserved, would act to deter insects. Phillips comments that "on this account it is used by the Germans to keep their chambers free from fleas".

The generic name was given because the foliage of many plants in the genus is similar to that of the peach tree (*Persica*).

OX EYE (greater daisy)

White – Patience

Reading Victorian gardening books, it becomes clear that the term 'ox eye daisy' was applied to a number of similar-looking plants including the common ox eye daisy (*Leucanthemum vulgare*), the greater daisy (*Gerbera jamesonii*) the giant daisy (*Leucanthemella serotina*) and the creeping daisy (*Leucanthemum paludosum*). Since AMC lists both ox eye daisy and greater daisy, it suggests that she was not limiting the meaning of 'patience' to a specific species.

In the 1754 edition of his *Gardener's Dictionary*, Philip Miller describes the common ox eye daisy as "very common in the Meadows in most Parts of England, from whence the Flowers are gathered, and brought into the Markets in London for medicinal Uses; but it is seldom cultivated in Gardens".

An author signing herself "ES" in the *Lady's Magazine and Museum* of May 1837 suggests why that might be. She complains that "the ugly ox-eye…grows on rubbish so plentifully, and flowers profusely… spreading its fennel-shaped leaves and ill-smelling blossoms on every side of the metropolis, as if it had a particular ambition of being admired by the citizens of London". While acknowledging that "it is wrong to dislike God's creature", she cannot help but call it "a fetid and unlovely flower". Having pointed out that it is poisonous "although its medicinal virtues, if properly applied, are said to be considerable" she states that it is the largest flower to grow naturally in or near London, "and seems as if it delighted in the impure and heavy atmosphere". She suggests that it has been given the meaning of 'patience' "because the more it is trod upon the more it grows".

P

PALM

Dark green – **Victory**

Loudon in his *Encyclopaedia of Gardening* (1824), tells us that palm trees are "of great interest... both as fruit trees and as supplying other products and of much grandeur of appearance. The cocoa, sago and date palms are well known; upwards of fifty other species have been introduced into this country."

Palm trees were cultivated in Mesopotamia and the Middle East over 5,000 years ago and, in ancient Egypt, the date palm was a symbol of immortality. In ancient Greece and Rome, palm branches were a symbol of victory and were presented to military leaders and successful athletes. Even today, the award given to the best feature film at the Cannes Film Festival is known as the *Palme d'Or* (golden palm).

There are numerous species, some of which can grow to a height of 70 feet or more, with the Quindio wax palm (*Ceroxylon quindiuense*), the national tree of Colombia, reaching between 160 and 200 feet.

As well as producing a variety of edible fruits including dates and coconuts, palms have provided building materials (their leaves making a useful thatch), wax for candles, oil for food, cosmetics and fuels, and, between the fifth century BCE and the 19th century, in South and South East Asia, dried leaves were polished and used as a form of paper.

PARSLEY

Green – **Feasting**

Parsley (*Petroselinum crispum*) was introduced into England from Sardinia in 1548 and, says Don, it is now "so common as to be naturalised in several places both in England and Scotland". He lists three varieties, the common plain leaved, which is seldom cultivated, the curled-leaved which is "the most esteemed variety" and the broad-leaved or large-rooted Hamburgh "which is cultivated for its carrot-shaped roots". The first two, he tells us, are used as pot-herbs and garnish, while the roots of the third are eaten like parsnips and are occasionally used as a remedy for "the gravel".

Barton says that, in ancient Greece, it was used to make the victor's crown for certain games, and was also strewn on the tomb at a funeral.

If sheep eat parsley, says Barton, it will "render their flesh more delicious". However, parsley is poisonous to a number of birds, particularly parrots.

PASQUE FLOWER (ANEMONE)

Pale pink – **Sickness, expectation**

The common pasque flower (*Pulsatilla vulgaris*) is usually purple but can also be pink. Don tells us that it is to be found growing wild on uncultivated fields, in exposed situations and in dry open chalky pastures. He warns that the plant is acrid and will easily cause blisters.

The generic name is from the Latin *pulsare*, meaning to sway, since its tendency to grow in exposed places means it is often caught by the wind.

PASSION FLOWER

White, blue, green & brown – **Faith & hope**

Glenny describes the passion flower genus (*Passiflora*) as very showy and beautiful climbers, some deciduous and some evergreen. Mrs. Loudon says of the common passion flower (*P. caerulea*) that it will "live in the open air in the climate of London, flowering abundantly, and ripening fruit every year". The fruit, she says, is edible but insipid.

It is probably *P. caerulea* that AMC is thinking of, since this species has flowers that are blue and white with a green and brown centre.

The generic name comes from the Latin *passio*, passion and *flos*, a flower. Traditionally, the flower is said to symbolise many aspects of Christ's passion, including the crown of thorns (the corona of filaments growing above the petals), the apostles who remained loyal to Jesus (the ten petals), the nails that held Jesus on the cross (the three stigmas), the wounds Jesus received (the five anthers), the spices and perfumes prepared by the women to embalm the body (the scent), the hand of man (the leaves) and the world (the fruit).

PEACH BLOSSOM

Pale pink – I am your captive

The peach tree (*Prunus persica*), says Don, has been cultivated from time immemorial in Asia and was probably brought to Europe from Persia in the first century CE. It was introduced to England in the mid 16th century. In Don's time, the best European peaches were grown in Italy, with those of Montreuil, near Paris, in second place. However, England was not without its successes – Don mentions a tree in Suffolk "which covers about 600 square feet of trellis under a glass case . . . and ripens annually from 60 to 70 dozen of peaches".

PENNY ROYAL

Dark green – **Flee away**

Penny royal (*Mentha pulegium*) is a member of the mint family and, according to Don, is found "in ditches and bogs, and other humid places". Barton, however, says that it "is not so frequently found wild in this country as cultivated in gardens". Its flowers are pale purple, so presumably AMC is referring to the leafy part of the plant.

It was used as a herb for seasoning by the ancient Greeks and, says Don, in his time it continued to be used in cookery and also for making pennyroyal water which, like peppermint water, was said to have medicinal qualities and which was also used for flavouring bitter medicines.

The specific name is derived from the Latin *pulex*, a flea, because the smell of the plant is said to repel fleas. And this, no doubt, is what led to its being given the meaning of 'flee away' in a number of floral dictionaries. It has also been called flea mint, pudding-grass, pulial-royal, and organy.

PEONY

Crimson – **Anger, gaudiness**
White – **Blushes, timidity**

Mrs. Loudon tells us that there are many handsome varieties of peony, which is quite hardy in the climate of London. The "most esteemed", however, is the tree peony (*Paeonia suffruticosa*), which has large white flowers and "a few years ago . . . sold at six guineas[1] a plant, but it may now be obtained from 3s. 6d to 5s". AMC's white peony may refer to this, or it may refer to the Chinese peony (*P. lactiflora*), a native of Siberia which was introduced into England in 1784. Phillips says that it has an agreeable fragrance and that the Mongols "boil the root in their soup, and grind the seeds to put it into their tea".

AMC's crimson peony may well be the common peony (*P. officinalis*), a native of Switzerland which has long been grown in England and which Phillips describes as superb.

Phillips tells us that only one species, the wild peony (*P. mascula*) is native to England, and that it was reported by Gerard as growing wild on a rabbit warren in Kent. However, this has purplish flowers and so does not relate to either of AMC's plants.

The generic name was given in honour of the physician of Greek legend, Paeon, who is said to have used the plant to cure Pluto, the god of the Underworld, after he had been wounded by Hercules.

---

1. £6 6s.

PERIWINKLE

Blue – **Pleasure of memory, early friendship**
Red – **Remember early friendship**
White – **Remember our childhood**

Both the greater and lesser periwinkle (*Vinca major* and *Vinca minor*) have flowers that range from purple to blue. Phillips declares that the lesser periwinkle, and especially the variety with double flowers "is exceedingly ornamental, as their fine blue colour is so desirable a mixture to the yellows and reds of other plants". Glenny comments that it is "well adapted for covering the surface of the ground in shady situations where little else will live".

The red species is the rose periwinkle (*Catharanthus roseus*) which, according to William Curtis in the *Botanical Magazine* of 1794, was first grown in England in 1757 by Philip Miller after he had been sent seeds by Antoine Richard, the gardener at Versailles. Richard, in turn, had received them from Madagascar, where the plant is indigenous. The white periwinkle is a variety of the lesser periwinkle, *V. minor*.

Glenny mentions the astringent properties of the plant and the fact that it has been used in tanning, "while amongst the French peasantry they are extensively used, in the form of poultices for contusions and swellings".

Early botanical works, says Barton, called it *pervinca*, from the Latin *pervincere*, to overcome. Some believe this name was given "because it resists the winter's cold" but, according to Phillips, it is because "it subdues other plants by its creeping, or binds them by its runners". He tells us that, in France, it is sometimes known as "*Violette des sorciers*, because the French considered it one of the plants which assisted the Sorcerers in their pretended magical operations", while, in Italy, "the peasants . . . generally call it *Fior di Morto*, flower of death, because it is used by them to make garlands for their dead infants".

PHEASANT'S EYE

Scarlet – **Sorrow, remembrance**

Don tells us that 10 species of the genus *Adonis* are known as pheasant's eye, but only three of these have red flowers. The autumn pheasant's eye (*A. annua*), a popular garden plant which is also found in cornfields throughout Europe, has flowers that are "an intense blood-red". The deep crimson summer pheasant's eye (*A. aestivalis*), which is indigenous to England, is also found in cornfields while the large pheasant's eye (*A. flammea*) is a native of Austria.

Mrs. Loudon is not a fan of them as garden flowers as the leaves are so bushy that "they would almost conceal the flowers were it not for their intensely deep blood-red colour".

Phillips tells us that the autumn pheasant's eye was being grown in British gardens by the late 16th century and, at the time he was writing, it could be found in Kent "in great plenty, in the fields sown with wheat". Large quantities of the flowers were brought to London each year, and sold under the name of Red Morocco.

Pheasant's eye has the alternative name of *flos adonis* (many floral dictionaries list it as 'Adonis') and Gerard records that, in his time, it was called red mathes and red camomile and that the women of London called it rose-a-rubie.

The generic name comes from a Greek legend which says that this is the flower that sprang up from the blood of Adonis, after he had been wounded by a boar.

PHLOX

White – **Unanimity**
Blue – **I agree to your wish**

Mrs. Loudon believes phlox to be one of the most beautiful of herbaceous plants, and recommends two white species, trailing phlox (*Phlox nivalis*) and creeping phlox (*P. stolonifera*), and the blue woodland phlox (*P. divaricata*). Glenny's favourites include garden phlox (*P. paniculata*) and meadow phlox (*P. maculata*) both of which are white.

Phillips tells us that the first of the genus to be grown in England was the smooth phlox (*P. glaberrima*), a pink species which Philip Miller was cultivating in the Chelsea Physic Garden in 1725.

The generic name is derived from the Greek *phlox*, meaning flame, and is said to relate either to the flame-like shape of the bud or to the bright colours of the flowers.

PIMPERNEL

***Chickweed, white* – An appointment**
***Scarlet* – Foretells tears**

AMC has muddled two plants here. The scarlet pimpernel is *Lysimachia arvensis*, whereas CHICKWEED belongs to a different genus and has the botanical name of *Stellaria media*. Mrs. Loudon calls the pimpernel "one of the prettiest of our common British weeds" and Phillips goes further, saying that even though it is a weed, it is "deserving of a situation on the parterre, its flowers being of a fine yellow scarlet, having a purple circle at the eye, which adds considerably to the beauty of this miniature flower".

At one time the pimpernel was used to treat epilepsy and melancholia. However, by the early 19th century it was being used mainly as a pot herb and, on the continent, was eaten as a salad.

A popular name for the pimpernel is the shepherd's weather-glass because, as Phillips explains, "the corollas never expand in rainy weather, or when the air is moist, but on the contrary when the atmosphere is dry and the sun shining, they display their scarlet and purple". Barton notes that, in addition, it is one of the *flores horologicae*[2], "its flowers expanding regularly about ten minutes past seven, and closing about a quarter past two".

---

2. Plants that open and shut at certain hours

PINE APPLE

Yellow – **Perfection**

The 1845 edition of Thomas Webster's *Encyclopaedia of Domestic Economy* tells us that the pineapple (*Ananas comosus*), which was introduced to Europe in the mid 17th century, was first grown in England by Sir Matthew Decker of Richmond, and that "in Kensington Palace there is a picture [of] Charles II . . . receiving a pineapple from his gardener, [John] Rose".

It is "the gardener's boast", says Webster, that pineapples grown in Britain, using artificial heat, are superior in both size and flavour to those grown in the West Indies. In Jamaica, he tells us, pineapples are used to flavour rum "and a wine is made from the fermented juice of the sweeter sorts nearly equal to malmsey".

The Family Magazine for 1836 contains an article whose author declares that the pineapple is thought to be the finest fruit in the world because of its "richness and fine aromatick flavour". Over 30 varieties, he says, are grown in England, including the queen-pine, New Providence, brown sugarloaf, striped sugarloaf, Montserrat, Antigua, king-pine and green-pine. Of these, the first two are "perhaps, the most esteemed", the queen-pine being the commonest in Europe and the most reliable. However, "the culture of the pineapple is very expensive and troublesome [and] fruit is seldom produced till after the lapse of two or three years". Be that as it may, Webster states that "At present, pineapples may be procured any day of the year in London with more certainty than in their native countries, and of late their price has been very much reduced".

The largest pineapple ever grown in Britain, says Webster, "was cut lately from the hot-house of John Edwards, Esq., of Rheda, Glamorganshire, and was presented to the king at Windsor[3]. It weighed 14 lbs. 12 oz. . . . was 12 inches high, exclusive of the crown, and 26 inches in circumference".

The juice of an unripe pineapple was said to have caustic properties, and to be able to corrode the knives used to cut it. Webster mentions that it is customary to cut a pineapple into horizontal slices in England, but into oblique slices in the West Indies, while the *Family Magazine* tells us that in the East Indies pineapples are so abundant that they are used to clean the inhabitants' swords.

The fruit got its name because its outer scales are thought to look like those of a pine cone.

PINK

White – Fair and pleasing
White, edged with pink – An offering
Carnation – Woman's love
Double, red – Ardent love

Glenny tells us that the majority of pinks (*Dianthus*) "are highly ornamental hardy perennials", while Mrs. Loudon says that the pink, the CARNATION (*D. caryophyllus*), and the SWEET-WILLIAM (*D. barbatus*) "are in every garden, and are universal favourites". Don lists 125 species of *Dianthus*, recommending that the rarer kinds be grown in pots.

Phillips compliments the florists for having transformed "an insignificant weed into one of the most delightful charms which the lap of Flora contains". The

---

3. Presumably Webster is referring to William IV, who was succeeded by Queen Victoria in 1837.

pink, he says, was unknown in the ancient world until the time of Augustus Caesar (63 BCE-14 CE), when it was found in Spain. By the 16th century, pinks were being grown in England in their "improved double state", as recorded by Gerard who calls them "Pinks, or Wild Gilloflowers". Phillips notes that London and Wise, who designed the gardens at Blenheim palace, "give more pages on the cultivation of the Pink than on that of any other plant" in their *Retired Gardener* (1706).

By the time Phillips was writing, it was being suggested that the pink "is degenerated into a mechanic's flower, because its cultivation is so carefully and successfully attended to in manufacturing districts... But... we have frequently noticed with what delight these flowers have been regarded by the most refined classes of society, when they have met with them in village gardens; for their own florists having of late years been so much engaged in the culture of rare plants, known ones have too frequently been neglected".

The pink, Phillips suggests, is "one of the most desirable flowers we possess as an ornament for apartments, since its odour is rather of a refreshing than a faint nature, and it retains its beauty longer ... than almost any other blossom, and as it is less affected by the steam of hot dishes than flowers in general, it is well calculated for the epergne[4] of the dinner table".

The generic name (*Dianthus*) comes from the Greek *dios*, divine and *anthos*, flower.

---

4. A table centrepiece that holds flowers

PLEURISY ROOT

Brown – **Cure for the heartache**

Unless she visited or lived in America, AMC may never have seen a pleurisy root plant (*Asclepias tuberosa*) since it is a native of North America and seems hardly to have been known in Britain. In fact, almost the only mention of it I could find was in American books, with the exception of a short paragraph by Mrs. Loudon in which she notes its various names – butterfly-weed "from its being generally covered with butterflies", the pleurisy plant "from its medicinal virtues, which are said to be very considerable" and ache-in-the-side plant "from its supposed efficacy in cases of pleurisy". Linnaeus named it the tuberous rooted swallow wort and it is also known as the orange flowered *Asclepias*, and in some places as silk weed.

J. E. Carter in his *Botanic Physician* (1837) gives it the additional name of flux root and describes it as "a beautiful plant, abounding in most parts of the United States; but . . . most abundant in the South, flourishing best in sandy or gravelly soil, along fences, and in old uncultivated fields". Its flowers, he says, "are of a most beautiful, brilliant, orange color".

In an article in the *Buffalo Medical Journal*, reprinted in the *Medical Examiner* of 1848, T. T. Lockwood tells us that "it is generally known in the country by the common name of Milk Weed". It needs, he says, great care in preserving the root which "should be collected about the first of October, cut in transverse slices, dried in the shade, and, as soon as sufficiently dried, pulverized and bottled". Since a dried root is likely to be brown in colour, it is possible that AMC may be referring to this.

Lockwood ascribes a wide range of therapeutic uses to the root. It "equalizes the circulation," he says, "produces copious expectoration . . . [and] in the treatment of measles . . . is often of essential service . . . [being] the most valuable medicine I have ever administered to bring out the rash in all eruptive diseases". In addition he declares that it is useful in the treatment of bronchitis, catarrh, chronic diarrhoea, chronic rheumatic affections, and "in all those low forms of fever in which there is a tendency to cerebral congestion" where it is preferable to the opium-containing Dover's Powder. Because it was used in the treatment of flatulence, it also acquired the name of wind root.

PLUM

Ripe, purple – **Independence, riches**

All varieties of garden plums, says Don, belong to the species *Prunus domestica*, which is "a native of or naturalized in Britain, very frequently found in hedges". In the early 1830s, nearly 300 varieties of plum, including greengages and damsons, were known in Britain.

Don quotes Thomas Martyn (1735–1825), Professor of Botany at Cambridge University, who observes that ripe plums in moderate quantity "are not unwholesome, but in an immature state they are more liable to produce diarrhoea and similar diseases than any other fruit of the class". That said, Don comments that plums make excellent pies, tarts, conserves, and sweetmeats and "a wholesome wine".

The wood of the plum has been used in turnery, cabinet work, and in making musical instruments.

POLYANTHUS

Brown and yellow – **Pride of riches**
Purple and white – **Worthy of confidence**
Crimson – **The mystery of the heart**

The polyanthus, Mrs. Loudon tells us, together with the AURICULA and the PRIMROSE, form the *Primula* genus and are some of the most popular and beautiful of florists' flowers.

Phillips says "it is a welcome inmate in every flower-garden, and in no part of the world is it so successfully cultivated as in England, particularly by the zealous florists of Lancashire and Cheshire", the finest specimens being produced in "the neighbourhood of Manchester and Macclesfield [which] is justly celebrated".

The English name comes from the Greek *polus*, many and *anthos*, flower, because both the polyanthus and its close relative, the auricula, produce many flowers on one stem.

POMEGRANATE

White and pink – **Folly**

In the opinion of Don, there is no tree more showy than the pomegranate in flower. Mrs. Loudon acknowledges it as "a very handsome deciduous shrub or low tree, which, in . . . London, thrives against a conservative wall, and produces fruit which attain their full size . . . but seldom ripen". It has been admired since ancient times and, in the 17th and 18th centuries "a double-flowered variety . . . was the most favourite plant in Continental and British orangeries next to the Orange and the Lemon". While pomegranate flowers are usually bright red, they can also be pink and white.

Don describes the flowers and the rind of the fruit of the common pomegranate (*Punica granatum*) as "powerful astringents . . . [that] have long been successfully employed as such . . . as gargles [and] in diarrhoeas".

The generic name comes either from the Latin *Punicus*, Carthaginian, because the plant is a native of north Africa, or else from *puniceus*, scarlet, referring to the colour of the flowers.

POPPY

White – Sleep, repose
Red – Consolation
Scarlet – Extravagance

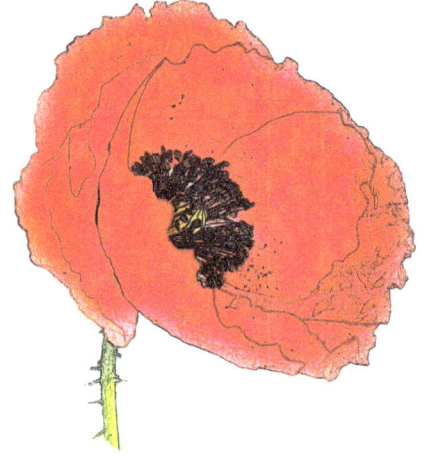

Here AMC is no doubt thinking of the common white, or opium poppy (*Papaver somniferum*) and the common red poppy (*P. rhoeas*) for the first two in her list. According to Don, there are a number of candidates for the scarlet variety including the horned scarlet poppy (*Glaucium corniculatum*), the rough poppy (*P. hybridum*), the long headed poppy (*P. dubium*), the oriental poppy (*P. orientale*) and the Persian poppy (*P. bracteatum*).

Glenny declares that many species of poppy "are weeds unworthy of a place in any garden" and Don describes the common red poppy as "a great pest in corn fields". But he allows that the oriental poppy is a "beautiful plant [which] is very frequent in gardens, where it is a great ornament", and the Persian poppy is "the most splendid of all the poppies, and . . . one of the greatest ornaments of borders".

The oriental poppy was discovered in Armenia by the French botanist Joseph Pitton de Tournefort (1656–1708) and, says Phillips, within six years it was being grown in England by the garden designer George London (c. 1640–1714). He describes it as magnificent "both in size and colour" with petals that are "generally of a bright red . . . but they sometimes vary to a reddish orange colour".

Mrs. Loudon describes various ways in which poppy seeds are used – in Italy, Germany, and Poland, they are used in confectionery, "in Germany they are boiled in milk, and eaten . . . like sago, . . . or made into a kind of open tart. In Poland they make a thick porridge of . . . buck-wheat, and strew poppy seeds over it" and in England and Germany the seeds make up "the principal part of that celebrated composition for [feeding] singing birds, called German paste".

Barton tells us that, in Poland and Russia, poppy seeds are used "as an ingredient in soups, and to make gruel and porridge", that the seeds of the opium poppy "yield a bland, nutritive oil . . . which may be substituted for that of olives or almonds in culinary and other processes" and that in Italy and Germany the seeds "are made into cakes . . . after the manner of the ancient Egyptians, Greeks, and Persians . . . [mixed] with flour, honey, and other substances".

However, the most important way in which the poppy was used, particularly in the 18th and early 19th century, was in the production of opium from *P. somniferum*. The best opium, says Mrs. Loudon, comes from Turkey and Asia Minor, although efforts have been made to grow it in Britain. "In 1796, Mr. John Bull, of Williton, obtained a reward from the Society of Arts for cultivating the poppy, and obtaining opium from it, 'in no respect inferior to the best Eastern opium' . . . [But] all attempts to grow opium on a large scale as a profitable speculation in Britain, have failed". However, some opium was grown commercially, mainly in Mitcham in Surrey. The ripening heads were gathered and brought to market in bags, each holding about 3000 heads, and sold to the druggists for around £4 10s a bag. From these, a liquid decoction was made which, under the name of syrup of poppies "was formerly much given to children to soothe them during the pains of teething". However, Mrs. Loudon warns us that this is "a very dangerous preparation" since the amount of opium it contains is so variable, and Wilkinson, commenting on this practice says "Lord Bacon . . recommends the introduction of the poppy-head into the food of little babies; and he certainly appears to have more consideration for his own peace and quiet on this occasion than for the health of the poor children".

In England, opium was usually taken in the form of morphine or of laudenum, which is made by steeping raw opium in purified alcohol or white brandy.

Provincial names for the poppy include corn rose, cop rose, cup rose, canker rose, red-weed, wind rose, head-wark, cheese bowls and thunder flower, this last because of a belief that if the petals fall off as it is being picked, the person picking it is more likely to be struck by lightning. Don tells us that the generic name comes from pap, the soft food given to small children, because of the habit of putting poppy juice into their food to make them sleep.

POTATOE FLOWER

White and violet – **Benevolence**

Don tells us that "The common potatoe varies much in the leaves, colour of the flowers, shape and colour of the roots". The first country in Europe to import it was Spain which received it from Ecuador in the early 16th century. Some decades later, Sir Walter Raleigh brought it back from Virginia.

William Camden, in the 1789 edition of his *Brittania* claims that "the potatoe was first planted by Sir Walter Raleigh on his estate at Youghall, near Cork" where it was grown for food long before it was common in England.

Towards the end of the 17th century, the Royal Society tried to encourage the cultivation of the potato, with the idea of preventing famine. Don quotes one writer on gardening who, writing some time before the great Irish potato famine of 1845-52, expresses the common view that "They are much used in Ireland and America as bread, and may be propagated with advantage to poor people". But they were not considered to be of value otherwise. In 1699, John Evelyn suggested that, if you did plant them, it should be "in your worst ground".

"It was near the middle of the 18th century," says Don, "before they were generally known over the country; since that time they have been most extensively cultivated. In 1796 . . . in the county of Essex alone about 1700 acres were planted with potatoes for the supply of the London market . . . The cultivation of potatoes in gardens in Scotland was very little understood till about the year 1740 . . . [but] since the middle of the 18th century . . . has made rapid progress, so that they are now to be seen in almost every cottage garden, and fields of them on every farm".

By 1817, the popularity of the potato was well established and Patrick Neill could write in his *Account of British Horticulture* that "so generally is it relished, and so nutritious is it accounted that on many tables it now appears almost every day in the year . . . [and] potatoe starch . . . is considered an equally delicate food as sago or arrow-root."

Apart from its value as a food, the potato was also used as a source of starch for cleaning woollen cloth or silk without damage to their colour and, by book-binders and shoemakers, as an adhesive. In addition, Don notes that "wine of considerable quality may be made from frosted potatoes".

POTENTILLA

Scarlet – I believe you

Potentilla forms a genus of herbaceous plants and shrubs, some of which, says Mrs. Loudon, are very ornamental. Why AMC specifies 'scarlet' for this plant is hard to tell, since most of the species have yellow flowers. However, there are some scarlet species, of which Mrs. Loudon considers *P. Russelliana* to be "by far the handsomest". (The illustration shows *P. atrosanguinea*.)

Don tells us that the generic name comes from the Latin *potens*, meaning powerful, and relating to the "supposed medical quality of some species".

See also cinquefoil

PRIMROSE

Sulphur – Early love, first flower of spring
Lilac – Youth, hope
Red – Unrequited merit

The primrose is a close relation of the auricula and the polyanthus, all of them being members of the *Primula* genus. It is to be found, says Phillips, "seeking the partial shade of hedge-rows, the banks of sheltered lanes, and the borders of woods or coppices".

Mrs. Loudon declares the common primrose (*P. vulgaris*) very ornamental as a border flower "but it has not sported so much as the *Polyanthus*, and there are therefore no florists' primroses". Even so, the garden varieties, most of which are double, are, she says, very showy and she believes that the double varieties of the flesh-coloured, white, brimstone, red, copper, dark purple, and violet, deserve a place in every garden. The single white and the single red are both found wild but these, too, says Mrs. Loudon, are much admired.

The generic and the English names are derived from the Latin *primus*, meaning first, and referring to the fact that these plants tend to flower in the early spring.

PRIVET

White – **Mildness, prohibition**

The privet (*Ligustrum vulgare*), which Mrs. Loudon describes as one of the most common but also most useful garden shrubs, is best known as an evergreen with white flowers. However, the wild version, which Don tells us can be found in hedges and woods around Britain, is deciduous. "The flowers are sweet scented, white at first, but soon changing to a reddish brown". The evergreen kind came originally from Italy, according to Mrs. Loudon, and "is preferable to all other plants for garden-hedges on account of the rapidity of its growth, and the nature of its roots, which never extend to a great distance from the plant". It is, she says "one of the best plants for verdant architecture and sculpture; because it grows compact, is of a deep green colour, and the leaves being small, they are not disfigured by clipping". An added advantage is that it grows "even in narrow courts amid coal-smoke".

Don lists five varieties of privet: the white-berried, the yellow-berried, the Italian or evergreen, the variegated-leaved and the narrow-leaved. The common privet has dark purple berries from which a reddish pigment can be made. "In times of scarcity," says Don, "they are eaten by different sorts of birds, particularly the bulfinch".

The generic name is said to be derived from the Latin *ligare*, meaning to bind, referring to its flexible branches. In the past its English names have included prim, print and primprint.

Q

QUEEN'S ROCKET

White – **You are a coquette**

Queen's rocket (*Hesperis matronalis*), which Phillips also refers to as garden rocket, is not to be confused with the popular salad leaf, *Eruca sativa*. Found in coppices and hedges throughout much of Europe, according to Don, it has white or purplish flowers that are usually sweet scented.

Phillips tells us that queen's rocket was imported from Italy some time before the end of the 16th century, "and its spikes of double corollas are ranked amongst the most ornamental of our garden flowers". However, "it will not endure the atmosphere of either Paris or London" because it needs pure air and a light, fresh soil.

It is, says Phillips, "much cultivated on the French coast, and may be seen in great perfection in most gardens between Calais and Abbeville". And Don tells us that "the ladies of Germany have pots of this plant placed in their apartments".

The generic name comes from the Greek *hesperos*, meaning evening, since that is when the scent of the flowers is strongest. In England, it has been known as dame's violets, queen's gilloflowers, and damask violets.

QUINCE BLOSSOM

White edged pink – **Temptation**

Don describes the quince tree (*Cydonia oblonga*) as "low, much branched, and generally crooked and distorted" and says that it "has never been very much cultivated". The fruit, however, makes an "excellent marmalade and syrup", and can also be stewed or put into pies or tarts. The juice has been used therapeutically to treat digestive disorders.

R

RANUNCULUS

Scarlet – You are rich in attraction
Golden – I am dazzled by your charms
Variegated – Aspiring
Globe, yellow – Jealous of honour
Wild, yellow – Youthful joy

Mrs. Loudon tells us that there are two kinds of *Ranunculus* – border flowers and florists' flowers. But, as Glenny points out, the genus also includes CROWFOOT and "the BUTTERCUPS of the meadows".

Originating in the Middle East, the Persian buttercup (*Ranunculus Asiaticus*) has spawned, according to Mrs. Loudon, "some hundreds of varieties", all of which have double flowers and which Don says may be white, yellow, orange, red, purple or variegated. The varieties, he says, are endless: "Maddock[1], in the end of the last century, had nearly eight hundred, ranged as purple, grey, crimson, red, rosy, orange, yellow, white, olive, coffee, striped, spotted, &c."

Phillips tells us that the *Ranunculus* was first brought to Europe by St. Louis of

---

1. The florist James Maddock (1718-1786)

France when he returned from the Crusades in the mid 13th century, but it had been cultivated in Constantinople before this. By the late 16th century it had reached England, and Gerard wrote that in his garden "they flourish as in their owne countrey." As a result of its popularity in England in the second half of the 18th century, says Phillips, "the English are said to have raised a greater variety [of *Ranunculus*] than any nation".

The generic name comes from the Latin *rana*, a frog, because most of the species live in damp places.

RASPBERRY

Red – **Remorse**

AMC may be referring here either to the flowering raspberry (*Rubus odoratus*) which has deep pink flowers, or to the fruit itself, the latter being produced by the red raspberry (*Rubus idaeus*) which has white flowers.

R. idaeus, says Don, is found in woods and hedges, especially parts of Wales and Scotland. Its fruit, he tells us, "is much esteemed when made into sweetmeats, and for jams, tarts, and sauces [and] . . . is much used in distilling, to make [a] cordial spirituous liquor". He goes on to say that raspberry syrup is second only to the strawberry when it comes to cleaning tartar off the teeth, and it has also been used to treat gout and rheumatism.

REED

Common, brown – **Desirous to please**
Split, brown – **Indiscretion**
Reeds, brown – **Harmony, music**

A number of plants in different genera are known as reeds. The giant reed (*Arundo donax*) was introduced into Britain in 1648, and Mrs. Loudon describes it as "a splendid bamboo-looking reed, [which] will grow to the height of ten or twelve feet in one year; producing a fine oriental appearance when standing singly on a lawn, or near water". *The Rural Cyclopedia* (1847) tells us that its leaves can sometimes be "as broad and long as the blade of a small sword". In Italy and the south of France it is used to make fishing-rods, fences, and stakes for vines. A variety with striped leaves is, says Mrs. Loudon, common in gardens and is known as ribbon grass in England, and gardener's garters in Scotland.

The Rural Cyclopedia tells us that the common reed (*Phragmites australis*) "grows wild in the ditches of Great Britain . . . [and] is used for protecting sea-embankments, thatching houses, ceiling cottages, constructing rustic verandahs, laying the bases of mortar-floors, and forming hot-bed covers for tender culinary plants". The wood reed (*Calamagrostis epigejos*) grows in damp woods, while the upright reed (*Calamagrostis stricta*) grows wild in the marshes of Scotland.

The Rural Cyclopedia also mentions the sea-reed, marrum, or mat-grass (*Ammophila arenaria*) which "grows in vast abundance on the sea-coasts of Britain, . . . pierces the sand banks of the shores with its tough subterranean stems, and in consequence converts them into powerful barriers against the inroads of the ocean". Because of their value in coastal defence, both a Scottish parliament "at a remote date" and a British parliament in 1742 passed laws to prevent sea-reeds from being cut.

RHUBARB

Light straw – **Advice**

Loudon, in the 1850 edition of his *Encyclopaedia of Gardening,* notes that rhubarb (*Rheum rhabarbarum*) is native to Asia and had been introduced into Britain by the late 18th century. It can, he says, be "formed into tarts and pies in the manner of apples and goose-berries".

Why AMC describes rhubarb as 'light straw' in colour is hard to say since, even after cooking, most rhubarb remains pink, . It is possible that she is referring to the flowers which can be a range of colours, including yellow or orange, but these are tiny. Or she may be referring to rhubarb which was dried and powdered to be used medicinally. However, even this is not quite right since George Richardson Porter in *The Tropical Agriculturist* (1833) tells us that "the powder should appear of a bright yellow colour".

Rhubarb was used therapeutically mainly for disorders of the bowels and was very popular. Robley Dunglison in his *General Therapeutics and Materia Medica* (1850) informs us that, in 1831, 40,124 lbs. of rhubarb was imported from Russia and the East Indies.

ROSE

Full blown, red – Happy love, beauty
Full blown, white – I am worthy of you
Full blown over two buds – Paternal approbation
Variegated, pink & white – War or peace
Faded, any color – Hope told a flattering tale
Faded, yellow – Decrease of affection
Rosebud, red – Declaration of love
Rosebud, white – A heart ignorant of love

The rose, more than any other flower, demonstrates clearly that the Language of Flowers could never be used in a practical way. AMC, together with a number of other floral dictionaries, lists 'rose' with one meaning and then various species of rose with a variety of other meanings. And it seems impossible that the recipient of a rose or bunch of roses could have determined their correct meaning using a book which lists (in a number of cases) over thirty possibilities, unless both she and the sender had a detailed knowledge of botany.

Mrs. Loudon tells us that over 100 distinct species of roses have been recognised and "there are above two thousand named varieties to be procured in the nurseries". They are natives of Europe, Asia, Africa, and America, "but none have yet been found in Australia".

Don comments that there is no agreement among botanists as to the number of original species of this genus, and "notwithstanding the labours of many scientific men the genus still remains a chaos". He adds that roses are cultivated commercially for the production of rose-water and attar of roses[2], and grown in every garden "from the most humble cottage upwards". However, he warns us that no rose thrives well in or near large towns "on account of the smoke or confined air".

Barton tells us that the Greeks and Romans used to strew roses on tombs and included requests in their wills for this to be done. There was a similar practice in England in the 17th century where, says Barton, "it was the custom to plant roses round the graves of lovers, and to strew the flowers upon the graves of friends, and the practice, we believe, is not yet quite obsolete". Wilkinson tells us that one Edward Barnes, who lived in London and died in 1653, left the sum of £20 to buy an acre of land for the use of the poor, "for so long a time as they should keep rose-trees fresh and flourishing on his grave".

Gerard thought that the rose hip "maketh the most pleasante meats and banqueting dishes, and tarts, and such-like" and Wilkinson notes that preserves of rose hips and rose flowers were to be found "in our own village confectionary". In China, she tells us, Sir John Davis, at "a feast given to him at Shangae" was served "a ragout of the flowers of the common China-rose dressed whole".

The rose was believed to have medicinal properties and Gerard goes so far as to suggest "the possibility of perfectly maintaining the health by a morning diet of a salad of rose-leaves".

Wilkinson relates a legend that the first rose grew when, simultaneously, Venus rose from the waves and Minerva, the Roman goddess of Wisdom, sprang from the brain of Jupiter. The rose was white until Venus, running to the wounded Adonis, trod on a rose thorn and dyed the flower red.

---

2. Also known as otto of roses – a fragrant oil derived from rose petals

ROSE, CABBAGE & MOSS

Cabbage, red – **Ambassador of love**
Moss, bud, pink – **Confession of love**
Moss, full blown, pink – **Superior merit**

The cabbage rose or Provence rose (*Rosa centifolia*) is, says Mrs. Loudon the best known and most common kind of rose, being very beautiful and very fragrant. Don speaks of 43 garden varieties while Mrs. Loudon, writing a little over 10 years later, says there are more than a hundred. William Paul in his *Rose Garden* (1848) comments that "the group has improved of late by the varying of the colours, [but] no individual variety has been raised to surpass the original".

As to the moss rose, American writer, Robert Buist, in his *Rose Manual* (1847) says this "is most probably an accidental sport or seminal variety of the common Provence Rose, as the Old Double Moss Rose, which was introduced to this country from Holland in 1596, is the only one mentioned by our early writers on gardening". This is confirmed by a modern source – the David Austin website – which states that moss roses are "centifolias that have developed a moss-like growth on the sepals of their flowers. This was the result of a sport or mutation . . .They were at the height of their popularity in Victorian times".

Buist tells us that the cabbage rose "has been an inhabitant of English gardens for nearly three hundred years" and, while "vague tradition says it comes from the east", its origins are obscure. It has, he says "been crossed and amalgamated with many others, [but] few of the progeny outvie the parent in size, beauty, perfection, and fragrance". It has been "the favourite ornament of English gardens" for many years, being found "around almost every cottage". Buist considers it likely that it is the same flower described by Pliny as the "hundred leaved rose", a favourite flower of the Romans. Philip Miller, head gardener at the Chelsea Physic Garden from 1722 to 1771, thought it to be the prettiest of all roses. William Paul describes it as "deliciously fragrant", branching, or pendulous, with "bold and handsome" foliage.

ROSE, DAMASK

York & Lancaster – **United in peace**

Don describes 50 garden varieties of the damask or perpetual rose (*Rosa Damascena*), while Mrs. Loudon speaks of over 100, "the most beautiful of which is Lee's Perpetual or the *Rose du Roi*". The petals of the damask rose were a favourite for the manufacture of rose water.

Robert Buist, in his *Rose Manual* (1847), says that the damask rose is frequently confused with the cabbage rose, having a "delicious odour" and producing flowers in clusters. It has "long spreading branches thickly set with prickles [and] the foliage is strong, of a pale green". The York and Lancaster variety "is often striped, and frequently one-half pink and the other half white".

Thomas Rivers, in *The Rose Amateur's Guide* (1840), comments that the damask rose has been eulogised in poetry more than any other rose "and its colour described with a poet's licence. [But] in these glowing descriptions the truth … has been entirely lost sight of; for … the original Damask Rose, and the earlier varieties … the roses of our poets … are most uninteresting plants". The original species, which had single flowers, he tells us, is said to have been introduced into Europe in 1573, from Syria. The newer varieties, he acknowledges, are both beautiful and fragrant.

ROSE, MAIDEN'S BLUSH

*Pale pink – **Will you love me***
*Bud, white – **If you love me you'll find me***

Modern sources say that this rose is a cultivar of *Rosa alba*, the white rose of York, and has been known since the 14th century.

The *Annals of Horticulture* for 1847 calls it a sweet, delicate rose, with a very pale blush colour. Thomas Rivers, in his *Rose Amateur's Guide*, (1840), describes it as "double and pretty, with fragrant leaves" and, the Rev. J. S. Henslow, in *Le Bouquet des Souvenirs* (1840) expresses his admiration of the maiden's blush and others, such as the cabbage rose, calling them "real Roses . . . to distinguish them from the crowd of varieties which swell the modern floral list". They bloom, he says, "in perfection" in cottage gardens.

ROSE, CHINA

Multiflora China, red – **Beauty with dignity**
Monthly, pink – **Thy smile I hope for**
China rose, a delicate pink – **Beauty ever new**

The China rose (*Rosa chinensis*) acquired the name of 'monthly rose' from its habit of continuous flowering. Mrs. Loudon mentions that it "may be made to flower all the winter by keeping it in a greenhouse". It is, she says "the parent of another large family of roses, comprising upwards of two hundred varieties and hybrids", the most interesting of which are the tea-scented roses, and the noisettes.

Don lists several varieties which could be AMC's 'delicate pink' – the rose-coloured *odoratissima* and *longifolia*, the pink *Fraseriana* and the 'pale blush' *Lawrenciana*. However, it seems more likely that she is describing 'Parsons' Pink China' which, according to Jerry Haynes' *History of Roses* on the American Rose Society website, was introduced to England in 1793 by Sir Joseph Banks, the Director of Kew Gardens, and was grown by a Mr Parsons in Rickmansworth, Hertfordshire. By 1823 "it was said to be in every cottage garden. From now on, when you ordered 'Monthly Roses' you would expect to receive . . . 'Parsons' Pink China' or one of its near relations". Haynes goes on to say that it could well be identical to the rose brought to England in 1751 by the Swedish naturalist Pehr Osbeck (1723-1805) which was propagated and sold under the name of 'Pale China Rose'.

ROSE, MUSK

Cluster of, red – **You are charming**

The original musk rose (*Rosa moschata*) is described by a number of authors as having white flowers and this seems to have remained the predominant colour, although pink and (less common) red varieties are mentioned. However, the American writer, Robert Buist, in *The Rose Manual* (1847) says that, while "it is true we have the Pink Musk Cluster, Red Musk Cluster, Frazerii, and some others . . . they are worthless". It is not clear, therefore, whether AMC is really referring to a red variety of musk rose or whether she has become confused by the profusion of rose species.

William Paul in his *Rose Garden* (1848) tells us that the musk rose is a rambling shrub, introduced into England around 1596 and now spread widely around the country.

According to Thomas Rivers, writing in *The Rose Amateur's Guide* (1840), a rose-tree known as the "Chinese Rose Tree," was discovered in Ispahan, by the zoologist Guillaume-Antoine Olivier (1756–1814). Olivier sent seeds from the plant back to Paris where it produced what is now the common musk rose and, says Rivers, was probably "the parent of nearly all their garden roses". The musk rose, he says, is "one of the oldest inhabitants of our gardens" and some very old and large plants are to be found in the gardens of old country houses.

The flower acquired its English name because of its scent, although Paul comments that it is "not so powerful as some authors would lead us to believe". Rivers observes that "it is much more fragrant in the evening, or in the cool weather of autumn, than at any other time or season".

Paul lists 12 varieties, ten of which have white or yellowish flowers. The other two are the pale red Blush (or Fraser's), and Rosine, which has flowers that are "clear rose". Rivers tells us that "the Blush Musk, or Fraser's Musk, . . . is not quite a pure Musk Rose; but as it is the only rose of this division of the colour, and also very fragrant, it has been much planted".

ROSEMARY

Green – **Remembrance, welcome**

Rosemary (*Salvia rosmarinus*) is, says Don, "a densely-branched and densely-leafy shrub" with flowers that are white or pale blueish-purple. Clearly, AMC is referring to the foliage and not the flower.

It grows best, says Don, on dry rocky soils, especially by the coast but, according to Barton, it has "long been a favourite tenant of the British garden", having been introduced into the country "in the dark ages".

Rosemary has been credited with various medicinal properties, particularly for stimulating and strengthening the nervous system. It has been used to treat headache, deafness, giddiness, and palsy and to improve the memory. It is this last, says Don, that made it an emblem of fidelity for lovers. "It was accordingly worn at weddings, and perhaps, on the same principle, at funerals."

In addition to its therapeutic properties, rosemary formed the main ingredient of Hungary water (the earliest European alcohol-based perfume) and was also used in the manufacture of other cosmetics and perfumes. It was (and, of course, still is) used in cooking. Barton tells us that it is used on the continent for flavouring hams, rice and other dishes and "has had the repute of greatly improving the flesh of sheep that feed on it"

The English and specific names come from the Greek *ros*, dew and the Latin *mare*, the sea, reflecting the place where it grows best.

RUE

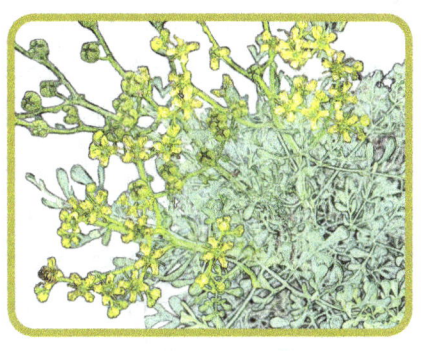

Dark green – **Herb of grace**

The common rue (*Ruta graveolens*) is a native of the "mountainous and sterile situations" of southern Europe, says Barton, but "has been cultivated in our gardens from time immemorial".

Mrs. Loudon describes it as "having a very unpleasant smell, and a bitter taste", with blue-green leaves and yellowish flowers. Don warns that "the leaves are so acrid as to irritate and inflame the skin, if they be much handled" and may excoriate the lips and nostrils if used incautiously to counteract bad smells and contagion.

However, rue has been used therapeutically as a tea and as an antiseptic and, says Don, "among the common people" was sometimes taken in treacle to get rid of worms. The oil was used to treat hysteria, febrile convulsions in children, and palsy.

The old name for rue was herb of grace, and, in 19th century Sussex, it was still known as ave-grace. Some writers believe that the name 'herb of grace' derived from it having been used in exorcisms.

RUSH

Green – **Docility**

G. W. Francis, in *The Little English Flora* (1842). describes the rush (*Juncus*) as "generally without leaves, consisting of a number of upright, round, pithy, smooth stems, and their flowers are borne in bunches on the side of these stems". He comments that "many are common, and extremely useful". However, in a paper presented to the Linnean Society of London in 1816, the naturalist James Ebenezer Bicheno described the genus as "obscure and uninviting".

Bicheno tells us that "the old herbalists seem to have had no other character for the *Junci* than their grassy appearance, and their internal spongy structure" and so included plants that rightly belonged in other genera. Admitting that the *Juncus* genus contains a great variety of species, he tells us that they can be subdivided into three groups – those with leafless stems, those with channelled leaves and those with jointed leaves.

He then goes on to list 21 species, including the spiny rush (*J. acutus*) – "one of those useful plants, which Providence has ordained to bind the loose sands of the shore together as a barrier to the ocean", the soft rush (*J. effusus*) – "cultivated in Japan for the purpose of making mats of an extremely delicate texture, which are used in the place of carpets", and the mud rush (*J. gerardi*) – "very plentiful in those places on the coast subject to be overflowed by the sea". Two species that he is particularly scathing about are the heath rush (*J. squarrosus*) – "this plant fully justifies the proverbial worthlessness of the Rush ... Lime is recommended ... as the means of destroying it", and the toad rush (*J. bufonius*) – "Sometimes it may be observed on a sandy coast not an inch high ... I could never perceive that it was worth much attention".

Among his 21 species, Bicheno also lists the compact rush (*J. conglomeratus*) which, he concedes, has some value, being used "to make the wicks of rush-lights, pith in toys, mats, little baskets, chair-bottoms, ropes and lines .... [and they] are employed by the cleanly peasantry to strew their floors".

Possibly the most widespread use of the common rush was as a substitute for candles. The manufacture of rush-lights is described in some detail by Gilbert White in his *Natural History of Selborne* (1789). The common rush, he says "is to be found in most moist pastures, by the sides of streams, and under hedges". They are gathered during the summer and autumn and immediately "must be flung into water, and kept there; for otherwise they will dry and shrink". The rind of the rush has to be stripped off – a job that is done, says White, by "decayed labourers, women, and children". After this, the rushes "must lie out on the grass to be bleached, and take the dew for some nights, and afterwards be dried in the sun". They are then ready to be dipped in scalding fat or grease. "The careful wife of an industrious Hampshire labourer ... saves the scummings[3] of her bacon-pot for this use" but, elsewhere, other animal oils are used. Adding a little beeswax or mutton suet will make the rushes burn longer.

White tells us that rushes provide a good light and are much more economical than candles. A single rush can burn for over an hour and a pound of rushes, ready for use, costs three shillings. He has calculated that this means that "a poor family will enjoy five and a half hours of comfortable light for a farthing" whereas a halfpenny candle will burn for only two hours.

---

3. The fat that rises to the top during cooking

S

SAFFRON

Golden yellow – **Hymen, matrimony**

While this may refer to the yellow spice, saffron, which is derived from COLCHICUM, AMC has already listed this, together with its vernacular name of meadow saffron. However, there is another possibility. Sarah Hale's floral dictionary, *Flora's Interpreter* (1836), identifies saffron as the common or dyer's safflower (*Carthamus tinctorius*), otherwise known as false saffron. Since this is bright yellow, it may well be the plant to which AMC is referring.

A. F. M. Willich, in *The Domestic Encyclopaedia* (1802), tells us that the common safflower is a native of Egypt and parts of Asia and is cultivated in various parts of Europe and the eastern Mediterranean, from where large quantities of the flower heads are imported into Britain.

Both flowers and seeds have been used medicinally but, by the time Willich was writing, the flowers were "principally employed for dyeing linen, woollen, silks, and especially cotton, which ... retains the volatile hue of the safflower much longer than any other stuff". A versatile dye, it could produce a variety of shades, from bright yellow to deep red, according to what it was mixed with.

An earlier book, the *Compleat Body of Husbandry* (1758), describes the safflower as "a kind of thistle, [that] has very much the appearance of a weed", growing to a height of about four feet. "The principal place where we have seen it in England," says the author, "is in Norfolk". The flowers, like those of true saffron, are picked as soon as they open so that they don't lose their colour. Their "right and honest use" is for dyeing but some people "when it was more cultivated in England . . . had a way of mixing it with saffron . . . [although] no art can so blend them together". Safflower is paler than saffron and so can be recognised when the two are mixed. "One reason why the foreign saffron is held in so much contempt in England," the author continues, "is, that there is too often *Carthamus* among it".

ST. JOHN'S WORT, SATIN FLOWER

(*No colour given*) – **Superstition, truth**

Satin flower is the name given to a number of different species. I have found it being used as a synonym for *Sisyrinchium striatum*, godetia (*Clarkia amoena*), HONESTY (*Lunaria annua*), CHICKWEED (*Stellaria media*), milkwort (*Polygaloides paucifolia*) and others, but nowhere other than in AMC's listing can I find it associated with St. John's wort.

Mrs. Loudon describes the genus of *Hypericum* or St. John's wort as consisting of pretty yellow-flowered shrubs and herbaceous perennials. Don tells us that the common St. John's wort (*H. perforatum*) is abundant in Britain, growing in groves, hedges, and thickets. The plant, he says, "has a powerful lemon-like scent when rubbed, staining the fingers with dark purple, from the great abundance of coloured essential oil lodged in the herbage, and even in the petals". Wilkinson lists some other British species including the creeping St. John's wort (*H. calycinum*) "which is so frequently cultivated in shrubberies", the square-stalked St. John's wort (*H. tetrapterum*) "which decorates the sides of streams, ditches, or other moist places" and the marsh St. John's wort (*H. elodes*) "which brightens our spongy bog-lands". Phillips relates that the creeping St. John's wort was introduced by Sir George Wheeler in 1676 from "the country near Constantinople . . . to illuminate the banks of our shrubberies".

Don tells us that St. John's wort has been used therapeutically as a diuretic and to get rid of worms while, according to Gerard, the leaves were used to treat burns, and an extract of the seeds taken for forty days was thought to cure sciatica. During the mediaeval period, it was believed to be effective in driving out insanity and was given the name *fuga daemonum* (banish demons). Barton reports that the plant has been "in great repute as a remedy for wounds", although its only economical use is to produce a yellow dye. However, Wilkinson tells us that it also makes an "excellent red varnish, which is frequently used by upholsterers for colouring woods".

A great deal of folklore is associated with St. John's wort, probably resulting from the name *fuga daemonum* which was interpreted literally as having to do with exorcism. Mrs. Loudon tells us that St. John's wort was frequently planted near houses to drive away evil spirits. Don adds that, in France and Germany, it is hung in the windows as a charm against storms, thunder, and evil spirits, and that in Scotland it used to be carried as protection against witchcraft, and to cure "ropy milk[1], which they suppose to be under some malignant influence". Wilkinson informs us that, in the Scottish highlands, children were taught to put

---

1. Milk that has thickened, often as a result of bacterial growth

leaves of St. John's wort between the pages of their Bibles.

Other names for the plant include St. John's grass, tutsan, touch-leaves, park-leaves, and grace of God. Tutsan, according to Wilkinson is a corruption of the French *tout sain* (all healing) or of *toute sainte* (all holy) which – like *fuga daemonum* – relates to the belief that it can aid exorcism. Barton believes that the association with St. John is because it tends to flower around St. John's day (24th June) but Wilkinson tells us that it is because on St. John's eve "demons were supposed to be unusually active".

Phillips, however, having told us that there are 39 species of St. John's wort, puts the name down to "modern bigotry" and ancient superstition which said that the plant was a defence against "phantoms and spectres and . . . devils". For the same reason, he says, the creeping St. John's wort has been given the name *sol terrestris* (terrestrial sun) because the sun chases away all the spirits of darkness. His preference, he says, is "to adopt this latter name to distinguish this flower from its thirty-eight relatives, as thirty-nine Worts are too many to dedicate to any one saint".

SAGE

Dark green – **Wisdom, domestic virtue**

Most species of sage, or *Salvia*, says Glenny, are herbaceous or half-shrubby perennials, and scores "are merely weeds". But both Glenny and Mrs. Loudon mention a number of species that are "highly esteemed for the brilliance of their flowers", including gentian sage (*S. patens*), scarlet sage (*S. splendens*) and golden sage (*S. aurea*), which have blue, scarlet and yellow flowers respectively. However, since AMC describes the sage as green, and is clearly referring to the leaves rather than the flowers, she is probably thinking of the common sage (*Salvia officinalis*) which, Barton tells us, is a native of southern Europe, and "has been much cultivated in our gardens, for an unknown period".

Writing about the uses of common sage, Don comments that the leaves "are used in stuffing and sauces for many kinds of luscious and strong meats, as well as to improve the flavour of various articles of cookery" and to make a "decoction called sage-tea". The tea, he says, with a little added lemon juice, can be valuable in the treatment of fevers.

The generic name comes from the Latin *salvo*, I save, and probably alludes to the plant's therapeutic properties.

S<small>EE ALSO CLARY</small>

SCABIOUS

Indian or sweet, dark purple or dark violet – **Widowhood, I have lost all**
Starry, dark purple – **I have lost all**
Corn flower, blue – **Plenty**

In the sixth edition of *Ladies' Botany* (1865) John Lindley describes the sweet, or Indian, scabious (*Scabiosa atropurpurea*) as "one of the most beautiful of our annual exotics" with intensely deep purple petals. Indeed, Phillips describes them as being "of so dark a purple that they nearly match the sable hue of the Widow's Weeds". But, he adds, it "frequently varies in the colour of its flowers, sometimes producing blossoms of a pale purple", while Elizabeth Kent, in her *Flora Domestica* (1831), comments on its rich colours and her belief that the "finest hue is a dark mulberry red".

Glenny says the scent is very like honey, while Phillips thinks it resembles musk, but it is "not powerful enough to be offensive to the most delicate person".

John Parkinson, writing in the early 17th century, mentions that the sweet scabious is common in English gardens. Maund believes it to be a native of the East Indies and "some of the southern parts of Europe", while Kent tells us that "botanists are uncertain of its native country; hesitating between Spain, Italy, and India".

Lindley mentions the starflower scabious (*S. stellata*) which, he says, is not very pretty but is often cultivated "for the sake of its curious heads of seed-vessels". Phillips tells us that 33 species of scabious have been cultivated at Kew, and 43 are listed in Miller's Gardener's Dictionary. Three of these varieties, he says, "are indigenous to our fields". One of these is the devil's bit scabious (*Succisa pratensis*), which has blue flowers. It may be this species to which AMC is referring with her third entry (although the true cornflower is a different plant entirely – *Centaurea cyanus*). However, another possibility is the deep blue pigeon scabious (*S. columbaria*) which, according to Don, is plentiful in England on chalky soils.

Therapeutically, the scabious has been used to treat skin conditions and gonorrhoea. The dried leaves have been used to produce a yellow or green dye.

The generic and English names come either from the Latin *scabiosa*, meaning itch (since the plant was said to be effective in treating skin conditions) or from *scaber*, meaning rough (since, according to Maund, "roughness is characteristic of the tribe"). The specific name *atropurpurea* is derived from the Latin *ater*, dark and *purpurea*, purple. The epithet 'devil's bit scabious', given to *Succisa pratensis*, relates to the stumpy form of the root which gave rise to a tradition that the devil, annoyed that the plant was so beneficial, bit a piece out of it.

SCARLET LYCHNIS

Scarlet – **Eyes bright as the sun**

Don is of the opinion that all species of the *Lychnis* genus deserve cultivating "for the brilliancy of their blossoms" and he identifies the scarlet lychnis as *L. Chalcedonica* "an old and much esteemed border-flower".

A native of eastern Russia, Mongolia and north west China, the scarlet lychnis has strong connections with the city of Bristol in south west England. One legend says that it was brought there by a crusader or Knight Templar during the Middle Ages, at a time when Bristol was a major trading port. Certainly, by the 17th century it was established as the city flower and is said to have influenced John Whitson, mayor of Bristol, who ordered that the girls attending the school that he had founded would wear red.

It is possible that the plant has been associated with the crusades and the Templars because its flowers are said to resemble the shape of a Maltese cross. Other names for it are Jerusalem cross, flower of Constantinople and nonesuch.

The generic name comes from the Greek, *lychnos*, meaning a lamp, and probably refers to the brilliant flowers of most of the species.

SHAMROCK

Green – Light heartedness

While shamrock is usually identified as white CLOVER, both Don and Wilkinson say that the true shamrock is the wood or wild SORREL (*Oxalis acetosella*). But in *Flower Lore* (1879), the author – identified only as Miss Carruthers – states that both plants are commonly worn on St Patrick's day. AMC may be referring to either, as she lists both clover and wild sorrel elsewhere in the book.

Wilkinson suggests that 'shamrock' is a corruption of '*shamroot*' and that this name was applied to a range of plants with similar characteristics.

SNAKE TONGUE

Olive green – Slander

John Craig, in his splendidly titled *New Universal Etymological, Technological and Pronouncing Dictionary* (1849), identifies the snake tongue as the fern *Ophioglossum vulgatum* (also known as adder's tongue) "and other plants of the same genera".

Richard Deakin, in *The Ferns of Britain* (1848) describes it as a "very curious little fern" which grows in most pastures and woods and, in some parts of the country, "is so abundant as to seem to usurp the place of the grasses in the meadow lands, and is thought greatly to injure the crops".

In the same year that Deakin's book was published, Thomas Moore brought out his *Handbook of British Ferns*, in which he tells us that snake tongue can be grown in pots but "is nothing more than a curiosity, and . . . would hardly be considered even that in the many localities where it grows naturally".

Boiled in oil, the leaves were traditionally used to produce an ointment to treat cuts and bruises but John Lindley in *The Vegetable Kingdom* (1847) is dismissive of its effectiveness, saying that it has about as much value as the "magical virtues" once ascribed to the plant.

The generic name comes from the Greek *ophios*, a serpent, and *glossa*, a tongue, since, as Moore informs us, "the fertile frond [bears] some resemblance to the tongue of a serpent".

SNAP DRAGON

Various – **A snare, take heed**

The common snapdragon (*Antirrhinum majus*) is, says Mrs. Loudon, in almost every garden and, in its wild state, is often found growing on the top of old walls. Phillips comments that it is "adapted for the bleak situations in which it grows naturally, as on the highest rocks, or out of the crevices of the most exposed cliffs, or the chinks of the loftiest towers" and may be considered a rustic rather than an elegant plant.

The snapdragon, says Tyas, has been cultivated in our gardens from time immemorial. The tendency of the flowers to sport led many a professional florist "to turn his attention to the improvement of the flower, and within the last few years it has been in a manner recovered from the waste places of the earth ... and admitted to ... the greenhouse and the conservatory".

Glenny comments on the wide range of colours of the flowers, which Phillips describes as "all the shades of a rich orange and yellow down to white, with the same varieties in reds and purple".

According to Phillips, although the snapdragon is now classed as one of the native plants of England, growing wild on the cliffs of Dover, "it is generally supposed not to have been originally belonging to our soil".

Phillips mentions the culinary use of the snapdragon: "The use of eating oil in this country [is] so confined to the wealthy and higher orders of society ... [but] most of the continental countries consume a great deal of oil ... and hence they seek plants whose seeds yield the best oil. In Russia the *Antirrhinum* is sown for the sake of the seed, which produces by expression an oil little inferior to that obtained from olives".

The generic name comes from the Greek *anti*, like, and *rhin*, a snout, relating to the shape of the flowers. It has also been called calves' snout, dog's mouth, lion's snap and toad's mouth.

SNOW DROP

White – **Confidence in the future**

The common British snowdrop, *Galanthus nivalis*, is, says Mrs. Loudon, well known both in its single and double state, and Phillips comments that the latter is "now nearly as common in our gardens" as the former.

The snowdrop, Phillips says, was "formerly held sacred to virgins [which] may account for its being so generally found in the orchards and gardens attached to old monastic buildings". Although claimed as a native plant, Phillips has his doubts and quotes Gerard as saying "These plants do grow wilde in Italie and the places adjacent, notwithstanding our London gardens have taken possession of them all, many yeeres past."

The generic name comes from the Greek *gala*, milk and *anthos*, flower. An old English name is fair maids of February.

SORREL

Garden, red – **Parental affection**

The common sorrel (*Rumex acetosa*) is, says Barton, found throughout Europe and "in this country abounds in meadows and pastures". Several of the "numerous species" are indigenous to Britain. The red colour specified by AMC relates either to the flowers or the red-tinted stems.

Barton tells us that, especially on the continent, sorrel is used in salads, broths and soups, and makes "an excellent sauce for stewed lamb or veal", while in parts of Ireland, it is eaten with fish.

The roots have been used in tanning and, when boiled with alum (a form of aluminum sulphate), produce a "fine red colour useful to painters".

SORREL, WILD

Green – **Ill timed raillery**

The wild sorrel, or wood sorrel (*Oxalis acetosella*) is described by Barton as "a very elegant plant . . . a native of Europe in woods, shady places, and alpine rocks . . . [and] very abundant in England, particularly in the beech woods". Wilkinson goes further, saying that "There are few woods or shady walks where, in early spring, its bright, half-folded leaves are not to be found".

Oxalis, says Barton, is a "curious, beautiful and extensive genus, containing upwards of 200 species" although only the wood sorrel (*O. acetosella*) and the creeping wood sorrel (*O. corniculata*) are indigenous to Britain. The first of these, says Wilkinson, "makes bright and beautiful our hedgerows; and copses; and dense woods; and broken banks in spring", while the second is to be found "in the south of Devonshire, and perhaps in Cornwall, as well as in Sussex". Most of the others, says Mrs. Loudon, come from the Cape of Good Hope.

Over the years, wood sorrel has found many uses – therapeutic, culinary and domestic. Wilkinson tells us that "the acid which abounds in the whole plant renders it of great use as a cooling drink in fevers" and she quotes the second century physician, Galen, who wrote "wood sorrell, used for green sauce, is good for them that have sick and feeble stomachs". Fourteen hundred years later, Gerard commented "of all sauces sorrell is the best, not only in virtue, but also in the pleasantness of his taste . . . it cooleth mightily any hot, pestilential fevers". This sauce, Wilkinson tells us, was still popular on the continent in the 19th century, as an accompaniment to fish dishes, and Barton is of the opinion that wild sorrel leaves "form a more elegant salad than those of Common Sorrel".

At one time, wood sorrel was essential to the manufacture of 'Salts of Lemon' which was used to take iron mould and ink stains out of linen. However, by the time Wilkinson was writing, the preparation was seldom, if ever, made from the plant "as it can be artificially prepared, at a much lower price".

The generic name comes from the Greek *oxus*, meaning sharp or acid. Its English names include alleluia, lujula, sour trefoil, wood-sour, stub-wort, cuckoo's meat, hearts, and woodsom. In Wales, according to Wilkinson, the plants are known as fairy-bells, a name "given to them by the peasantry . . . who believe that they are especially favoured by the 'good people'".

SEE ALSO SHAMROCK

SOUTHERNWOOD

Green – **An old man, jesting**

Southernwood (*Artemisia abrotanum*) is a dwarf, hardy shrub which, according to Barton, "is frequently cultivated in gardens, and endures our severest winters". Glenny believes it is one of the most desirable plants of its genus, while Mrs. Loudon says it is "valuable for bearing want of air, and smoke, without injury". Barton tells us that it is a native of Italy, France, Spain, Syria and Asia Minor, "growing in open mountainous situations".

Traditionally its foliage has been used to repel moths, and the smell of the plant was also said to drive off snakes. Other names are garde-robe and old man (the latter, no doubt, explaining why AMC offers this as one of the meanings).

SPEEDWELL, VERONICA

Speedwell, blue – Faithful, true, celerity
Veronica, blue, white or pink – Patience

Once again, AMC has listed a single plant under two different names and with different meanings. The speedwell or *Veronica* is, says Mrs. Loudon, a genus of "very pretty perennial and annual plants, generally with blue flowers, natives of Europe, and many of them found wild in Britain".

Phillips claims 17 species as being indigenous to Britain although the tall speedwell (*V. longifolia*), which was being grown in London before the end of the 16th century, is a native of Germany, Austria, and Russia. Don lists a number of indigenous species, including the spiked speedwell (*V. spicata*) which is found on high dry chalky pastures, the alpine speedwell (*V. alpina*) which grows on the margins of rivulets on Scotland's highest mountains, and the ivy-leaved speedwell (*V. hederifolia*) which is found growing in rubbish in gardens and fields. The common speedwell (*V. officinalis*), says Barton, grows "in woods, on dry barren pastures, commons and hedge-banks . . . and the simple subdued brilliancy of its flowers, has a pleasing effect".

Several species of speedwell, says Phillips, have been "greatly celebrated by old medical writers as being efficacious against . . . many disorders". He also recommends aquatic veronica or brook-lime (*V. beccabunga*) as a substitute for water cress, being milder and more succulent, and only slightly bitter. Spiked speedwell, he suggests, can be an alternative to tea, tasting "somewhat astringent like the green tea of China", although Barton considers it inferior to "foreign tea". The leaves of the common speedwell, says Barton, when "in decoction with iron filings . . . yield a black dye, which may be used for staining leather".

Gerard considers the germander speedwell (*V. chamaedrys*) to be of use in the treatment of wounds and rashes, including smallpox and measles. In addition, he recommends it as a poultice to treat inflamed eyes and believes the root to be effective in fevers and (when distilled in wine) in inflammation of the lungs. Speedwell has also been used to treat dropsy, jaundice and gout.

Alternative names are Paul's betony and fluellen.

SPIDER WORT

Blue with yellow – **Esteem but not love**

Mrs. Loudon identifies the spiderwort as *Tradescantia*, a genus of "handsome herbaceous plants". Glenny comments that the common spiderwort (*T. virginiana*) can have blue, red, or white flowers, and he also mentions the blue-flowered zigzag spiderwort (*T. subaspera*).

Maund, writing about the common spiderwort, says it was imported from Mexico "by G. Barker, Esq. of Springfield, near Birmingham; and named by Messrs. Knowles and Westcott, who published it in the *Floral Cabinet*". He describes it as having "spikes of numerous flowers branching out from the main stem, and not overshadowed by foliage".

STAR OF BETHLEHEM

Yellow – Guidance, reconciliation

Mrs. Loudon identifies star of Bethlehem as the white-flowered *Ornithogalum*, but says that in the Midlands the name is also applied to the large yellow *Hypericum* (St. John's wort). However, there is another plant, *Gagea lutea*, which is known as the yellow star of Bethlehem and it seems likely that this is the plant to which AMC is referring. Like some of the other plants that she lists, it was not common at the time.

George Bentham in his *Handbook of the British Flora* (1865) tells us that *Gagea lutea* was to be found "in meadows and fields especially in sandy soils over the greater part of Europe and Russian Asia except the extreme north" but was found only rarely in England and the lowlands of Scotland, and not at all in Ireland. Robert Thompson and Thomas Moore in *The Gardener's Assistant* (1878) agree that it is rare in Britain (although a native) but say that it is "well worth cultivating".

According to the botanist Thomas Green, in *The Universal Herbal* (1820) "the Swedes eat the roots of this species in times of scarcity."

STAR WORT

Michaelmas daisy, yellow – Late blossoms
Violet – Welcome to strangers
Red and blue – Cheerfulness in old age

Here again, AMC has listed a plant in two places, although the entry for MICHAELMAS DAISY specifies violet and yellow, and white and red.

Starwort is another name for the aster, a genus which John Lindley tells us, in *Edward's Botanical Register* (1832), "has long been the disgrace of Botanists". There is, he says "no instance in the whole range of Natural History of such imperfect descriptions, unscientific arrangement, false species, confused synonyms, and multiplied names, as that genus presents". However, he is encouraged by the appearance of a work on asters by the German botanist, Dr. Nees von Esenbeck (1776-1858), which is "the most remarkable instance of scientific research applied to systematic Botany that we are acquainted with".

Glenny simplifies matters by telling us that while there are hundreds of perennial asters, "those in general cultivation are the numerous varieties known as Michaelmas daisies, which only require to be planted, and will stand half a century, spreading, and seeming in nowise the worse for neglect".

However, other writers detail a number of asters, or starworts, although several of these have since been transferred to other genera. Maund mentions the alpine aster (*A. alpinus*), a very hardy plant, with blue, purple or pink flowers, introduced from the Alps in the 17th century. The majority of asters, however, are natives of North America. Lindley tells us that the smooth blue aster (*Symphyotrichum laeve*) "has been a long time in our Gardens, where it is a great ornament of the outskirts of Shrubberies . . . increasing rapidly by its spreading roots". He also mentions a pale blue species, the heartleaf aster (*Symphyotrichum cordifolium)* which is "common in our Gardens".

Among the handsomest of the genus, says Lindley, and having masses of bluish flowers, is the purple stem aster (*Symphyotrichum puniceum var. puniceum*) which, he says, has long been known in English gardens. He also describes a number of purple or violet species, several of which fall into the loose 'Michaelmas daisy' classification. These include the showy aster (*Eurybia spectabilis*) "among the most beautiful of the tribe", the New York aster (*Symphyotrichum novi-belgii*) "found in marshes and by the sides of ditches, from New York to Carolina ... and also in Canada" which has "bright lilac flowers" and the smooth blue aster which is "among the most distinct of the species of this difficult genus" with gaily coloured flowers, and a neat appearance.

As to AMC's yellow Michaelmas daisy, Wilson Flagg in his *Studies in the field and forest* (1857) writes "The prevailing color of the autumnal flowers is yellow; yet there is not a single yellow aster among their whole extensive tribe". However, this is not strictly true. Christ's eye inula (*Inula Oculus Christi*), which the illustration depicts, although not a member of the aster genus, is a member of the wider aster family and has yellow flowers. It was being cultivated in Britain in the late 1750s, so it may be this to which AMC is referring.

The only red asters that I can find mention of at this time (assuming AMC means red *or* blue) are some varieties of the China aster and the New England starwort (*Symphyotrichum novae-angliae*) which has dark red flowers.

STOCK

Gilly flower, red – **Lasting beauty**
Purple – **Bounty**

Phillips tells us that the stock (*Matthiola*) "is now become the pride of every British parterre from the gay palace to the humble cottage", having been "one of the earliest inmates of our gardens". Within the last two centuries, he says, what was in the time of Queen Elizabeth "but one degree removed from a small mountain or sea-side flower" has been transformed by the art of the florist into "a shrub . . . whose branches are covered with blossoms . . . forming, on the whole, a mass of brilliant beauty".

At meetings of the London Horticultural Society he has seen carmine stock with "the appearance of ropes of Roses", and has himself grown specimens "of extraordinary size and beauty". But the largest he has come across was in 1822 in the garden of a Mr. Stockdale of Notting Hill, "which measured eleven feet nine inches in circumference when in flower".

The double flowers, says Phillips, seem to have been unknown until the early 17th century and "only within the present century [has] its high state of perfection . . . been achieved".

Gerard, in the late 16th century, mentions only purple and white varieties but Parkinson, in the following century, describes crimson and red stocks.

At the start of the 18th century, London and Wise, who, says Phillips, were "the celebrated nurserymen and florists of that age" described stocks as "one of the principal ornaments of our garden from the variety and number of its flowers". Mrs. Loudon mentions the purple flowered Grecian stock (*M. Graeca*) as having been "long in cultivation in British gardens".

Stock is not the only plant to be known as a gillyflower, sharing the name with the WALLFLOWER, the CARNATION and others. Chaucer, Phillips tells us, spells it Gilofre, while William Turner, in his *History of Plants* (1568), calls it gelouer but adds the word stock "as we would say, Gelouers that grow on a stem or stock to distinguish them from the Clove Gelouers and the Wall Gelouers".

SEE ALSO TEN WEEKS STOCK

STRAWBERRY

Scarlet – **Perfection**
Leaf, green – **Love and esteem**

The common strawberry (*Fragaria ananassa*) is, says Barton, very abundant in woods and thickets in this country and may be considered as truly indigenous to Britain, having formerly been cultivated "in what is now the heart of London". It yields many of the best varieties, with others deriving from the hautbois (*F. eliator*).

Strawberries have not always been as popular as they are today. Barton comments that "it is astonishing that so delicious a fruit . . . should have been neglected by the ancients . . . Pliny scarcely mentions it, and Ovid and Virgil only speak of it as a wild fruit". Don tells us that strawberries are "very nourishing, and may be safely eaten in quantity . . . [since] there are few constitutions with which strawberries, even when taken in large quantities, are found to disagree". Not only that, they have beneficial properties – such as being able to "dissolve the tartarous incrustations of the teeth . . . promote perspiration" and relieve the symptoms of gout and kidney stones, while "Hoffmann[2] states he has known consumptive people cured by them".

The generic name comes from the Latin *fragro*, to be fragrant, while the specific name *ananassa* means pineapple. The English name, according to Don derives from "the ancient practice of laying straw between the rows, which keeps the ground moist and the fruit clean", but Barton says it is a corruption of stray-berry, "so called in allusion to the trailing runners, which stray, as it were, in all directions, from the parent stock".

SUNFLOWER

Tall, yellow – **Constancy, pride**
Dwarf, yellow – **Adoration, I turn to thee**

The common sunflower (*Helianthus annuus*) is an annual, native to Peru, while the perennial sunflower (*H. multiflorus*) is a native of North America and, specifically, Virginia. Both species have dwarf varieties.

Glenny describes the sunflower as a "very ancient ornament of the British gardens", and Phillips tells us that it is a favourite "with rustic gardeners". But it seems that it was also grown in London, since Phillips points out that it "is remarkable for not being affected by the smoky atmosphere ... and is one amongst the small number of plants that will flourish in our overgrown capital".

---

2. Probably Friedrich Hoffmann (1660-1742) who was professor of medicine at the University of Halle

The sunflower was cultivated by Gerard in the late 16th century, and he records that one plant in his Holborn garden grew to a height of fourteen feet and had flowers that were sixteen inches across. He refers to it as "the flower of the sun", and "the great marigold of Peru".

Mrs. Loudon tells us that the Incas regarded the sunflower as sacred. On a more practical level, she notes that Mr. Taylor, a London seedsman, has many acres of it, from which he produces "oil from the seeds, thread and paper from the fibre, and potash from the ashes of the refuse". Phillips mentions that the sunflower is cultivated on a large scale in the United States, mainly for the seed oil "which is good-tasted and fit for salads, and all the purposes for which olive-oil is used".

SWEET PEA

White or pink – **Respect and love**
Purple or dark pink – **Respect and friendship**
A bunch, all colours – **Dependence**

Describing the sweet pea (*Lathyrus odoratus*) as a universal favourite, Mrs. Loudon tells us that there are six varieties in constant cultivation – the purple, the white, the blue, the violet, and the new and old 'painted ladies' the first of which is pink and the second white and pink.

The sweet pea was imported into England from southern Europe at the start of the 18th century, and was grown by the horticulturalist, Dr. Robert Uvedale (1642-1722) in Enfield in 1701. By 1713 it was being included in the Chelsea

Physic Garden's list of ornamental flowers.

If well trained, says Mrs. Loudon, they are very ornamental "but few plants have a more disorderly and untidy effect if they are neglected. They are thus well suited for the culture of a lady, as they require continual watering, tying up, and cutting off of dead flowers or bruised branches".

She goes on to tell us that huge numbers of sweet peas are grown in pots by florists, and sold to the public in the London markets at prices ranging from a shilling to half-a-crown a pot.

Glenny declares that "there is not among the annuals a better nosegay flower than the sweet-pea", and Phillips reports "we now meet with it in every garden, from the palace of the monarch to the cottage of the peasant... [and it decorates] the balconies of the mansions of the metropolis". However, he adds a word of caution, pointing out that although its perfume is "delightful in the open air, [it] is found rather oppressive than reviving when confined to close apartments".

SWEET SULTAN

Yellow – Gallantry

Sweet sultan is the English name for two species of *Amberboa*. The common sweet sultan (*A. moschata*) has purple or lilac flowers, while the yellow sweet sultan (*A. amberboi*) has – as its name suggests – yellow flowers.

Both species were introduced into England from their native Persia during the 17th century, *A. moschata* coming via

Turkey in the 1620s and *A. amberboi* in 1689. Both have a honey scent and Mrs. Loudon describes that of *A. moschata* as "so overpowering . . . that it is almost impossible to bear it in a room", but she acknowledges that the scent and beauty of *A. amberboi* "have long made it a favourite in gardens".

Parkinson, writing about it in 1629, says "The Turks themselves, as I understand, do call it the Sultan's Flower, and I have done so likewise".

SWEET WILLIAM

Variegated – **Gallantry**
Dark red – **Maturity**
Double, white – **Finesse**

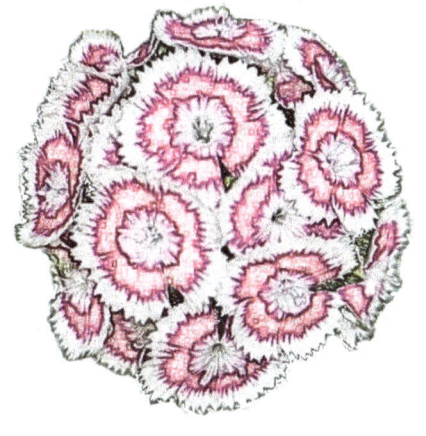

Sweet William (*Dianthus barbatus*) is, says Phillips, "a species of PINK that is indigenous to Germany, from whence it has been scattered over all parts of Europe". Glenny comments that "the varieties of different colours . . . are now numerous", while Don tells us that, by the beginning of the eighteenth century, there were nearly 100 varieties.

Phillips reports that the first writer to mention sweet William seems to have been D. Rembertus Dodoneus, physician to the Holy Roman Emperor Charles V, in the 16th century. Towards the end of that century, however, Gerard mentions it as being a common garden flower, known – among other things – as 'London Tuftes'. The name sweet William was also being used at that time but, says Phillips, "on what account they were so named we are left to surmise".

SYRINGA

Primrose – **Disappointment**

Confusion, says Glenny, sometimes arises from the fact that Syringa is both the common name of the mock orange (*Philadelphus*) and the botanical name of the LILAC tree. Samuel Wood in *The Tree Planter* (1880) agrees: "if you send for a Syringa to a nurseryman, probably he might send you a Lilac, and they are two things quite different, both in character and in quality".

It seems likely that AMC is referring to the mock orange, since she has already listed lilac elsewhere, although the colour she gives doesn't tally with either plant – the flowers of the mock orange are white, and a primrose coloured lilac was not developed until the mid 20th century.

Don lists 12 species of mock orange and tells us that they are all "very desirable plants for shrubberies, the flowers being showy, and ... [mostly] sweet-scented". But Loudon in his *Encyclopaedia of Trees and Shrubs* (1842) says that "the species are in a state of utter confusion: there are probably only three: one a native of the South of Europe ... one of North America and one ... of Nepal".

An article in *The Horticulturist* of May 1848 tells us that "all the Syringas are highly ornamental in their thick foliage and abundant white blossom", while an American publication, *The Ladies' Wreath* (1850), comments that the common mock orange (*P. coronarius*) has a strong perfume "which at a distance nearly resembles orange flowers, but is too powerful for most persons on nearer inspection".

T

TANSY

Yellow – **Resistance**

Tansy (*Tanacetum vulgare*) is, says Barton, well known in gardens as well as being found wild "on hilly pastures, borders of fields, and roadsides, generally in large patches". It has been credited with a wide range of therapeutic effects, including the treatment of hysteria, toothache, gout, urinary problems, and worm infestations. Culpeper says that it is "very profitable for such women as are given to miscarry in child-bearing, to cause them to go out their full time", but Dr. Charles T. Hildreth, writing in the *American Medical Magazine* for November 1834, takes the opposite view, telling us that oil of tansy can produce abortion, and going on to relate a case where administration of this oil caused fatal poisoning.

William Woodville in the second edition of his *Medical Botany* (1810) tells us that the leaves and flowers "have a strong, not very disagreeable smell, and a bitter somewhat aromatic taste". Ildrewe mentions that its bitter flavour has led to tansy traditionally being eaten at Easter, as a reminder of the bitter herbs which Jews were commanded to eat at the Passover.

Barton lists a number of domestic uses for tansy. It can be shredded and used to give colour and flavour to puddings, omelets and cakes and it has been used as a substitute for hops. Rubbing meat with the herb is said to protect it from flies, while putting tansy in a bed will drive away bugs. In Finland, the juice is used to dye cloth green.

Dolby gives several recipes for tansy including a pudding consisting of eggs, cream and flour, coloured with spinach juice and flavoured with tansy juice, salt and nutmeg, all baked in puff pastry and garnished with slices of Seville orange.

TEN WEEKS' STOCK

Red – **Promptitude**

Ten week stock (*Matthiola annua*), also known as hoary stock, is the annual version of the STOCK or gillyflower which AMC has already listed. A native of Southern Europe, it was introduced into England in 1731, and Mrs. Loudon tells us that it is the only annual kind known in British gardens. However, there are "perhaps few species of which there are more varieties".

AMC's red version could be one of several varieties described by Mrs. Loudon. Some of the so-called German stocks are, she says "very curious, particularly the brick-red variety". There are, in addition, among the double kinds, crimson, scarlet and rose-coloured varieties.

THISTLE

Blue – **Austerity**
Scotch, purple – **Retaliation**

There are numerous types of thistle. However, AMC's blue version is likely to be one of the many species of globe thistle (*Echinops*), while the purple Scottish thistle is, according to Wilkinson, either the milk thistle (*Silybum marianum*) or the musk thistle (*Carduus nutans*). Those who support the claim of the latter to be the Scottish thistle, she says, point out that although the milk thistle is very common in England, it is extremely rare in Scotland. and almost the only place it grows is near Dumbarton Castle where it is said to have been planted by Mary, Queen of Scots.

The 17th century diarist John Evelyn noted that the milk thistle was often to be found in food markets, being sold as a suitable vegetable for wet-nurses (which, presumably, is how it got its English name). Wilkinson tells us that "it is as a fodder for cattle that the thistle is most valued" and that a tax on thistles sold at St. Boswell's fair in Scotland has never been repealed. "Few, if any, of our ordinary fodder plants", she says "afford so much nourishment, in the same bulk, as the thistle". In addition, the oil derived from thistle seeds "is admirably adapted for cooking purposes, [and] is also excellent for burning".

The thistle probably became the emblem of Scotland in the early 16th century and by the middle of that century was being stamped onto the coinage.

THRIFT

Crimson – **Mutual sympathy**

Mrs. Loudon describes thrift (*Armeria*) as consisting of hardy perennials, most of which are ornamental. It is, says Phillips, frequently found in the "mud or ooze mixed with the shingles of the sea beach" and so is often called the sea pink. But he recalls that in times gone by, when geometrical flowerbeds were the fashion, the thrift was an important and necessary plant for this style of gardening. As an edging, he believes it is more attractive than box, and "in undulating lawns . . . it adds to the beauty of the turf without injury to its neatness". The name thrift, he suggests, refers to "the rapid manner in which it propagates itself". In the 16th century, thrift was also known as ladies' cushion and sea gilloflower.

THROAT WORT

Pale blue – **Neglected beauty**

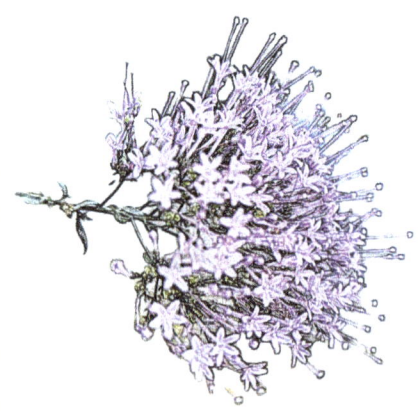

Wilkinson identifies the throat wort as *Campanula*, giving the alternate names of bell-flower, witch's thimble, BLUEBELL and HAREBELL. However, plants of the genus *Trachelium* are also known as throat wort and some of them, too, have blue flowers so, since AMC has already listed both the bluebell and the harebell, it is probably *Trachelium* that is referred to here.

According to Mrs. Loudon, the blue throat wort (*T. caeruleum*) is the most common species. Phillips describes it as "a plant of such a graceful elegance . . . whose flowers . . . seem dyed with the finest tint of its native Italian sky". But it has, he says, been neglected by the British florists and "is rarely to be found on the English parterre" even though it was introduced here almost 200 years previously and "is a perennial plant sufficiently hardy to endure our winters". It seems likely from this that the meaning of 'neglected beauty' for *Trachelium* originated with Phillips (as did quite a few meanings in the Language of Flowers).

Don tells us that the generic name comes from the Greek *trachelos*, meaning neck, relating to its supposed therapeutic value in diseases of the throat.

THYME

Violet – **Activity**

Thyme, says Mrs. Loudon, is a genus of fragrant dwarf shrubs. Don tells us that the flowers are usually purplish and that the common thyme (*Thymus vulgaris*) and the lemon thyme (*T. citriodorus*) are used in soups, stuffings and sauces. Although the broad-leaved variety of the common thyme "is generally preferred . . . the flavour of the lemon thyme is much liked in peculiar dishes".

Don dismisses the "common notion" that sheep fed on wild thyme and other aromatic plants produce mutton of a superior flavour. Sheep, he says, do not eat these plants, but the soil which is favourable to their growth also produces "a short sweet pasturage, best adapted to feeding sheep".

According to Barton, the generic name comes from the Greek *thymos*, meaning strength, since the plant's aromatic qualities are said to strengthen the animal spirits. Wild thyme is sometimes known as mother of thyme, pulial mountain, and creeping thyme.

TRUE LOVE

Red – **True love**

There is a plant known by this name, but it is more commonly called herb paris (*Paris quadrifolia*) and it has inconspicuous greenish-yellow flowers. Since I can find no other floral dictionary that lists 'True Love', I wonder whether AMC meant to list another plant, which is red and has a meaning of true love?

Herb paris, which grows in woods and shady places, seems to be hardly mentioned in 19th century books on flora, other than those dealing with the medical aspects of plants. Barton tells us that it has been used as a poultice to treat tumours and swellings of all kinds, and that the juice of the berries was considered beneficial in the treatment of eye diseases. The 1636 edition of Gerard's *Herbal* recommends it as an antidote to poisons such as arsenic or mercury.

A modern source – the Royal Botanical Gardens website – tells us that the generic name comes not from the city of Paris but from the Latin *par*, meaning pair, and refers to the symmetry of the plant, while the specific name is the Latin for four leaves.

TUBER-ROSE

Pink – **The further the dearer**

The botanist Richard Anthony Salisbury FRS, in a paper read to the London Horticultural Society in December 1806, said of the tuberose (*Agave amica*) "I know no ornamental plant which seems to me more deserving of cultivation... or that would repay the labour attending it with greater profits, than the tuberose". Thirty years later, an article in the Boston publication *The Horticultural Register and Gardener's Magazine* echoes this sentiment: "they will, by their beauty, add to the gaiety and grandeur of the house, and shed around their fragrant odours, every even and morn when the house is closed, such that cannot be conceived but by those whose fortune it is to grow them well".

The tuberose was thought, at various times, to be a native of the East Indies, of Italy and of Mexico. Nowadays, it is said to have come originally from Mexico, although its history is not entirely clear. It was believed to be related to the hyacinth and was given the name of Indian tuberous hyacinth (tuberous relating to its bulbous roots). From this came the French name *tubereuse* and the English corruption of this, tuberose.

When it was first imported into Britain is unclear, but Miller, in the first edition of his *Gardener's Dictionary* (1731), described it and declared it to be a different genus from the hyacinth. Salisbury tells us that Miller "describes the variety with double flowers, now so common, but then only to be seen in M. de la Court's garden, near Leyden, whose memory is... consigned to infamy... for destroying many hundreds of the roots, rather than part with a single one to any person".

The tuberose had certainly established itself in Britain by the early 19th century. Thomas Mawe and John Abercrombie, in *Every man his own gardener* (1818), describe it as having "many white flowers of great fragrancy" (AMC's 'pink' probably relates to the buds). Salisbury mentions that it "continues to maintain its superiority" with roots being imported from North America and Italy, although he has cultivated it for many years in Yorkshire. He adds that "in the East Indies it is distinguished by the poetical title of *Sandal Malam*, or Intriguer of the Night".

TULIP

Red – **Pride with jealousy**
Yellow – **Hopeless love**
Variegated, gold and brown – **Beautiful eyes**

Most of the tulips grown in gardens are, says Mrs. Loudon, varieties of *Tulipa Gesneriana*, a native of the Levant. However, there are other species, and "one of the most beautiful of these is the wild French Tulip, *T. sylvestris*, which is . . . a beautiful yellow, and very fragrant, and which is occasionally found wild in England". Phillips describes tulips as "gaily painted and enlivening", while Mrs. Loudon tells us that "Mr. Groom, of Walworth, is the principal Tulip grower in the neighbourhood of London; and he has an exhibition of them every year".

The tulip first started to attract notice when the Swiss naturalist and writer, Conrad Gessner (1516-1565) wrote about the plant he had seen growing in a garden in Augsburg in Germany, having apparently originated in Constantinople.

In 1582, the English writer and geographer Richard Hakluyt (1553-1616) wrote "we are told that now within these four years there have been brought in England, from Vienna in Austria, divers kinds of flowers, called Tulipas." By the early 17th century, the tulip had become all the rage and, says Phillips, "was carried to such an excess both in Holland and in France, as to produce bankruptcy and ruin to many families". In Haarlem in a period of three years in the mid 1630s this obsession was "said to have yielded . . . a sum not less than ten millions sterling, for the price of these bulbs rose higher than that of the most precious metal". Single tulips could sell for more than 10,000 florins and eventually the Dutch government "were obliged to issue a proclamation to suppress this ruinous excess". (Alexandre Dumas' novel *The Black Tulip* is set in the Netherlands at this period.)

At the beginning of the 18th century, the tulip was still one of the most popular flowers in English gardens but in the 1730s its popularity started to decline. Phillips, ever the snob, laments that since then it has "become neglected by the higher classes, and descended into the gardens of tradesmen and operative manufacturers".

The English and generic names come from the tulip's supposed resemblance to the Turkish turban or *tulipan*. The specific name is a homage to Conrad Gessner.

TULIP TREE

White – Fame

Liriodendron tulipifera is, says Don, "a tall elegant deciduous tree, very commonly cultivated, particularly in the South of Europe, in avenues" but it "is well adapted to grow singly on lawns". Its flowers are yellow and

orange, not the white stated by AMC. Ildrewe calls it a magnificent flowering tree, while Mrs. Loudon comments that it is "very ornamental from its flowers . . and its curiously-shaped leaves" although it usually needs to reach a considerable size before it will flower.

Don tells us that there are two varieties of tulip tree, known as white-wood or white poplar, and yellow-wood or yellow poplar. Ildrewe says that the white-wood variety (also known as canon-wood) has fragrant flowers and "surpasses almost every other in America in height as well as beauty".

The bark, says Don, has been used to treat intermittent fever and, in the United States, was prescribed by doctors for "chronic rheumatism". The smooth, fine grained wood was used for carving, joinery and coach building.

The generic name comes from the Greek *leirion*, lily, and *dendron*, tree, while the specific and English names are based on the fact that the flowers resemble tulips rather than lilies. Other names include tulip-bearing lily tree and saddle tree.

TURNIP

Yellow – **Charity**

The turnip (*Brassica rapa*) is a biennial plant that, Don tells us, grows wild in some parts of England but is "better known as an inhabitant of the gardens or the farm". He lists six types of "round yellow turnips" but says that the white turnips (of which there are nine types) are "by far the best and most generally cultivated".

The turnip is used, says Don, "in broths, soups, and stews" all over Europe while the shoots can be "gathered whilst tender and dressed as spring-greens or spinach". He also notes that the turnip is used by "the London manufacturers of imitations of foreign wine" and has also been used to make "a kind of bread".

Dolby gives recipes for turnip mash and turnip soup, and notes that a turnip will draw out the strength of onions if boiled with them. He also recommends using a piece of raw turnip to help a pastry case keep its shape while baking (much as we would use baking beans today).

The main use for turnips was as animal fodder. But in 1847, two years into the great potato famine in Ireland, Professor James F. W. Johnston wrote in the preface to David F. Jones' *Turnip Husbandry* "the culture of the Turnips as a profitable substitute for the potato is at present of more importance to Ireland, than at any previous period".

V

VALERIAN

Scarlet – **Accommodate to reconcile**

There are many species of valerian but it seems likely that, here, AMC is describing red valerian (*Centranthus ruber*). Don describes it as being "cultivated in almost every garden" and found "on chalk cliffs, on walls, and among rubbish" having, he believes, escaped from gardens. But Phillips thinks that wild valerian, growing "on the old walls of colleges, or on the ruins of monastic buildings" is a legacy from the days when these were the only places where medicinal plants were cultivated.

The therapeutic properties of valerian have been recognised for millennia and it is still a common ingredient in herbal sleeping remedies. In the past it has also been used for anxiety, migraine, digestive problems, epilepsy and plague and, in the Middle Ages, it was believed to be an aphrodisiac.

The English name comes either from the physician Valerius, said to have been the first to use it therapeutically, or from the Latin *valere*, meaning to be healthy.

VENUS'S LOOKING GLASS

Pink – **Flattery**

Venus's looking-glass is the name usually associated with *Legousia speculum-veneris*, which Mrs. Loudon describes as a well-known and pretty annual, grown in English gardens since the late 16th century. However, she also mentions the small Venus's looking-glass (*Legousia falcata*), which was introduced from the area around the Mediterranean in 1820 and has rose-coloured flowers that "grow so close to the stem, and are so intermingled with the leaves, as to form a kind of leafy spike". Don tells us that both species "are showy border annuals" and Phillips describes them as "a great ornament to the parterre".

The English name relates to the seeds which are shaped like a hand mirror.

VERBENA

Rose – **Sensibility**
Scarlet – **Brilliant talents**
White – **Modesty, content**

"Only a few years ago", says Mrs. Loudon, verbena (or vervain) was "scarcely known in flower-gardens . . . [but] in 1827, the beautiful *Verbena melindres** [Peruvian vervain] . . . was introduced from Buenos Ayres, and it directly became a favourite. Since that time, numerous other species have been introduced . . . and it is now rare to see a garden or a balcony without them".

Peruvian vervain, says Mrs. Loudon, is "the most brilliant scarlet", and while Glenny believes that it has been equalled in colour by other species "its creeping habit cannot be excelled, nor can its abundant bloom". However, since its introduction, "far more beautiful sorts have sprung up under the florist's superintendence". The beauty of verbena, he says is that "they are as close to the ground as a carpet, and last in full bloom for months".

Barton tells us that common vervain (*V. officinalis*), which is dismissed by Glenny as "a mere weed", is not uncommon in England by the road side and on waste ground, but he doubts if it is truly a native since it is rarely found at any great distance from human habitation.

According to Phillips, the ancient magi of Persia used vervain in their worship of the sun and "the magicians also employed the Vervain in their pretended divinations, and affirmed that by smearing the body over with the juice of this plant, the person would obtain whatever he set his heart upon, and be enabled to reconcile the most inveterate enemies, make friends with whom he pleased, gain the affections and cure the diseases of whom he listed". The Romans also used it in religious rituals and believed it would keep evil spirits out of their houses. The Greeks were of a similar mind and called it *hierabotane*, meaning sacred herb.

At the time Phillips was writing "the shepherds in the northern provinces of France, still continue to gather the Vervain under different faces of the moon, using certain mysterious ejaculations known only to themselves . . . they profess to charm both the flocks and the rural belles with this plant".

Gerard gives alternative provincial names including holy herb, Juno's tears, Mercury's moist blood and pigeon's grass.

VERNAL GRASS

***Green* – Poor, but happy**

In his *Practical Observations on the British Grasses* (1798), William Curtis tells us that sweet vernal grass (*Anthoxanthum odoratum*) is valuable because it is one of the earliest of English grasses to flower and also because it will grow in a wide variety of soils and situations. It is found, he says "in bogs, in woods (especially such as are of low growth, or have had the underwood cut down), in rich meadows, and in dry pastures".

It is the only English grass that is scented – bruising the leaves will scent the fingers, and the smell of new-made hay is entirely due to vernal grass. It is, says Curtis, well liked by cattle but, in dry seasons, can become blighted.

In *Concise Notices of British Grasses* (1850), David Moore tells us that vernal grass is considered one of the most common grasses throughout the whole of Europe, as well as in the most northern parts of North America. And he notes that, as an agricultural commodity, the average price of vernal grass is one shilling and sixpence a pound. This seems a tiny amount now, but in 1850 it was roughly what an agricultural labourer would earn in a day.

VINE

Purple – **Rural joy**
Leaf green – **Friendship**
Wreath with grapes, purple – **Intoxication**

In his *Practical Treatise on the Cultivation of the Grape Vine* (1841), Clement Hoare relates that, in England, vines are grown "only against walls… and under glass" but comments that the walls of a medium sized cottage could produce enough grapes to pay half its rent.

Mrs. Loudon, focusing more on the ornamental value of the plant, suggests that the common vine (*Vitis vinifera*) is ideal for "covering a bower or veranda, or training round the window of a breakfast-room" where it can form a framework to the garden beyond "with its beautiful leaves looking almost transparent in the morning sun".

The vine is said originally to have been a native of Persia from where it spread across Europe. In *A Treatise on the Vine* (1830), William Robert Prince gives us a potted history. In the ancient world, he says, the vine was probably taken to Greece, Italy and France by the Phoenicians. By the latter part of the eighth century CE, the Emperor Charlemagne had a vineyard attached to each of his palaces, and some of the later French royal residences, including the Louvre, have had vines since the 12th century. Burgundy became associated with wine at an early period, with the first Dukes of Burgundy (in the 9th and 10th centuries) often being given the title "prince of good wines". By the time William Robert Prince was writing, some two million agricultural labourers were employed in French vineyards.

It is uncertain when the vine arrived in Britain, but it was probably brought by the Romans. The Venerable Bede (672-735), in his *Ecclesiastical History of the*

English People, mentions vineyards established in several places in Britain. Soon after the Norman conquest, the Bishop of Ely was receiving between 750 and 1000 gallons of wine a year as tithes from his diocese, and the Normans dubbed the Isle of Ely "the isle of vines".

However, the culture of vines declined over the years. Various theories have been put forward as to the reason. Among these are the unpredictable English weather, the availability of cheap wine from France, and the dissolution of the monasteries in the 16th century since, as Prince tells us, "it was the religious fraternities of the dark ages . . . that carried with them the knowledge of agriculture and gardening, and . . . vineyards were common appendages to abbeys and monasteries from their first establishment".

Around the start of the 19th century, vines started to come back into fashion "both among the scientific horticulturists and among the numerous amateurs . . [so that] grapes of the finest quality for the table . . . are a regular article of sale in the London markets for nine months in the year".

The vine can live for centuries – Pliny speaks of one 600 years old and, in more recent times, the botanist Professor Louis Bosc (1759–1828) identified vines in Burgundy that were over 400 years old. They can also become very large – one growing in Yorkshire in the late 18th century was recorded as having a stem circumference of nearly four feet and covering an area of 137 square yards, while the Hampton Court vine, planted as a cutting in 1768 by the landscape architect Capability Brown, now has a circumference of 13 feet and is officially the largest vine in the world. It can produce 600 lbs or more of grapes a year and, in 2001, it produced a record 845 lbs.

One of the largest bunches of grapes ever grown may have been that presented to the Marquis of Rockingham by the Duke of Portland in 1781. According to William Robert Prince, it weighed just over 19 lbs. and was four and a half feet in circumference and nearly two feet in length.

VIOLET

Blue – **Faithful**
White – **Candour**
Purple and white – **Perseverance, modesty**

Don lists 170 species of *Viola*, which includes both violets and pansies. The sweet violet (*V. odorata*) is shown as having a number of varieties in white, purple and blue. Barton tells us that it grows in woods and pastures and on hedge-banks, while Mrs. Loudon says that white violets are usually found growing on chalky soils. This is backed up by Phillips who recalls that in the spring of 1823, he found the banks between Preston and Clayton, near Brighton, covered with white violets. And Mrs. Loudon tells us that the sweetest white violets she ever smelled were those growing among the limestone rocks in the woods of Dudley Castle.

Phillips mentions the dog violet (*V. canina*) which has no scent and is to be found in more exposed situations than the sweet violet, "often covering large spaces on heaths and downs with its fine blue flowers". It is, he says, "one of the most ornamental of our creeping plants, yet it is seldom to be seen in the flower garden".

Don tells us that violets are grown commercially in Stratford upon Avon for their therapeutic and chemical properties: "a syrup made from the infusion . . . is said to be an agreeable and useful laxative for children, but it is chiefly valued as a delicate test of the presence of uncombined acids or alkalies, the former changing its blue to a red, and the latter to a green".

Phillips records that, in Syria and Turkey, violets are used to make violet sugar and violet sorbet or sherbert, while Wilkinson says that the French use the flowers to make conserves, ices, syrups "and numberless confections of a similar character".

Dolby gives a few recipes for violets, including violet syrup, candied violets and violet marmalade, the last of these consisting of violets "bruised to a pulp" and added to apple marmalade together with boiled sugar.

Vitruvius, the Roman author who lived in the first century BCE, wrote of violets being used to cure ague, inflammation of the lungs and insomnia, and to diminish anger. The flowers were also worn as protection against 'falling sickness' and headaches, and were believed to counteract the effect of a scorpion sting. Pliny recommended a liniment of violet roots and vinegar as a treatment for gout and "disorders of the spleen".

Wilkinson tells us that, mixed with milk, the dog violet "forms a highly-prized cosmetic".

W

WALLFLOWER

Brown with yellow – **Fidelity in misfortune**

Don expresses the opinion that some varieties of wallflower (*Erysimum cheiri*), especially the double kinds, are very ornamental, "and the flowers of all possess an agreeable odour". Mrs. Loudon comments that their "principal beauty is displayed at a season when there are few hardy plants in flower" and their "brilliant yellow and dark orange . . . give a peculiar brilliancy and liveliness to gardens". Of the ten or twelve varieties known to her, some have "rich dark reddish brown flowers, called the Bloody Wallflowers, and others [have] light yellow, with nearly all the intermediate shades".

Phillips tells us that, originally, the species came from southern Europe "and we may presume that it was one of the earliest flowers which was cultivated in our gardens, from its being so constantly found on the ruins of our oldest buildings". The double wallflower, he says, has been grown since the beginning of the 17th century. Don mentions that it is sometimes sown in pastures, together with parsley and thyme, "as a preventive of the rot in sheep".

William Turner, writing in the 16th century, calls the wallflower wall-gelouer or hartis ease. Towards the end of that century, Gerard refers to it as wall-flower, yellow stocke gillo-flowers, and wall gillo-flower.

WALNUT

Straw – **Stratagem**

The 1807 edition of *Miller's Gardener's and Botanist's Dictionary* tells us that the walnut (*Juglans regia*) is not native to Europe and most likely came from "some part of Asia" to Greece and then to Italy. Barton is more specific, saying that it is generally considered to be a native of Persia.

Samuel Fullmer, in *The Young Gardener's Best Companion* (1781), describes the walnut tree as "growing to a vast magnitude, with a large widely spreading head . . either in orchards or around the outer boundary thereof, and in avenues, fields, [and] hedge-rows". Miller comments on the very strong but not unpleasant smell of the leaves.

John Evelyn, in *Sylva or a Discourse of Forest Trees* (1670), describes the trees as forming "most graceful Avenues". Burgundy, he tells us, "abounds with them, where they stand in the midst of goodly Wheat-lands" and are considered to benefit the crop by keeping the ground warm. And at several places in Germany "no young Farmer whatsoever is permitted to Marry a Wife, till he bring proof that he hath planted . . . a stated number of Walnut-trees".

Walnut was, for many years, widely used for furniture-making but, in the mid 18th century, the fashion changed as mahogany began to be imported in large quantities from abroad. Miller laments the fact that, while there used to be large walnut plantations in England, particularly in Surrey, these have gradually diminished, with old trees being cut down and not replaced. Barton tells us that "it is now chiefly used in this country for gun-stocks, being lighter in proportion to its strength and elasticity than any other", although on the continent it is still used for furniture "as it is beautifully veined and admits of a fine polish".

Evelyn considers walnut wood greatly superior to "the more vulgar Beech, [which is] subject to the worm, weak, and unsightly" but which can be washed over "with a decoction made of the Green husks of Walnuts" to deceive the unwary.

Barton describes the culinary uses of the walnut fruit – for pickling, as an adulteration of soy sauce, and made into a confection with sugar. Incisions in the trunk will yield a sap that, when fermented, "constitutes a pleasant wine" and, if evaporated, produces a sugar "equal to that from beet-root". Evelyn mentions that the nut oil is used for frying and, in central France, as a substitute for butter.

The oil, says Evelyn, is also of value to painters. A decoction of the husks and leaves will kill worms in bowling greens, and will also make a dye to colour wool, wood and hair.

Miller informs us that the walnut is of value therapeutically as a laxative, and is also used to treat mouth ulcers and sore throats. The vinegar in which walnuts have been pickled, he adds, "is a very useful gargle".

Two somewhat unusual properties are described by Evelyn who claims that rubbing a walnut kernel on a crack in a leaking vessel will stop it "better than either Clay, Pitch or Wax" and that a distillation of walnut leaves with honey and urine "makes Hair spring in bald-heads".

Miller claims that the English name was originally Gaul-nut, implying that the tree originally came from France. But Barton suggests that it derives from the German *walschnuss*, meaning foreign nut.

WEEPING WILLOW

***Green* – Sympathy in trouble**

"One of the most graceful objects on the face of the earth" is how James Grigor describes the weeping willow (*Salix Babylonica*) in *The Eastern Arboretum* (1841). It is, he says, "a tree of serene weather, and associated in the mind with the soft stirring breezes of the milder months of the year". In France and Germany, he tells us, it is often planted in cemeteries, although he believes that the yew is far more suitable "for if the solemnity of the grave is to be preserved, it must surely be by trees of a sombre hue".

The weeping willow was long thought to be a native of Asia and, particularly, the banks of the Euphrates river, but modern authorities believe it originated in China. It was introduced into England in 1730 and Grigor tells us that a century later there was scarcely a Thames-side villa in Twickenham, Hammersmith, Richmond, or Fulham, without a specimen of considerable size. It can grow very quickly – Mrs. Loudon tells us that it has been known to attain a height of twenty feet in ten years.

One very fine specimen was planted by the poet Alexander Pope (1688-1744) at his house in Twickenham, but it was cut down in 1800 because, says Grigor, the then owner of the house was annoyed that people kept asking to see it.

Barton tells us that the bark of the weeping willow is useful in tanning, while the wood, which is very white, tough, light and pliable, is used for flooring, for making boxes, milk-pails and hoops for casks, and for conversion into excellent charcoal for gunpowder.

The generic name, says Barton, comes from the Celtic *sal*, near, and *lis*, water.

WHEAT

***Straw* – Prosperity**

The vast majority of 19th century books on wheat (*Triticum*) focus on its cultivation. However, Henry Phillips (whose gardening books have been quoted extensively elsewhere in this work) gives a lot of background material in his *History of Cultivated Vegetables* (1822).

He offers extracts from the Bible to show that wheat has been known for millennia and says that many people believe it to be a native of Egypt. And he quotes Pliny who wrote of the "wonderful fruitfulness of wheat in Africa" and of wheat being imported into Italy from there as well as from France, Lombardy, Sardinia, Alexandria and Greece. Sicily, says Phillips, is believed to be the first country in Europe where grain was cultivated. But it is not known when it was first grown in England. Julius Caesar "found corn growing on the coast, but of what kind we are not informed".

Certainly wheat was an important crop by the time of Henry III (1216-1272) since, in 1270, a wet season which affected the harvest resulted in a famine and, at some time during his reign, wheat was so scarce that it was being sold for "£6 8s a quarter" (a quarter is 494 lbs), meaning that one pound of wheat was being sold for what a skilled tradesman could earn in 15 days.

Phillips notes that both ancient and modern writers have observed that wheat can be cultivated almost anywhere in the world. The inhabitants of the New World, he says, not only grow enough for their own needs but "are always ready to pour their surplus into every European kingdom where scarcity requires it to be imported".

England came to the forefront of wheat cultivation in the early 18th century thanks to Jethro Tull who developed a horse-drawn seed drill which would sow seeds in neat rows, making sowing both easier and more productive.

Phillips quotes the French agriculturalist, Henri-Louis Duhamel du Monceau (1700-1782) who urged his countrymen to adopt the drill, saying that it could double the amount of grain produced.

Wheat, like most plants, is subject to various diseases. Phillips tells us that Dr. Edmund Cartwright (who is better known for inventing the power loom), while investigating the effects of salt on vegetables, found that sprinkling wheat with a salt solution would combat mildew within 48 hours. He recommended this as being very economical since, with one man mixing the solution and two men spreading it, more than four acres could be treated in a day.

According to Phillips, the art of bread making was not known in Rome until around the second century BCE, although it was practised in "eastern countries" long before this. Leavened bread, made with yeast, he says, "is of great antiquity, and originated with the French and Spaniards".

Even in the 18th century, the value of fibre in the diet was understood. The physician Dr. Robert James (1703–1776), says in his *Medicinal Dictionary* that bran is a purgative, so bread "which is made of flour not thoroughly cleansed from the bran ... seems to us to be more wholesome, and also more savoury, than that which is made of pure flour." Phillips considers bread beneficial for other reasons, telling us that dry food, such as bread, stimulates saliva to flow: "To effect this, we eat bread with meat, which would otherwise be swallowed too quickly. Bread serves as a medium to blend the oil and water of food in the stomach".

According to Phillips, wheat has also been used therapeutically. He tells the story of Sextus Pompeius (c.67-35 BCE) who suddenly developed an attack of gout while sitting in his barn watching the corn being winnowed. "He thrust his legs above the knees into the heap of wheat, either by accident, or in a rage from the extreme pain, where he soon found himself wonderfully eased ... from which time he never used any other remedy".

X, Y & Z

XANTHIUM

Yellow – **Rudeness**

There is remarkably little in the literature about *Xanthium*. The 1807 edition of *Miller's Gardener's and Botanist's Dictionary*, tells us that the only native English native species is *X. strumarium*, the common cocklebur. And Sir James Edward Smith, in *The English Flora* (1828) tells us that this grows in the south of England, in rich moist ground or near dunghills, but is rare. Miller describes the flowers as pale straw colour, and says that a decoction of the whole plant "affords a showy yellow colour, but it is better if only the flowers are used".

Smith tells us that, in the past, xanthium was thought to be of value in the treatment of scrofulous disorders but it is no longer used.

The generic name comes from the Greek *xanthos*, meaning yellow.

YEW

***Dark green, crimson berry* – Melancholy**

Mrs. Loudon dismisses the common yew (*Taxus baccata*) as being too large for a garden but acknowledges that the slow-growing Irish yew "makes a very handsome plant, which . . . may for a long time be almost considered a shrub".

Barton tells us that the common yew is "indigenous to the mountainous woods of Cumberland, Westmorland [and] Herefordshire" and is also found in southern England. It has, for centuries, been planted in churchyards "as a symbol of immortality; and from its sombre aspect it is well suited". And, says Barton, it is still customary in some parts of Wales and Ireland to throw yew twigs into the grave at a funeral.

The yew can live a long time and attain "a prodigious magnitude". Barton mentions the Crowhurst yew near Hastings, which was thirty feet in circumference, and a yew that once grew in Fortingal church-yard in Scotland which had a circumference of over 56 feet. It used to be the fashion to clip yews "into all sorts of shapes and forms [but] when allowed to take its natural shape, it is one of the handsomest of the British evergreens, and a good shelter for tender trees and shrubs".

Yew wood, which Barton describes as "hard, heavy, and smooth, beautifully veined with red streaks" has, over the years, been used by both turners and cabinet makers, while its strength and durability has led to its being used for mill wheels, axle trees and flood gates. But perhaps the most important use it has had was in the manufacture of bows when these were one of the main instruments of warfare. A statute passed in the reign of Edward III (1327-1377) demanded that every Englishman must possess a bow of his own height, and, says Barton, "the supply in this country being far too scanty, Yew was largely imported from abroad [and] every ship trading with Venice was obliged to bring home ten bow-staves with every butt of malmsey".

The generic name may come from the Greek *toxos*, meaning poison, while the English name comes from the Celtic word *iw*, meaning green.

ZINNIA

Yellow – **Absence**

Mrs. Loudon tells us that the *Zinnia* genus consists of beautiful annual flowers that are natives of Mexico. Glenny describes them as being "all the colours from scarlet to light pink and to dark crimson, and all the shades from dark chocolate to light purple and lilac". However, he considers the most ornamental species to be the elegant zinnia (*Z. elegans*).

Mrs. Loudon agrees that the elegant zinnia is "by far the handsomest of all the Zinnias". She describes one variety as being a very pale yellow, and it may be this to which AMC is referring. The alternative, also described by Mrs. Loudon, is a yellow variety of *Z. peruviana* which has "been common in British gardens since 1770".

The generic name was bestowed in honour of Johann Gottfried Zinn (1727-1759) who was both director of the botanical garden and professor of medicine at the University of Gottingen.

GROUPS AND MESSAGES

After the dictionary itself, AMC has a page of 'Groups and Messages'.

A rose, a pink and a heartsease – *Love offering heartsease*

A rose, sweet-briar, a geranium and ground ivy – *Love offers marriage, a home and domestic comfort*

St John's wort and a fennel leaf – *Truth. I only live for you*

Garden yarrow and the yellow flag – *I shall quarrel. I am jealous*

Scotch thistle, snap dragon and apple blossom – *Retaliation, a snare, beware*
(This would be hard to put together since the thistle and snapdragon bloom at least a month after the apple blossom has finished.)

A snowdrop and a rose – *Confidence in future love*
(This is another difficult one, since snowdrops usually finish blooming in March while roses do not start blooming until April or May.)

Flax, scarlet potentilla and a narcissus – *I feel much obliged. I believe you admire yourself*
(This would only be possible in May, when flax and potentilla are just starting to

bloom and narcissi are just finishing.)

A blue iris and a fig – *I have a message to you. I do not care for you.*

BOTANICAL NAMES

While some of the names that occur in quotations are still the currently accepted names, others are not. These have not been corrected but are marked with an asterisk and the current name is shown here:

Dracocephalum canescens is now *Lallemantia canescens*
Scilla non-scripta is now *Hyacinthoides non-scripta*
Dicranum glaucum is now *Leucobryum glaucum*
Bryum hornum is now *Mnium hornum*
Polyanthus narcissus is now *Narcissus tazetta*
Verbena melindres is now *Glandularia peruviana*

ACKNOWLEDGEMENTS

All the illustrations in this book are based on photographs. The publishers would like to thank the creators of these photographs for permission to use them:

ACACIA: JHenryW (CC BY-SA 3.0, via Wikimedia Commons); ACANTHUS & COLCHICUM: Meneerke bloem (CC BY-SA 3.0, via Wikimedia Commons); ACONITE: Kor!An (CC BY-SA 3.0, via Wikimedia Commons); ALL HEAL: Consultaplantas (CC BY-SA 4.0, via Wikimedia Commons); ALMOND BLOSSOM: Manfred Heyde (CC BY-SA 3.0, via Wikimedia Commons); ALOE: Diego Delso (CC BY-SA 3.0, via Wikimedia Commons); AMARANTH & FILBERT: Michal Svit (CC BY-SA 4.0 via plantnet.org); AMARYLLIS (DAY LILY): Risssa at English Wikipedia (Public domain, via Wikimedia Commons); ANEMONE: lopezlacasa (CC BY-SA 2.0 via plantnet.org); ANGELICA, DRAGON WORT, HYSSOP & MOONWORT: Krzysztof Ziarnek (CC BY-SA 3.0, via Wikimedia Commons); APPLE BLOSSOM: R J Higginson (CC BY-SA 3.0, via Wikimedia Commons); APPLE, THE CRABB: John Severns (Severnjc, CC BY-SA 3.0, via Wikimedia Commons); APPLE (THORN APPLE): Ian Sutton (CC BY-SA 2.0 via Flickr; ASPHODEL, CLARY, MILFOIL & ORANGE BLOSSOM: Zeynel Cebeci, (CC BY-SA 4.0, via Wikimedia Commons); ASPEN, BACHELOR'S BUTTON & ZINNIA: Agnieszka Kwiecień, Nova (CC BY-SA 4.0, via Wikimedia Commons); AURICULA: Primrose (via Pixabay); AZALIA: Zbigniew Niepokój (CC BY-SA 4.0, via Wikimedia Commons); BALM: Quinn Dombrowski (CC BY-SA 2.0 via Flickr); BALM OF GILEAD: Maurice Hoffmann (CC BY-SA 2.0 via plantnet.org); BALSAM: David J. Stang (CC BY-SA 4.0, via Wikimedia Commons); BARBERRY & EVENING PRIMROSE: gailhampshire from Cradley, Malvern (CC BY 2.0 via Wikimedia Commons); BASIL, GLOBE AMARANTH & IVY: Mokkie (CC BY-SA 3.0, via Wikimedia Commons); BAY: Brian Arthur (CC BY 2.5 via Wikimedia Commons); BEE ORCHIS: Charlie Jackson (CC BY 2.0, via Wikimedia

Commons); BEGONIA: Rom Sei (via plantnet.org); BELLADONNA LILY: EOL – Donna Pomeroy (via plantnet.org); BILBERRY & CELANDINE: Andrew Curtis (via Geograph.org.uk); BINDWEED: Andrzej Konstantynowicz (via plantnet.org); BIRD'S FOOT, BLUEBELL, CEDAR & GROUND IVY: Anne Burgess (CC BY-SA 2.0 via Geograph.org.uk); BITTERSWEET: huy HO (via plantnet.org); BLACKTHORN: Michael Bosch (via plantnet.org); BLUE BOTTLE: FlowerPowerH2020 (CC BY-SA 4.0, via Wikimedia Commons); BORAGE & SENSITIVE PLANT: Kai Best (CC BY-SA 2.0 via plantnet.org); BRAMBLE: Emi F (via plantnet.org); BRANCH OF THORNS & OATS: W.carter (CC BY-SA 4.0, via Wikimedia Commons); BROOM: U.S. Department of Agriculture (Public domain via Flickr); BUGLOSS: Gloria Signor (via plantnet.org); BULRUSH: Bill Nicholls (via Geograph.org.uk); BUTTERCUP, CHICKWEED, SPEEDWELL & TANSY: Robert Flogaus-Faust (CC BY 4.0, via Wikimedia Commons); BUTTERFLY ORCHIS & PIMPERNEL: Rossen Vassilev (via plantnet.org); CABBAGE: Bayer CropScience UK (CC BY 2.0 via Wikimedia Commons); CACTUS: Toni Gürke (Public domain, via Wikimedia Commons); CALYCANTHUS: Gmihail at Serbian Wikipedia (CC BY-SA 3.0 RS, via Wikimedia Commons); CAMELLIA: mlvanzeler (via plantnet.org); CAMOMILE & DODDER: anna_485 (via plantnet.org); CAMPION, ROSE: ju li (via plantnet.org); CANARIENSIS: Денис (via plantnet.org); CANDYTUFT: Marie-Reine Raison (via plantnet.org); CANTERBURY BELLS: nicolaas johannes fransen (via plantnet.org); CARDINAL FLOWER: Judy Gallagher (CC BY 2.0, via Wikimedia Commons); CARNATION, CLEMATIS, CROWN IMPERIAL, CURRANTS, DAHLIA, FRENCH HONEYSUCKLE, GRASS, MALOPE, MUSHROOM, MYRTLE & NASTURTIUM : via PxHere (CC0); CASSIA: Noleander (CC BY-SA 4.0, via Wikimedia Commons); CATCHFLY & COLLINSIA: ALAN SCHMIERER (CC0 via Flickr & Wikimedia Commons); CHINA ASTER: Rameshng, (CC BY-SA 3.0, via Wikimedia Commons); CHINA PINK: Niralee Gupta (via plantnet.org); CHRYSANTHEMUM: Satdeep gill (CC BY-SA 3.0, via Wikimedia Commons); CINQUEFOIL: Maria Los (via plantnet.org); CITRON: Johann Werfring (CC BY-SA 3.0, via Wikimedia Commons); CLARKIA: marlin harms (CC BY 2.0, via Wikimedia Commons); CLOVER: ☐☐☐☐ masaki ikeda (CC BY-SA 3.0, via Wikimedia Commons); CLOVES: Cheha M'madi Daoud Hadidja (via plantnet.org); COBAEA SCANDENS: Michael Wolf (CC BY-SA 3.0, via Wikimedia Commons); COLUMBINE: Irmgard Groß (via plantnet.org); CONVOLVULUS: delirium florens (CC BY 2.0 via Flickr); COREOPSIS: Carl Lewis (CC BY 2.0 via Flickr); CORIANDER: Rajesh S Balouria (via Pexels); CORONILLA: Martin Cooper (CC BY 2.0 via Flickr); COWSLIP: Amanda Slater (CC BY 2.0 via Flickr); COXCOMB: sylisa (via plantnet.org); CRANBERRY: Kaz Andrew (CC BY 2.0 via

Flickr); CRANESBILL: Jonathan Billinger (via geograph.org.uk); CROCUS: mina258 (via plantnet.org); CROWFOOT: Enrico Blasutto (CC BY-SA 3.0, via Wikimedia Commons); CUCKOO FLOWER, GORSE & PASQUE FLOWER: Bernard DUPONT (CC BY 2.0 via Flickr & Wikimedia Commons); CUCKOO PINT: Pier52 (via Pixabay); CUCUMBER: WiseMan42 (CC0, via Wikimedia Commons); CYCLAMEN: hamon jp (CC BY-SA 3.0, via Wikimedia Commons); CYPRESS: Darekk2 (CC BY-SA 3.0, via Wikimedia Commons); DAFFODIL, FUCHSIA, HEARTSEASE & HEATH: via Pickpik (CC0); DANDELION: Bach Carme (via plantnet.org); DARNEL: Arthur Chapman (CC BY 2.0, via Wikimedia Commons); DEAD LEAVES: Gabriela Reyna (via Pexels); DITTANY: Babij (CC BY 2.0 via Flickr); DOG'S BANE & HAREBELL: Ryan Hodnett (CC BY-SA 4.0, via Wikimedia Commons); DOGWOOD: www.ForestWander.com (CC BY-SA 3.0 US, via Wikimedia Commons); EGLANTINE: Jackcoralimes (CC BY-SA 3.0, via Wikimedia Commons); ELDER: Alain Bigou (via plantnet.org); ELECAMPANE: Paul Herrington (via plantnet.org); ENCHANTER'S NIGHTSHADE & SPIDERWORT: KP Laer (CC BY-SA 2.0 via plantnet.org); ENDIVE & WALLFLOWER: David Monniaux (CC BY-SA 3.0, via Wikimedia Commons); ERYNGO: Pierre LEON (via plantnet.org); EVERLASTING FLOWER & RUE: Plenuska (CC BY-SA 4.0, via Wikimedia Commons); EVERLASTING PEA & ROSE (CABBAGE): Dieter Albrecht (via plantnet.org); EYEBRIGHT: Natalie-S (CC BY-SA 4.0, via Wikimedia Commons); FAIR MAID OF FRANCE: Bernd Haynold (CC BY-SA 3.0, via Wikimedia Commons); FENNEL: Forest & Kim Starr (CC BY 3.0, via Wikimedia Commons); FIG: CC0 via Rawpixel; FIR TREE: Bill Harrison (via geograph.org.uk); FLAX & LILY: Swallowtail Garden Seeds (CC BY 2.0 via Flickr); FLAX LEAVED GOLDEN LOCKS: Muscari (CC BY-SA 3.0, via Wikimedia Commons); FLOS AERIS: StarWrong (CC0, via Wikimedia Commons); FLY ORCHIS: Michel Pansiot (via plantnet.org); FORGET ME NOT: sannse (CC BY-SA 3.0, via Wikimedia Commons); FOXGLOVE: Evelyn Simak (via Wikimedia Commons); FRENCH MARIGOLD: Jim Evans (CC BY-SA 4.0, via Wikimedia Commons); FRENCH WILLOW: manuseitz (via plantnet.org); GERANIUM: Lalit Bali (via Pexels); GOATS' RUE: Uleli (CC BY 3.0, via Wikimedia Commons); GOLDEN ROD: Calimo (CC BY-SA 3.0, via Wikimedia Commons); GOOSEBERRY: Rafał Has (via plantnet.org); GOURD: nociveglia from Appennino Emiliano, Italy (CC BY 2.0, via Wikimedia Commons); GRAPES: walknboston (CC BY 2.0, via Wikimedia Commons); GUELDER ROSE: Grigoriy (via Pexels); HAWKWEED: Tela Botanica – Thierry Pernot (via plantnet.org); HAWTHORN & MICHAELMAS DAISY: David Wright (CC BY 2.0 via Flickr); HELIOTROPE: David Anstiss (CC BY-SA 2.0, via Wikimedia Commons); HELLEBORE. HOLLY & POLYANTHUS: Annemarie Ahrens-Stehle (CC BY-SA 2.0 via plantnet.org);

ANNA MARIA CAMPBELL'S FLORAL DICTIONARY 353

HEMLOCK: Dona Hilkey (CC0 via Flickr); HEMP: K-State Research and Extension (CC BY 2.0 via Flickr); HENBANE: Matt Lavin (CC BY-SA 2.0, via Wikimedia Commons); HEPATICA: Uoaei1 (CC BY-SA 4.0, via Wikimedia Commons); HOLLYHOCK: Bernard Spragg. NZ (CC0 via Flickr); HONESTY: ɒɒ HQ (CC BY-SA 2.0, via Wikimedia Commons); HONEY FLOWER: JMK (CC BY-SA 3.0, via Wikimedia Commons); HONEYSUCKLE: Marysia Kay (via plantnet.org); HOPS: Diana via Pexels; HOREHOUND & VERNAL GRASS: Harry Rose from South West Rocks (CC BY 2.0, via Wikimedia Commons); HORSE CHESTNUT: ИринаЯ (CC0, via Wikimedia Commons); HOUSELEEK & SORREL (WILD): William Coville (CC BY-SA 2.0 via plantnet.org); HOUSTONIA: Alvin Kho (CC BY 2.0 via Flickr); HYACINTH: WerbeFabrik-1161770 (CC0, via Wikimedia Commons); HYDRANGEA: MJJR (CC BY 2.5, via Wikimedia Commons); ICE PLANT: juliettadeep (via plantnet.org); INDIAN CRESS: Emőke Dénes (CC BY-SA 4.0, via Wikimedia Commons); INDIAN PINK: Dagmar Haggerty (via plantnet.org); IRIS: Pamwik (CC BY-SA 4.0, via Wikimedia Commons); JASMINE: Joël Macé (via plantnet.org); JONQUIL: Gerhard Müller (via plantnet.org); JUNIPER: Peter O'Connor aka anemoneprojectors (CC BY 2.0 via Flickr); KINGCUP: Wolfmann (CC BY-SA 4.0, via Wikimedia Commons); KNOTGRASS: New York State IPM Program at Cornell University (CC BY 2.0 via Flickr); LABURNUM: Beate Riedel (via plantnet.org); LADIES' BEDSTRAW: Phil Sellens from East Sussex (CC BY 2.0, via Wikimedia Commons); LADY'S SLIPPER: Franco Colnago (via plantnet.org); LARKSPUR: Vivien Kingl (via plantnet.org); LAUREL: Killarnee (CC BY-SA 4.0, via Wikimedia Commons); LAURUSTINUS, SHAMROCK & ST JOHN'S WORT: Fabrice Rubio (via plantnet.org); LAVENDER, POTATO & STOCK: Jacques Zuber (CC BY-SA 2.0 via plantnet.org); LEMON: FASTILY (CC BY-SA 4.0, via Wikimedia Commons); LETTUCE: Dwight Sipler from Stow, MA, USA (CC BY 2.0, via Wikimedia Commons); LICHEN: Umberto Salvagnin from Italy (CC BY 2.0, via Wikimedia Commons); LILAC & PRIVET: via Pixabay; LILY, DAY: Epibase (CC BY-SA 3.0, via Wikimedia Commons); LILY, JERUSALEM: Mickael Loth (via plantnet.org); LILY OF THE VALLEY: Аська Добрая via Pexels; LILY (WATER): Snowdrift (via Pixabay); LIME TREE & OLEANDER: Alvesgaspar (CC BY-SA 3.0, via Wikimedia Commons); LIQUORICE: Chérif-Jacques Allali (via plantnet.org); LOBELIA: Les Meloures at Luxembourgish Wikipedia (CC BY-SA 1.0, via Wikimedia Commons); LOCUST TREE: Famartin (CC BY-SA 4.0, via Wikimedia Commons); LONDON PRIDE: Caroline Thomas (via plantnet.org); LOTUS: Koorakula Divya (CC BY-SA 4.0, via Wikimedia Commons); LOVE IN A MIST: Wildfeuer (CC BY-SA 3.0, via Wikimedia Commons); LUCERNE: Patrice Bracquart (via plantnet.org); LUPIN: Si Griffiths (CC BY-SA 3.0, via Wikimedia Commons);

MADWORT: antonio_334 (via plantnet.org); MAGNOLIA: hermaion (via Pexels); MAIDENHAIR: Schnobby (CC BY-SA 3.0, via Wikimedia Commons); MALLOW: Lucarelli (CC BY-SA 3.0, via Wikimedia Commons); MARIGOLD & OLIVE: Ввласенко (CC BY-SA 3.0, via Wikimedia Commons); MARJORAM & WALNUT: Ivar Leidus (CC BY-SA 4.0, via Wikimedia Commons); MARVEL OF PERU: LucaLuca (CC BY-SA 3.0, via Wikimedia Commons); MEADOW LYCHNIS: KENPEI (CC BY-SA 3.0, via Wikimedia Commons); MEADOWSWEET: Evgeniya (via plantnet.org); MEZEREON: Jutta Gems (via plantnet.org); MIGNONETTE: papazachariasa (via Pixabay); MILK VETCH: USFWS Mountain-Prairie (CC BY 2.0, via Wikimedia Commons); MIMOSA: Lensational (CC0 via Pixahive); MINT: LeahReiter (via Pixabay); MISTLETOE, THYME & VIOLET: Hans (via Pixabay); MOSS: Laura C (via Pexels); MOUNTAIN LAUREL & PHLOX: Fritzflohrreynolds (CC BY-SA 3.0, via Wikimedia Commons); MUGWORT & POTENTILLA: Vinayaraj (CC BY-SA 4.0, via Wikimedia Commons); MULBERRY: Geo Lightspeed7 (CC BY-SA 4.0, via Wikimedia Commons); MULLEIN: Теменужка Минева (via plantnet.org); MUSTARD SEED: Edal Anton Lefterov (CC BY-SA 3.0, via Wikimedia Commons); MYRRH: Axel Strauß (CC BY-SA 3.0, via Wikimedia Commons); NARCISSUS: w-mue (via plantnet.org); NEMOPHILA: Cliff Hutson (CC BY 2.0 via Flickr); NETTLE: J Brew (CC BY 2.0 via Flickr); NIGHTSHADE: Puusterke (CC BY-SA 4.0, via Wikimedia Commons); OAK APPLE: Dazzii (CC BY-SA 4.0, via Wikimedia Commons); OAK LEAF & ACORN: pasja1000 (via Pixabay); ORCHID: Eleonora Sky (via Pexels); ORIENTAL PERSICARIA: ThierryB (CC BY-SA 3.0, via Wikimedia Commons); OX EYE: Arun Prakash Ambathy (via plantnet.org); PALM : ThousandImages (via Pixabay); PARSLEY: JACLOU-DL (via Pixabay); PASSION FLOWER: Kuribo (CC BY-SA 3.0, via Wikimedia Commons); PEACH BLOSSOM: John Freshney (CC BY 2.0 via Flickr); PENNYROYAL & VENUS LOOKING GLASS: Stefan.lefnaer (CC BY-SA 4.0, via Wikimedia Commons); PEONY: Sunset Magazine (CC BY-SA 4.0, via Wikimedia Commons); PERIWINKLE: Maxime Simon (via plantnet.org); PHEASANT'S EYE: C T Johansson (CC BY 3.0, via Wikimedia Commons); PINEAPPLE: Schwarzenarzisse (via Pixabay); PINK: sylviahsc (via Pixabay); PLEURISY ROOT: (□□□□ □□□□CC BY 4.0, via Wikimedia Commons); PLUM: Glysiak (CC BY-SA 4.0, via Wikimedia Commons); POMEGRANATE: Christian Poma (via plantnet.org); POPPY: Uschi_Du (via Pixabay); PRIMROSE: Dr Richard Murray (via geograph.org.uk); QUEEN'S ROCKET, SAFFRON & XANTHIUM: Peter Schmitz (CC BY-SA 2.0 via plantnet.org); QUINCE BLOSSOM: Olivier Chiodi (CC BY-SA 2.0 via plantnet.org); RANUNCULUS: Ralphs_Fotos (CC BY-SA 2.0 via plantnet.org); RASPBERRY: Agnieszka (CC BY-SA 2.0 via plantnet.org); REED: Marin Marin Lisek (CC BY-SA

ANNA MARIA CAMPBELL'S FLORAL DICTIONARY

2.0 via plantnet.org); RHUBARB: Dieter Weber (CC BY-SA 3.0, via Wikimedia Commons); ROSE (CHINA) & SOUTHERNWOOD : annemarieah (CC BY-SA 2.0 via plantnet.org); ROSE, DAMASK : Emmanuel Bouchard (CC BY-SA 2.0 via plantnet.org); ROSE, MAIDEN'S BLUSH: ᴅᴅ (CC BY-SA 4.0, via Wikimedia Commons); ROSE, MUSK: fanny.papile (CC BY-SA 2.0 via plantnet.org); ROSEMARY: Víctor Gonzalez (CC BY-SA 2.0 via plantnet.org); RUSH: Jiří Vilím (CC BY-SA 2.0 via plantnet.org); SAGE: photosforyou (via Pixabay); SCABIOUS: Sergio costantini (CC BY-SA 2.0 via plantnet.org); SCARLET LYCHNIS: Tuukka Haapaniemi (CC BY-SA 2.0 via plantnet.org); SNAKE TONGUE: Dominique Wernert (CC BY-SA 2.0 via plantnet.org); SNAPDRAGON: ignartonosbg (via Pixabay); SNOWDROP: satynek (via Pixabay); SORREL: Pleple2000 (CC BY-SA 3.0 via Wikimedia Commons); STAR OF BETHLEHEM: Zsuzsanna Lázár-Tóth (via plantnet.org); STARWORT: HermannSchachner (CC0, via Wikimedia Commons); STRAWBERRY: Rick888chen (CC BY-SA 4.0, via Wikimedia Commons); SUNFLOWER: Jardin Botanique (via plantnet.org); SWEET PEA: Frank Vincentz (CC BY-SA 3.0, via Wikimedia Commons); SWEET SULTAN: Provincial Archives of Alberta via Wikimedia Commons); SWEET WILLIAM: D LaMack (via plantnet.org); SYRINGA: Haggeswood (CC BY 4.0, via Wikimedia Commons); TEN WEEKS' STOCK : nekanesh92 (via plantnet.org); THISTLE: Timothy A. Gonsalves (CC BY-SA 4.0, via Wikimedia Commons); THRIFT: Dinkum (CC BY-SA 3.0, via Wikimedia Commons); THROAT WORT: M Mary (CC BY-SA 2.0 via plantnet.org); TRUE LOVE: Anatas (CC BY-SA 2.0 via plantnet.org); TUBEROSE: Swaminathan from Gurgaon, India (CC BY 2.0, via Wikimedia Commons); TULIP: Jessie Emslie (CC BY-SA 2.0, via Wikimedia Commons); TULIP TREE: Sdkb (CC BY-SA 4.0, via Wikimedia Commons); TURNIP: thebittenword.com (CC BY 2.0, via Wikimedia Commons); VALERIAN: Landschaftsgärtner (via plantnet.org); VERBENA: Cephas (CC BY-SA 4.0, via Wikimedia Commons); VINE: jean-marc lallemand (via plantnet.org); WEEPING WILLOW: Christine Westerback (CC BY-SA 2.0 via Wikimedia Commons); WHEAT: donauwood (via Pixabay); YEW: uroburos (via Pixabay).

COVER IMAGE: The painting on the cover is by Annie Louisa Pressland (1862-1933) via Wikimedia Commons.

www.ingramcontent.com/pod-product-compliance
Lightning Source LLC
Chambersburg PA
CBHW071951070526
44583CB00015B/1145